Pulpit and Politics

Pulpit and Politics

Clergy in American Politics
at the Advent of the Millennium

edited by

Corwin E. Smidt

Baylor University Press
Waco, Texas 76798

Cover Design: Bob Bubnis

Library of Congress Cataloging-in-Publication Data

Pulpit and politics : clergy in American politics at the advent of the millennium / edited by Corwin Smidt.
    p. cm.
  Includes bibliographical references and index.
  ISBN 1-932792-13-9 (pbk. : alk. paper)
  1. Religion and politics--United States. 2. Clergy--United States. I. Smidt, Corwin E., 1946-

  BL2525.P85 2004
  261.7'0973--dc22

                                        2004014280

Printed in the United States of America on acid-free paper

To my father, the Rev. Esdert W. Smidt, and to my uncles,
the Rev. Ralph H. Cordes and the Rev. Kenneth M. Cordes,
faithful and tireless workers in the Lord's vineyards.

Contents

Acknowledgments

This effort draws upon the assistance and cooperation of many individuals, without whom this volume would not be possible. First of all, I need to thank the various scholars who participated in the Cooperative Clergy Study Project; your enthusiastic response to the idea of this research project and your wonderful cooperation in conducting the surveys made the proposed project a reality. Expressions of appreciation also need to be extended to the more than 8,800 clergy who took time from their busy schedules to answer the rather long, time-consuming survey; your willingness to respond to the survey provided the foundation for the chapters contained in the volume. Thanks, too, need to be extended to Ellen Hekman, my coworker in the Henry Institute, for her extensive and excellent assistance in preparing this volume; without your able assistance I never would have been able to meet the publisher's deadlines. An expression of gratitude is also owed to James Guth and Lyman Kellstedt for their helpful comments and suggestions, particularly in regard to the concluding chapter of this volume; though not every suggestion was followed, the final chapter, whatever its limitations, is nevertheless far better because of your comments. Finally, I want to express my appreciation to Carey C. Newman, Director, Baylor University Press, for the confidence he exhibited in this volume when I suggested the idea to him; I trust this completed volume merits the faith you placed in my proposal.

Contributors

Kedron Bardwell is a professor of political science at Grand Valley State University in Allendale, Michigan.

Linda Beail is an associate professor of political science at Point Loma Nazarene University in San Diego, California.

Timothy C. Coburn is an associate professor of mathematics at Abilene Christian University in Abilene, Texas.

Sue Crawford is an associate professor of political science at Creighton University in Omaha, Nebraska.

Greg Crow is a professor of mathematics at Point Loma Nazarene University in San Diego, California.

Melissa Deckman is an assistant professor of political science at Washington College in Chestertown, Maryland.

Paul Djupe is an assistant professor of political science at Denison University in Granville, Ohio.

Beverly Gaddy is an assistant professor of political science at the University of Pittsburgh at Greensburg in Greensburg, Pennsylvania.

Donald Gray is an emeritus professor of sociology at Eastern University in St. Davids, Pennsylvania.

John C. Green is a professor of political science and director of the Ray Bliss Institute at the University of Akron in Akron, Ohio.

James L. Guth is the William R. Kenan Jr. professor of political science at Furman University in Greenville, South Carolina.

Mel Hailey is a professor of political science at Abilene Christian University in Abilene, Texas.

Dan Hoffrenning is an associate professor of political science at St. Olaf College in Northfield, Minnesota.

Ted Jelen is a professor of political science at the University of Nevada in Las Vegas, Nevada.

Lyman Kellstedt is an emeritus professor of political science at Wheaton College in Wheaton, Illinois.

L. DeAne Lagerquist is an associate professor of religion at St. Olaf College in Northfield, Minnesota.

Eric McDaniel is a doctoral candidate in the department of political science at the University of Illinois Urbana-Champaign in Champaign-Urbana, Illinois.

Steve Montreal is an associate professor of justice and public policy at Concordia University Wisconsin in Mequon, Wisconsin.

Brent Nelson is a professor of political science at Furman University in Greenville, South Carolina.

Laura Olson is an associate professor of political science at Clemson University in Clemson, South Carolina.

James Penning is a professor of political science at Calvin College in Grand Rapids, Michigan.

Janelle Sagness was an undergraduate student at St. Olaf College in Northfield, Minnesota at the time the chapter was written.

Corwin E. Smidt is the Paul B. Henry professor of political science and director of the Paul B. Henry Institute for the Study of Christianity and Politics at Calvin College in Grand Rapids, Michigan.

Anand Sokhey is a graduate student in the doctoral program in political science at Ohio State University in Columbus, Ohio.

Sherrie Steiner is an assistant professor of sociology at Eastern University in St. Davids, Pennsylvania.

Jeff Walz is an associate professor of political science at Concordia University Wisconsin in Mequon, Wisconsin.

William (Beau) Weston is an associate professor of sociology at Centre College in Danville, Kentucky.

Part 1

INTRODUCTION

Chapter 1

Theological and Political Orientations of Clergy within American Politics: An Analytic and Historical Overview

Corwin E. Smidt

The advent of the new millennium provides an important opportunity to examine afresh the theological and political positions expressed by clergy within contemporary American life. Clergy have long been important forces in American politics, whether one considers their public pronouncements during the Revolutionary War, their championing of benevolent societies during the Second Great Awakening, their involvement in the abolitionist movement of the mid-1800s, or their efforts in the civil-rights era of the 1960s. Thus, the new millennium provides an important symbolic marker for a survey of the theological and political landscape within which contemporary clergy operate.

There are, however, more vital analytical grounds for examining the theological and political positions of clergy. First, clergy have important resources at their disposal to shape the political thinking and actions of their parishioners, and they enjoy ample opportunities to do so. Such resources and opportunities would be of limited political importance if clergy did not convey political messages or become engaged in the political arena. But, in fact, clergy do participate in political cue-giving activities (as well as in other kinds of political action) both in and out of the pulpit (Guth et al. 1997).

A second analytical reason for examining clergy orientations is that neither denominational life nor politics is static in nature. Old patterns of clergy involvement in politics may no longer be evident, and new patterns may emerge. Changing environmental conditions (whether in terms of varied economic conditions, deteriorating social structures, increasing global interdependence, etc.) may affect both religious and political life, altering the way in which the two spheres interrelate. Changes in the nature of the clergy ordained by each denomination (or in the candidates nominated by political parties) may affect the theological emphases advanced by clergy (or the political agendas advanced by candidates for public office). And changes in the nature of their constituents may change the ways religious and political leaders choose to relate to those whom they both serve and lead. Accordingly, the theological and political orientations of clergy at the turn of the millennium may well diverge from patterns discovered only a decade or two previously.

Finally, there are special historical reasons for examining clergy politics at the turn of the millennium. The specific features of the presidential race of 2000 provide an important basis for reevaluation. The election was highly contested and controversial and was unique in that it was the first time a Jew, Joseph Lieberman, was part of a national ticket. Moreover, religious themes, messages, and concerns were clearly evident from start to finish. For example, a leader of a Christian Right organization, Gary Bauer, sought the GOP nomination for president. George W. Bush and John McCain skirmished over the Catholic vote in both the South Carolina and Michigan presidential primaries. But religious considerations were not confined to the GOP nomination process. During the general election campaign, Republicans talked of restoring morality and integrity to the White House. Bush and Gore debated whether the government should provide vouchers for poor parents to send their children to private (even religious) schools, and both raised the issue of faith-based government programs. Thus, religion presented a much more public face in the 2000 campaign than in previous contests; as a result, the election serves to provide an important context for the study of clerical politics.

This volume contains chapters that examine the theological and political orientations of clergy in the election year of 2000. Each chapter analyzes the theological and political beliefs expressed by clergy of one denomination or religious body, their assessments about what constitute appropriate political activities for clergy, and the extent to which clergy in contemporary American political life are actually engaged in politics. Before beginning this examination, it is helpful to assess some of the different ways in which clergy can serve as political actors, discuss the potential importance of that role, and provide some historical background of clerical involvement in politics.

CLERGY AS POLITICAL ACTORS

The Political Roles of Clergy

Members of the clergy can be active in politics in a variety of roles. They may choose to make contributions to particular candidates or parties, join political associations, and exercise their democratic rights at the polls. In such matters, ministers enjoy the same privileges of citizenship as other American citizens.

Second, ministers may be political activists as a result of their leadership roles in local churches. The fact that many congregational members gather weekly enhances pastors' ability to politicize and mobilize their flocks, by expanding the opportunities both to educate church members politically and to advance their particular agendas. Whether or not a minister can shape the views of his or her congregants depends upon a variety of factors: the nature of the congregation, the pastor's personality, and the pastor's skill in dealing with the congregation (Vidich and Bensman 1968, 239). But recent research has suggested that pastors and local congregations can be important factors in explaining the political attitudes and behaviors of those who attend church. Clergy, in fact, recognize the potential influence they have over their congregations; ministers report that they could exert much political influence over their congregations, should they desire to do so (Djupe and Gilbert 2001b; Guth et al. 1997).

Third, ministers may also be political activists by virtue of their roles as "religious professionals" who help shape ongoing political debates. Clergy are professionals and, as a result, associate and interact with their colleagues within regional, state, and national denominational and interdenominational agencies and organizations. As religious leaders, ministers may collectively issue pastoral letters, statements, or declarations. Likewise, they may work to secure official denominational pronouncements or become involved in lobbying activities. Thus, as members of a particular profession, clerics may collectively seek to influence and shape the course of political affairs, whether with regard to matters that directly affect their profession (e.g., clergy liability in terms of pastoral counseling) or matters that are shaped by their religious convictions (e.g., speaking out on behalf of the dispossessed).

The Potential Importance of Ministerial Political Activism

Regardless of the particular role adopted, ministers constitute political actors of some potential import because of two major factors: they possess important political resources, and they enjoy important opportunities to influence others.

Resources

Clergy possess important resources on which they can draw should they try to mobilize others for political ends. First, ministers tend to be highly educated, possessing important verbal and analytical skills. As a result, they are not only more likely to engage in ideological thinking than many of their parishioners with less schooling (Guth et al. 1997), but they are better able to frame issues within broader systems of thought of their own particular choosing.

Second, clergy have access to important resources that can be used for political purposes. Church rooms and auditoriums can be used for political gatherings, bulletin announcements can solicit volunteers, and church buses can transport church members to the polls (Wald 1991).

Third, ministers are expected to be models of high moral character. Honesty in language and deed are expected. Clergy are generally viewed as individuals who are aware of, and concerned about, the moral conditions of the world around them. They are not expected, therefore, to sit passively while moral standards decline; rather, it is assumed that pastors should take a stand and draw lines between that which should be embraced and that which should be shunned.

Fourth, ministers have traditionally been accorded a certain respect within American culture, by both those within and outside the church. Given this relatively high esteem in which clergy are held, not only will the political messages they transmit likely be given a respectful hearing, but they may be accorded substantial credibility as well (Wald et al. 1988).

Opportunities

In addition to possessing important political resources, pastors also enjoy significant opportunities to mold the political attitudes and behavior of others. Most Americans claim church affiliation, and approximately 40 percent report attending worship services on a weekly basis (Wilson 1989, 363). When parishioners are at church, ministers may be able to transmit political messages through sermons, adult-education classes, church bulletin announcements, and poster displays. These opportunities to provide political perspectives and guidelines to parishioners are no small matter. Given their numbers and the frequent interaction of members, religious congregations probably constitute "the most vital voluntary organization in a country that puts a premium on 'joining up'" (Wald 2003, 8).

In addition, clergy often have audiences receptive to the political cues they transmit. If those attending worship services thought it inappropriate for ministers to address political issues, political cue-giving messages could largely be dismissed. But church attendees appear, at least under certain circumstances, to be receptive to such messages. Biblical passages or church teachings can be given a variety of interpretations, and parishioners may have difficulty interpreting the political ramifications of their religious beliefs, leading to church members relying on pastors for political guidance. Moreover, studies have shown that parishioners, particularly those who attend regularly, not only perceive, but are receptive to, political messages from their pastors (Leege, Kellstedt, and Wald 1990).

The Political Significance of Clergy

Given the political resources and opportunities enjoyed by clergy, scholars have paid considerable attention over the past several decades to the role that ministers play in American politics (e.g., Hadden 1969; Quinley 1974; Guth et al. 1997; Crawford and Olson 2001). These studies have revealed that clergy can indeed be political actors of some significance.

Cue-Giving Activities

First, clergy often provide political cues to their parishioners. Many of the millions who attend church do so not only to worship but to hear what their pastors have to say. Those who observe and listen carefully receive certain messages from the pulpit about issues and concerns they should pay attention to, care about, and act upon; often these cues are not ignored (Crawford and Olson 2001; Wald, Owen, and Hill 1988; 1990). This is especially true when clergy address certain issues regularly and when they speak to concerns that are salient both to their congregations and to society (Djupe and Gilbert 2001b). Under such circumstances, these messages and cues are not usually ignored (Crawford and Olson 2001; Fetzer 2001; Penning and Smidt 2001; Wald, Owen, and Hill 1988, 1990).

Moreover, congregation members may give greater credence to stances taken by their pastor than they would to a position heard or read about in some news medium (Buddenbaum 2001). It is true that clergy may often be preaching to the converted. But, even under such circumstances, ministers can still influence their congregational members by intensifying their attachments and reinforcing their preferences, thereby encouraging activism (Jelen 2001b). Thus, it is probably not too surprising, as a number of studies have shown (e.g., Wald et al. 1988; 1990; Gilbert 1989; Jelen 1990), that congregations frequently serve as "contexts for the transmission and reinforcement of political attitudes" (Welch et al. 1993, 3).

Finally, clergy may well move beyond exhorting or merely offering political cues to their congregations to more direct forms of activity. Some pastors have led their congregations in political actions intended to achieve political and social change. They may also mobilize their flocks into political action on behalf of particular candidates (e.g., Hertzke 1993) or particular issues (e.g., Tays 1990).

Relationship between Theology and Politics

Clergy are also politically significant in that they are in the business of connecting particular theological and religious beliefs to political attitudes and orientations. Ministers operate within the domain of religious beliefs and are steeped in theology, which is central to their belief systems, providing them with a worldview within which they understand and approach all of life.

Parishioners also hold theological beliefs, but given their relative lack of theological training, members vary more than clergy in theological sophistication. Moreover, even if parishioners express the same religious beliefs as clergy, they are less likely to understand and fully appreciate the social and political ramifications of these tenets. Hence, to understand how particular religious beliefs may shape specific political attitudes and behavior, the analyst may be better served to examine such relationships among clergy than among parishioners.

Possible Erosion of the "Two-Party System"

Finally, the theological and political orientations of clergy today are also directly related to the issue of how and to what extent religious differences may be manifested politically. As recently as a decade or two ago, the politics of many clergy were still strongly influenced by theological disputes that arose in the late nineteenth century. These profound disagreements ultimately served to form what Martin Marty (1970) called the "two-party system" in American Protestantism.

Although the contours of this division are complex and remain far from static, by the end of the twentieth century, most Protestant clergy and denominational leaders could be largely placed within either the evangelical tradition, comprising denominations and churches dominated by orthodox forces, or the mainline tradition, in which modernists were much more prevalent, at least among clergy and denominational leaders (Kellstedt and Green 1993).

Other analysts, however, have argued that such a two-party division tends to obscure important features of American religious life. As Wuthnow notes, "To state that American religion is divided neatly into two communities is to ride roughshod over the countless landmarks, signposts, hills, and gullies that actually constitute the religious landscape" (1989, 23). In so doing, the bipolar division of American religious life fails to give attention "to the nuances and complexities of American religion" (Jacobsen and Trollinger 1998, 7). Therefore, to place the chapters of this volume within the context of this broader debate, it is necessary to provide a brief historical overview of shifting cleavages within American religious life.

THE HISTORICAL CONTEXT

As the twentieth century began to dawn, important tensions and divisions were emerging in American Protestantism that affected the nature and level of clergy involvement in American social and political life. The emerging bifurcation of American Protestantism was related, in part, to changing intellectual perspectives. By the end of the nineteenth century, two major intellectual challenges confronted American Protestantism: the teachings of Charles Darwin and the contentions of German higher criticism of the Bible. Darwin's thesis about the origin of species, which flooded America following the Civil War, seemingly stood in opposition to scriptural teachings about the origin of man and challenged the integrity of the Bible. German higher criticism of the Bible argued that the biblical texts must be interpreted in terms of the social and historical contexts in which they were written. From the perspective of German higher criticism, the gospel was much more complex than the "simple gospel" of the Bible as read by the laity; this perspective challenged not only literalism in biblical interpretation but also the inerrancy of biblical texts in historical and scientific matters.

As a result of these intellectual challenges, there arose within Protestantism a new "liberal" theology that sought to reconcile the Word of God with modern, scientific understandings. Rather than assuming a divine authorship of the biblical texts, liberals adopted a more naturalistic stance in understanding its origin. Instead of emphasizing the particular revelation of God in Jesus Christ, these liberals focused on the general revelation of God in nature and history. And, in the place of stressing God's transcendent nature, they taught immanence, the presence of God in the midst of the world.

The emergence of this new liberal theology created strong divisions within American Protestantism but did not initially result in schisms. Some accepted it, while others rejected it. Most, however, tended to adopt viewpoints somewhere between the extremes (Hoge 1976). By the advent of the new century, liberal theology had simply permeated many seminaries and larger churches within existing denominations.

In addition to the theological challenges confronting American Protestantism, there were also major social challenges to the dominant Protestant culture. In particular, the rise of industrialization, with its attendant social changes, brought increasing pluralism to American society. Industrialization led to greater urbanization. The growing demand for cheap labor contributed to the immigration of Catholic and Jewish ethnic groups into American cities. New forms of transportation not only enabled the distribution of mass-produced goods, but also increased mobility out of smaller, more local, communities into larger, more cosmopolitan, settings. Associated with this growth in industrialization was the rise of the robber barons, the marginal existence of laborers, the abuse of child labor, and the squalor of industrial towns.

In response to these problems, a strong "social gospel" element emerged within Protestantism that rejected traditional revivalism as the basis of social reform. Rather than focusing on the need for spiritual conversion, social-gospel advocates stressed education, ethics, and social change. The human condition was viewed to be less a function of human depravity and more the result of deprivation. Reflecting the generally optimistic mood of the times, advocates of the social gospel generally advanced a more optimistic view of human nature: sin was something that either education could mitigate or social reform could prevent (Hoge 1976).

These differences between an "individual gospel" and a "social gospel" served to create a fault line in American Protestantism that coalesced into a "two-party system" (Marty 1970, 179). Those who advocated the former contended that the task of Christians was to save souls and that, by changing the hearts of individuals, social problems would dissipate. Those who espoused the latter view contended that social and economic forces were so oppressive that redemption of individuals could not take place without social reform (Hoge 1976).

Nevertheless, a spectrum of theological positions continued to be evident within American Protestantism until the 1920s (Handy 1955), when theological conservatives began to launch a strong attack against liberal forces. But when their efforts to oust modernists from the major denominations failed, many of these fundamentalists withdrew and regrouped. As a result, the character of fundamentalism changed dramatically over the course of the next two decades (Marsden 1975). In the early 1920s, fundamentalism had been a movement located within the Protestant mainstream; it aspired to control both denominational life and American culture. However, by the early 1940s, its locus and goals had shifted significantly. Having lost the major denominations, a "doctrine" of separation was increasingly stressed as a test of fidelity. This change in perspective prompted fundamentalists to create and operate within independent congregations, agencies, and institutions, while major denominations and established institutions were left largely, by default, to modernist forces. And, for the most part, this movement rejected politics in favor of efforts aimed toward individual conversion and sanctification.

Consequently, when scholars studied the political activism of the clergy during the 1960s and early 1970s, it was not surprising that political participation by the clergy seemed the domain of theological liberals from mainline denominations (Hadden 1969; Quinley 1974) or of African American pastors who were involved in the civil-rights movement (Morris 1984). Salvation, for these clerical activists, was not to be attained by adhering to theological doctrines, but "in the giving and involvement of oneself in this life" (Hadden 1969, 98). Accordingly, their theology moved them outside the doors of the church and prompted them to demonstrate God's love through their concern for the world, particularly the underprivileged, and through their desire to change those social structures that contributed to injustice.

In contrast, theologically conservative Protestant ministers, who were located in evangelical denominations and fundamentalist churches, largely shunned social and political activity during the 1960s and early 1970s (Koller and Retzer 1980; Nelsen and Baxter 1981). Indeed, so rare was their political involvement that some analysts contended that only "sounds of silence" emanated from conservative pastors; they attributed this lack of involvement to their "otherworldly" theology: that conservative clergy were committed to "miraculous and otherworldly" solutions to human problems (Stark et al. 1970).

By the 1980s, things had changed: theologically conservative Protestant ministers appeared to be very much engaged in political battle. Pastors from churches who in the past had espoused separation from the world now appeared to be deeply embroiled in political activity. This increased political involvement was evident both in preaching from the pulpit and in actual weekday political activity (Guth 1984; Beatty and Walter 1989; Guth et al. 1997).

Of particular concern to these conservative pastors were issues relating to traditional social morality and "the family." So great was the increase in political involvement among conservative clergy that some studies found little, if any, difference between liberal and conservative clergy with respect to the extent of their political and social involvement (Koller and Retzer 1980; Beatty and Walter 1989). No longer did it appear that clerical political activism was linked to particular theological perspectives.

Thus, by the mid-1980s, new questions were being raised about the nature, extent, and impact of clerical political involvement, and the evidence, based on analysis of clergy from eight Protestant denominations, suggested that there tended to be two basic constellations of values, beliefs, and attitudes, running from religious theology to political participation, that served to divide Protestant clergy (Guth et al. 1997). While two distinct parties were largely present, there was, however, no longer any distinct gap between evangelical and mainline clergy in terms of their willingness to engage the public sphere. The issues that galvanized the two groups were different, as were their proposed solutions to public problems. But significant numbers of both groups were now equally involved with both public and private concerns. Those clergy who held orthodox theologies were likely to endorse individualist social theologies, support moral reform political agendas, be ideologically conservative, and vote Republican. In contrast, those ministers who adhered to modernist theologies were more likely to advance communitarian social theologies, support social-justice political agendas, be ideologically liberal, and vote Democratic.

THE COOPERATIVE CLERGY STUDY PROJECT

Given the vital role that clergy can play in American politics, the Henry Institute for the Study of Christianity and Politics at Calvin College invited a number of scholars to a planning meeting in the summer of 2000 to discuss a possible study project focusing on clergy. The project was to be a cooperative endeavor, with each participant surveying clergy from a single denomination; usually the researcher was either a member of that denomination or very familiar with it. The effort was unprecedented in the breadth of denominations and religious faiths examined—namely, various evangelical, mainline, and black Protestant denominations, the Roman Catholic Church, as well as Jewish rabbis.[1]

The participants in the planning meeting decided to construct a common, rather extensive, questionnaire that could be used across almost all denominations, with one page of each church's survey devoted solely to denominationally specific questions. After the instrument was forged, each scholar mailed the questionnaire to a random sample of clergy from the appropriate denomination. The sample size varied from denomination to denomination. Larger religious bodies tended to have larger sample sizes; indeed, the whole clergy population in some smaller denominations was less than the sample size drawn in larger ones. Not surprisingly, the response rate varied by denomination, with smaller religious bodies tending to have higher response rates.[2]

OVERVIEW OF VOLUME

Each chapter in this volume examines clergy from one particular denomination or faith tradition, and each is relatively brief and largely descriptive. All the chapters employ the same outline and address the same questions—permitting comparative analysis of clergy across all denominations. The tables in each chapter are also identical[3] in the questions analyzed and the data presented. However, not all the data collected are presented in these tables. Where authors comment on data not found in the tables, they are drawing on data gathered from the full survey.

Each chapter begins with the denomination's historical background, along with some basic information about its size and number of clergy. The chapters then shift to an analysis of the survey data, beginning with the social characteristics of clergy such as educational attainment, age, gender, and racial composition, and the size of the communities in which they minister.

The theological positions held by clergy of the denomination are examined next. These stances relate both to theological beliefs histori-cally tied to the Christian faith as well as to issues related to the inerrancy[4] of Scripture, the historicity of Adam and Eve, and the relative importance of the church emphasizing individual sanctification versus transforming the social order.

The focus of each chapter then shifts to the norms clergy hold about their own involvement in politics. As the analyses reveal, clergy have very different assessments about whether it is legitimate to engage in a variety of political actions. Ministers in some denominations are more approving of clerical political activity than those of others, and some types of action are viewed to be much more legitimate than others. The forms of political engagement assessed span a spectrum of activities, from contributing money to political causes to delivering sermons on some political issue, from forming an action group within one's congre-gation to engaging in acts of civil disobedience.

After this, the focus shifts to an examination of the attitudes of the denominational clergy on eight issues related to public policy. A wide spectrum of topics is addressed—including the role of government in addressing social problems, health-care policy, affirmative action, gay rights, abortion, and the Middle East.

Finally, the clergy's own reports regarding their actual activities in the 2000 election are assessed. These include actions that occurred both in the pulpit (e.g., taking a stand from the pulpit on some political issue or praying about an issue) and out of the pulpit (e.g., contacting a public official about an issue). In addition, the self-professed partisan identifi-cations of the clergy are examined, along with their reported pattern of voting for president in the 2000 election.

The chapters of this volume are organized under three major head-ings. Following this introduction, the initial six chapters examine clergy in mainline Protestant denominations. The second set of chapters ana-lyzes clergy in nine evangelical Protestant religious bodies, and the last group of chapters examines religious leaders within denominations, faiths, and religious organizations that stand outside of the "two-party," white, Protestant world.

In the concluding chapter, these particular denominational studies are placed within a broader context of examining patterns of theological and political change over time. The analysis and conclusions assess the nature and direction of such change and discuss their implications for the future with regard to American politics.

Part 2

Politics of Mainline Protestant Clergy

Chapter 2

American Baptist Convention

Sherrie Steiner and Donald Gray

The American Baptist Convention is an association of churches that highly values individual religious freedom and local church autonomy. In light of this emphasis, American Baptist clergy seek to guide their congregations toward responsible civic behavior and attitudes within the context of individual and church freedom. These fundamental values shape the social organization, theology, and political engagement of Baptist clergy and laity alike.

American Baptist clergy tend to be theologically and politically conservative; these two tendencies are strongly related. In part, this conservatism stems from seminary education, which for the majority occurs in evangelical, rather than mainline, seminaries. Clerical conservatism also stems from congregational autonomy, as a conservative laity has considerable influence when it comes to pastoral selection.

HISTORICAL BACKGROUND

Baptists are a diverse, if not contradictory, group of Christians. Even Baptists often have difficulty defining who they are. As Goodwin so aptly put it,

Jesse Jackson is a Baptist. So is Jesse Helms. Baptists are right, left, and center on almost every issue, and if there are other positions, Baptists are there too. We are high church and low church, liberal, conservative, fundamental, open, closed, restrictive, inclusive—and always in process. We love constitutions and ignore them at every opportunity. We love the Bible and believe its every word to be from God, but there has never been a Baptist who did not feel entitled to edit some of its rougher parts and interpret (authoritatively) some of its more confusing texts. But somehow we are bound together in ways not even our most heated controversies can fully disconnect. Invite us to sing a favorite hymn, remind us of a Baptist witness, call us to a prophetic task, challenge us to an urgent mission, and we will, by the miraculous grace of God, respond in unity and joy. (1997, 1)

This diversity is the challenging side of Baptists' greatest gift to American culture: the high value they place on freedom of the soul. Whether it be freedom from oppression, freedom from confusion, or freedom *for* full religious expression, Baptists have consistently emphasized the importance of protecting integrity of both mission and individual belief. Consequently, they have consistently refused to organize around patriarchs, ecclesiological plans, theological frameworks, or institutional structures. Baptist culture is "deeply suspicious of institutions and leaders"—a value that promotes traditional diversity of organization and belief (Goodwin 1997). Baptists are keenly aware that even contexts of toleration can promote religious persecution (Brackney 2000).

This diversity should not be mistaken for lack of denominational identity and cohesion. Baptists share at least five unshakable commitments (Goodwin 1997; Ohlmann 2000):

1. Preservation of individual spiritual freedom
2. Preservation of local congregational autonomy
3. Primacy of mission over institutional preservation
4. Power of the Holy Spirit to conform Baptists and Baptist purposes to the will and work of God
5. The supreme authority of Scripture

Although various Baptist groups may apply or adhere to these convictions differently, the general principles of freedom and decentralized polity are defining Baptist characteristics (Ohlmann 2000).

Baptists want more than to be left alone—they want to believe freely and exercise that belief publicly. Baptists tend to favor religious free expression as an inalienable right rather than as a protected civic obligation. This places religious expression beyond the reach of politics—

whether derived from government or religion. While politics may inevitably influence Baptist life, religious expression is not subject to the political realm (Novak as quoted in Flowers 2000, 304–5):

> If this way of looking at our tradition is correct, the operational meaning of a phrase like "In God We Trust" is: Don't trust anyone with too much power, on the one hand, and, on the other hand, open the spiritual way for ordinary Americans of any and every background. In a word, keep the shrine of transcendence empty. People with different conceptions of God will fill that place as each sees fit. And others, in place of the symbol of God, will fill it with something like the courage to doubt, an insistence on free inquiry, or a capacity to question any institution and any arrangement whatever. A constitution by which the state does not insist upon filling that shrine, but keeps it empty so as to injure the consciences of none, is an operationally sound fulfillment of "In God We Trust." It allows transcendence according to each human conscience.

Given this understanding, Baptist identity takes on increasingly diverse expressions that challenge unethical hegemonies of every shape and size imaginable (Jones 1999). This fierce commitment to soul freedom is expressed within a religious culture in a variety of forms that are anti-institutional in nature. For example, Baptists tend to be very committed to the separation of church and state: if the state is to be held accountable to God, the church must maintain its separate identity so that the church might speak authoritatively to the practices of the state.

But Baptists also distrust *Baptist* organization and leadership. Indeed, they are on the lookout for politics in *any* form, including religious motivations that might influence political activities (Goodwin 1997). Baptists are sensitive to a long history of institutionalized religious corruption. Hence, they are inclined to forgo the increased social power that accompanies ecumenical unity in favor of individual integrity.

In keeping with this principle, Baptists have a history of organizing in a manner that promotes institutional isolation, institutional independence, and individual spiritual freedom (Goodwin 1997). For example, the first major Baptist organization in the United States was the Philadelphia Baptist Association, founded in 1707. But such Baptist churches joined together only for the express purposes of promoting mission and defending against common enemies; organization around building a common institutional life was deemed unacceptable. To those most committed to the principles of association, such as Isaac Backus—leader among the Massachusetts Separatists—common institutional life was to be defended *against* (Goodwin 1997). For Baptists, the problem is one of establishing a commonly lived moral life that is not constituted by legalistic moralities. Soul freedom is *not* confessionalism.[5]

This cultural heritage has worked against development of a strong, enduring, cohesive, and monolithic American Baptist denomination and identity. If preservation of individual and local freedom is their greatest strength, "defining appropriate responsibility by which they can live and work together" is their greatest challenge:

> Baptists are more easily defined by their grand visions and their individual, personal beliefs than they are by their intermediate institutions, programs, and priorities. Baptists find it hard to maintain that balance. Baptists have always found it hard to maintain balance. (Goodwin 1997, xvii).

As a result of their unique cultural heritage, Baptist history is riddled with divisions of various sorts.[6] One of the more marked divisions is known as the fundamentalist-modernist controversy. On the one hand, Baptists have promoted increased education as an important component in becoming responsible citizens. However, Baptists have been concerned that too much education might liberalize the denomination to the extent that Baptists lose their identity *and* forget their fundamental moorings (Torbet 1969). As society greatly increased in complexity during the modern era, this concern over the liberalizing effects of higher education reached a breaking point. While Baptists markedly advanced and strengthened their educational institutions, this significant growth was also torn by dissension over increasing national and international Baptist organization, threats to local autonomy, and distrust of the liberalizing influences of higher education.

After 1900, several seminaries were founded in an attempt to preserve an identity that promoted higher education with evangelical theological moorings (Torbet 1969). This changed the clergy pool from which local churches could draw. More conservative Baptist congregations could now encourage promising young preachers to obtain education in seminaries they trusted, and churches could draw from a pool of Baptist-trained clergy who were both educated and evangelical. By 1945, the number of clergy who had no college education was significantly reduced, and the new seminaries were beginning to provide alternative educational institutions for those seeking standard college and seminary training (Torbet 1969).

Nevertheless, the American Baptist tradition of combining institutional mistrust and local autonomy continues to result in Baptist churches having a comparatively large percentage of their clergy trained in non-Baptist schools. Since Baptist identity is problematic to begin with, this unusually large percentage of clergy trained in non-Baptist seminaries is considered a threat to "the maintenance of a strong denominational emphasis" (Torbet 1969, 449). Several more conservative seminaries have been made available in response to the demand of local churches, and it is hoped that the percentage of non-Baptist, seminary-trained clergy will decrease, subsequently reducing this additional "threat" to Baptist identity.

This tension between increased education and feared liberalization is but one example of how Baptist identity hangs in the balance between freedom and responsibility (Goodwin 1997). Many other areas of life and belief follow the same pattern.

NATURE OF THE STUDY

In mid-January of 2001, a twelve-page questionnaire and cover letter were mailed to a systematic sample of 1,498 American Baptist pastors who were selected from a commercially supplied list.[7] A second mailing and postcard reminder followed at three-to-four-week intervals, resulting in 530 returned surveys yielding a response rate of 35 percent. The response rate validity varied by region and state.

SOCIAL CHARACTERISTICS
OF AMERICAN BAPTIST CLERGY

In terms of social background, clergy in the American Baptist sample bear a strong resemblance to the traditional pastors in mainstream Protestant denominations. As seen in Table 2.1, they are predominantly male (93 percent) and Euro-American in ethnicity (93 percent).

Almost all (98 percent) are (or have been at one time) married, while only 14 percent have ever been divorced in a society where about half of all marriages are dissolved. Most are middle-aged or older; only 2 percent are younger than 35 years of age, while 38 percent are older than 55 years of age (mean age = 53 years).

Compared to past generations, American Baptist clergy today are well educated. Within the group, 97 percent are college graduates, 88 percent graduated from seminary, and 33 percent have received at least some post-graduate education. Among these seminary graduates, only 30 percent received their education at one or more of the evangelical American Baptist seminaries established since 1900, with 18 percent educated at the more established mainline American Baptist seminaries,

46 percent at other evangelical seminaries, and 7 percent at other main-line denominational seminaries. Thus, while a strong majority of American Baptist clergy may have received an evangelical theological education (a substantial move toward the goal cited by Torbet [1969]), less than half of those receiving such an education have pursued it at American Baptist institutions of any kind.

Table 2.1

Social Characteristics of American Baptist Clergy

	% of Clergy
Gender: Male	93%
Race: White	93%
Marital Status: Married, never divorced	79%
Education	
College Graduate	97%
Seminary Graduate	88%
Age	
Under 35 years of age	2%
Over 55 years of age	38%
Community Size	
Farm or small town	40%
Small or medium-sized cities	29%
Large cities	31%

This educational pattern may have other institutional consequences as well. For example, it may account in part for the tenuousness of denominational ties. Half of the clergy in our sample have changed denominational affiliation at least once, and 17 percent at least twice. Slightly more than half (56 percent) do not feel the denomination should be an important factor in selecting a local church.

Pastors in the sample tend to serve in relatively small churches located in small towns and rural areas. Median adult church membership as estimated by the clergy is 130, while the median estimate of attendance at Sunday worship is 100. Only 40 percent of the churches served are in urban areas of 50,000 or more, where 75 percent of all Americans live. The median number of years the responding pastors have been in the ministry is twenty-one, suggesting a high degree of occupational stability. On the other hand, they would also seem to be fairly mobile, having served their present congregations a median of five years.

In terms of demographic characteristics such as age, gender, ethnicity, and residence, the American Baptist clergy respondents are concentrated in categories that are traditionally more socially and politically conservative. This demographic profile may provide a partial explanation of other conservative tendencies discussed below.

THEOLOGICAL POSITIONS HELD
BY AMERICAN BAPTIST CLERGY

It is apparent from Table 2.2 that American Baptist clergy strongly affirm the classic creeds of orthodox Christianity. Strong majorities of the respondents adhere to four basic tenets—Jesus' second coming, his uniqueness as mediator, the virgin birth, and the literal existence of the devil—at levels ranging from 86 to 91 percent. Beliefs regarding biblical inerrancy and the existence of Adam and Eve received a significantly lower level of support, at 62 and 66 percent respectively. Although many twentieth-century conservatives have considered the latter two beliefs to be essential to orthodoxy, they have been among the first to be challenged by modern critical scholarship and seem to be less directly implied by early Christian creeds.

Table 2.2

Theological Views Held by American Baptist Clergy

	% Agreeing
Jesus will return to earth one day.	91%
Jesus was born of a virgin.	89%
The devil actually exists.	86%
There is no other way to salvation but through belief in Jesus Christ.	88%
Adam and Eve were real people.	66%
The Bible is the inerrant Word of God, both in matters of faith and in historical, geographical, and other secular matters.	62%
The church should put less emphasis on individual sanctification and more on transforming the social order.	13%

A comparison with clergy in other Protestant denominations studied in the late 1980s (Guth et al. 1997) suggests that American Baptists tend to be theological moderates. They are more orthodox than most other mainline denominations, where affirmation of these same tenets by clergy usually does not exceed 70 percent. On the other hand, their level of agreement does not reach that of the most conservative evangelical denominations (e.g., Assemblies of God and Southern Baptist), where agreement on the first four points in Table 2.2 tends to exceed 95 percent. Overall, affirmation levels seem very close to those of moderate evangelical denominations (e.g., Evangelical Covenant and Christian Reformed). Consistent with the views of clergy in most other denominations, only a small minority (13 percent) feel that the Church should give priority to social transformation over individual sanctification.[8]

POLITICAL ENGAGEMENT
OF AMERICAN BAPTIST CLERGY

American Baptist clergy, a largely conservative group, seem to vary widely in their approval of clerical activism, depending upon the nature of the activity. Overall responses to actions listed in Table 2.3 range from 96 percent who approve of taking a stand from the pulpit on a moral issue to only 42 percent who would agree that clergy may commit civil disobedience.

The relative degree of visibility of the activism seems to be one consideration: contributing money to a political organization receives more support (70 percent) than publicly supporting a candidate (43 percent), perhaps in part due to the potential reaction from members of one's congregation. Whether the minister acts as a private citizen or brings politics into the church may also matter. Participating in a protest march, despite its somewhat unconventional character, is slightly more approved (62 percent) than forming an action group in the church (55 percent). The low overall approval for civil disobedience, even for a worthy cause, probably reflects norms concerning what is appropriate for clergy as community role models.[9]

Table 2.3

Political Norms of American Baptist Clergy

	% Approving
Take a stand while preaching on some moral issue	96%
While preaching, take a stand on some political issue	58%
Publicly (not preaching) support a political candidate	43%
Contribute money to a candidate, party, or political-action committee	70%
Form an action group in one's church to accomplish a social or political goal	55%
Participate in a protest march	62%
Commit civil disobedience to protest some evil	42%

American Baptists have not been known for making denominational pronouncements on social and political issues. Table 2.4 suggests that this may be due in part to a general lack of consensus on such issues. Of the eight positions listed, overall agreement on seven varies between 40 and 60 percent. A denomination that emphasizes individualism, congregational autonomy, and democratic processes at higher levels of association would be hard pressed to give legitimacy to pronouncements at such low levels of overall agreement.[10]

Table 2.4

Policy Positions of American Baptist Clergy

	% Agreeing
The federal government should do more to solve social problems such as unemployment, poverty, and poor housing.	54%
Education policy should focus on improving public schools rather than on encouraging alternatives such as private and religious schools.	48%
Sex-education programs included in the curricula of public high schools should be abstinence based.	82%
We need government-sponsored national health insurance so that everyone can get adequate medical care.	44%
African Americans and other minorities may need special governmental help in order to achieve an equal place in America.	40%
We need a constitutional amendment prohibiting all abortions unless to save the mother's life, or in cases of rape or incest.	55%
Homosexuals should have all the same rights and privileges as other American citizens.	60%
A lasting peace in the Middle East will require Israel to make greater concessions to the Palestinians.	40%

Given these differences on issues, it is not surprising that American Baptist clergy also vary widely in party identification and voting choices. Pastors as a whole (see Table 2.5) are twice as likely to identify themselves as Republicans (40 percent) rather than Democrats (20 percent).[11] Similarly, all clergy were twice as likely to have supported Bush over Gore in the 2000 presidential election.

Ninety-eight percent of all American Baptist clergy report having voted in the 2000 election, and this does not seem to vary across the theological spectrum. However, other forms of political activism indicate that participation varies widely, depending upon the activity (see Table 2.5). Pastors are most likely to engage in what might be called nonpartisan politics, which involves praying publicly about issues (61 percent) and for candidates (42 percent) as well as urging church members to vote (60 percent). This is predictable, given role expectations for clergy. Conventional political activity, which includes taking public stands on issues (28 percent) and contacting public officials (41 percent), tends to be the next most popular form of engagement. Least popular is the unconventional—and perhaps publicly stigmatized—politics of protest, civil disobedience, and church organization for political reasons, where participation rates are 10 percent or less. It is also interesting to note that, in general, approval rates for political activities as shown in Table 2.3 are substantially higher than actual performance rates documented in Table 2.5.[12]

Table 2.5

Political Activities of American Baptist Clergy in the Election of 2000

	% Reporting
Urged their congregation to register and vote	60%
Contacted a public official about some issue	41%
Prayed publicly for political candidates	42%
Took a stand from the pulpit on some political issue	28%
Prayed publicly about an issue	61%
Party Identification	
Strong Democrat	13%
Weak Democrat	7%
Independent, lean Democrat	12%
Independent	13%
Independent, lean Republican	15%
Weak Republican	19%
Strong Republican	21%
Vote Choice in the 2000 Election	
Al Gore	32%
George W. Bush	63%
Pat Buchanan	0%
Ralph Nader	2%
Other	*
Did not vote	2%

* = less than 1 percent

CONCLUSION

Throughout their history, American Baptists have nourished a tradition that stresses individual freedom and local congregational autonomy. These emphases have allowed for greater diversity, but at times have strained efforts to maintain denominational cohesion. Two historical occurrences that have exacerbated this tension are the fundamentalist-modernist controversy of the early twentieth century and the social movements of the latter part of the century (civil rights and the Christian Right movement).

American Baptists accommodated to the fundamentalist-modernist controversy by establishing evangelical seminaries and preserving a high degree of congregational autonomy in the selection of pastoral leadership. Today, about three-fourths of American Baptists who are seminary trained have received their education at evangelical institutions. Consequently, while there is a wide divergence in theological views among American Baptist pastors, orthodox beliefs tend to be predominant.

The contemporary controversy over social issues is rooted in theological differences. Theological conservatives strongly support the moral-reform agenda of the Christian Right, while this agenda is largely opposed by theological liberals. Conversely, the social-justice agenda of liberals receives support from only a minority of conservatives. In an age in which denominations are prone to make social pronouncements, there does not seem to be sufficient consensus on most issues to allow American Baptists to have a prophetic voice.

This controversy is reflected in the political arena, first of all by the fact that conservatives overwhelmingly vote Republican, liberals predominantly vote Democratic. Beyond voting, liberals are more politically active than conservatives except on nonpartisan political actions (e.g., public prayer for issues and candidates), which may be seen as a legitimate part of the pastoral role by Baptist clergy of all major theological persuasions. Recent studies of other denominations suggest that conservative clergy may be gradually abandoning their traditional reluctance regarding political involvement and moving toward a more aggressive agenda which opposes that of their liberal colleagues. Should American Baptist conservatives embrace such a strategy, it is inevitable that tensions between conservative and liberal factions will be exacerbated.

Whether American Baptists can accommodate their differences on social issues as amicably as they have on theology remains to be seen. To do so in a way that maintains denominational cohesion will be a major challenge to their founding principles. Much will depend upon how the relationship between individual freedom, local autonomy, and the primacy of mission plays itself out in the first part of the twentieth-first century.

Chapter 3

Disciples of Christ

Sue E. S. Crawford, Melissa M. Deckman, and Laura R. Olson

Clergy are paradigmatic of other elites who hold leadership positions in nongovernmental social institutions. The primary responsibility of such leaders is not political participation, yet their profession places them in a position where they may find politics relevant to the community-leadership role bestowed upon them by their status as organizational leaders. At the same time, though, clergy are unique in American society in that their views and pronouncements carry the force of moral suasion, as they hold a role representing a social institution (organized religion) that is explicitly entrusted with providing moral guidance.

The first studies of clergy involvement in politics (Hadden 1969; Quinley 1974; Stark et al. 1971) were designed to document and explore the radicalization of mainline Protestant clergy during the civil-rights movement. Taken together, these early works came to represent the benchmark of scholarship in the area of clergy and politics for two decades. Only recently has scholarly attention again turned to the political involvement of clergy. James Guth and colleagues (1997; see also Guth 1983, 1996, 2001; Guth et al. 1991; Penning and Smidt 2001) have amassed and analyzed the results of thousands of surveys exploring ministers and their political beliefs and practices. Paul Djupe and

Christopher Gilbert (2003) build upon this work by incorporating analysis of the interplay of community, denominational, and congregational influences on clergy choices. Other scholars (Cavendish 2001; Day 2001; Jelen 1993; Olson 2000) have undertaken pioneering ethnographic work by interviewing clergy and visiting their churches. In this chapter, we continue this endeavor as we analyze the political attitudes and activities embraced by the pastors of one mainline Protestant denomination: the Christian Church (Disciples of Christ).

HISTORICAL BACKGROUND

The Christian Church (Disciples of Christ) is a mainline Protestant denomination that claims approximately 825,000 members in the United States and Canada and supports 3,700 congregations. Its current covenant statement emphasizes the need for Disciples to be "an anti-racist/proreconciliation church" that works to:

> Strengthen relationships among all manifestations of the church, share mutually and more fully the stewardship of God's gifts of our life in Christ, encourage our growing diversity within our church family and community, [and] work with our many ecumenical and global partners to heal the brokenness of the body of Christ and the human community.[13]

The denomination was born in 1832 when two religious movements of the American frontier—the Christians, led by Barton Stone, and the Disciples of Christ, led by Thomas and Alexander Campbell—merged. This union set the tone for the denomination's longstanding emphasis on repairing rifts within Christianity and emphasizing the unity of all believers. An oft-repeated saying in Disciples circles is "In essentials, unity; in nonessentials, liberty; in all things, charity." This theological principle is buttressed by themes that emerge from the denomination's social history. The Disciples emerged out of the Restoration Movement in American religion. Two of the leaders of this movement were Disciples founders Barton Stone and Thomas Campbell, Presbyterian ministers who protested against practices in the Presbyterian Church that emphasized denominational exclusiveness and adherence to creed.[14] As such, the Disciples honor no creed except faith in Jesus Christ as Lord and Savior.

The core theme of Disciples theology is acceptance of diversity. Disciples stress that they have "no creed but Christ," and they embrace elements of the diverse traditions of Presbyterians, Baptists, Methodists, and Roman Catholics. The Disciples' theological essentials, which differ to some extent from those of other mainline Protestant traditions, include the importance of accepting Jesus Christ as one's personal Lord and Savior. Disciples share much with Baptist traditions in this emphasis: the denomination practices adult baptism by immersion and often offers an altar call at the end of worship services, when those who have not accepted Christ as their personal Savior are invited to do so. The denominational mission statement also sounds an evangelical theme: "To be and to share the Good News of Jesus Christ, witnessing, loving and serving from our doorsteps 'to the ends of the earth'." Thus, it would be very possible for an evangelical (although not a fundamentalist) to feel theologically at home in a Disciples church.

The Disciples of Christ also share commonalities with some other religious traditions. They are similar to the Roman Catholics in that they place a very strong emphasis upon Holy Communion. Every Disciples worship service centers on the communion service, which "celebrates and makes real Jesus' sacrifice of self-giving love as the presence of God's own love and grace" for believers. In fact, the denominational symbol, a red chalice bearing a St. Andrew's cross, depicts this emphasis on communion (as well as the Scottish and Presbyterian roots of the denomination). Like their Presbyterian cousins, Disciples churches call their own pastors, and like the United Church of Christ, there is an emphasis on local congregational governance. The Disciples also resemble a wide range of Protestant traditions with their emphasis on the ministry of the laity.

For the Disciples of Christ, affirmation of unity through diversity does not mean ignoring the needs of other people in society. Disciples stress that their "covenant of love" with God means that they are "one with the whole people of God." This emphasis on unity smoothes the way for a social theology that is consistent with the 1920s social-gospel approach (Niebuhr 1951) that is still relevant in much of mainline Protestantism, which stresses the need to empathize with the poor because they (even those who are not Christian) are part of the whole people of God. Thomas Campbell's assertion of the gospel as the core ethical standard, as opposed to literalism (Williams 1991b), provides a further basis for a social theology that enunciates care for the poor. Jesus' actions are seen as illustrations to stress the importance of caring for the weak and oppressed.

NATURE OF THE STUDY

Using the Disciples of Christ 2000 Yearbook Directory that contained the most recent listing of the denomination's ministers, a stratified, random sample of 1,000 Disciples clergy was drawn from those who serve as pastors (or associate pastors) in recognized congregations.[15] The first mailing of questionnaires was sent shortly after the general election in November 2000. Following a second wave of mailings, we received 524 usable responses, for a response rate of 52 percent.

SOCIAL CHARACTERISTICS
OF DISCIPLES OF CHRIST CLERGY

As can be seen from Table 3.1, the responses received from Disciples clergy include a fairly high percentage of women pastors (23 percent), which is not surprising since the denomination was one of the first Protestant traditions to ordain women, beginning to do so in the late nineteenth century (Chaves 1997). Disciples ministers are predominantly white (93 percent), and an overwhelming majority (86 percent) are married, with approximately two-thirds (65 percent) reporting being currently married and never divorced. The mean age of the clergy surveyed is fifty-one. On average, these clergy have spent twenty-one years in the ministry and seven years with their current congregation. Geographi-cally, those surveyed were concentrated in the Midwest, especially Indiana and Missouri, which has been the base of the denomination since its early days.

The Disciples clergy are well educated, with 95 percent reporting that they hold at least a college degree, 89 percent having graduated from seminary, and more than one-third indicating that they possess a postgraduate degree such as a D.Min. or a Th.D. A little more than half the ministers (51 percent) attended non-Disciples seminaries: although the Disciples clergy are quite uniform in the level of education attained, they obtained their seminary education from diverse sources. However, none of the seminaries listed by ten or more pastors fell outside of the list of Disciples seminaries or other prestigious interdenominational seminaries, except for fourteen clergy who listed Claremont School of Theology, an institution associated with the United Methodist Church.

Table 3.1

Social Characteristics of Disciples of Christ Clergy

	% of Clergy
Gender: Male	77%
Race: White	93%
Marital Status: Married, never divorced	65%
Education	
College Graduate	95%
Seminary Graduate	89%
Age	
Under 35 years of age	6%
Over 55 years of age	28%
Community Size	
Farm or small town	35%
Small or medium-sized cities	28%
Large cities	37%

THEOLOGICAL POSITIONS HELD
BY DISCIPLES OF CHRIST CLERGY

In light of the openness of Disciples theology, it is unclear whether Disciples clergy are likely to answer specific theological questions in ways that will reveal the existence of certain identifiable core beliefs or the prevalence of theological pluralism more generally.

Table 3.2 reveals the stands taken by Disciples clergy in response to seven key theological questions. Only two statements produced "agreement" among 75 percent or more of the clergy surveyed, as less than one-quarter of the ministers (24 percent) assert that Adam and Eve were real people, while only about one-fifth (21 percent) believe the Bible to be the inerrant Word of God. We would expect to find few Disciples clergy agreeing with this statement, since the denomination does not embrace theological conservatism. At the same time, it is noteworthy that in both cases at least one in five Disciples ministers took a theologically conservative view, illustrating the church's diversity of beliefs. While the Disciples of Christ is not a conservative denomination per se, theologically conservative clergy as well as theologically liberal pastors work within the church.

Table 3.2

Theological Views Held by Disciples of Christ Clergy

	% Agreeing
Jesus will return to earth one day.	62%
Jesus was born of a virgin.	53%
The devil actually exists.	47%
There is no other way to salvation but through belief in Jesus Christ.	42%
Adam and Eve were real people.	24%
The Bible is the inerrant Word of God, both in matters of faith and in historical, geographical, and other secular matters.	21%
The church should put less emphasis on individual sanctification and more on transforming the social order.	33%

Further evidence of the theological pluralism inherent among Disciples clergy appears when respondents are asked whether the church should put less emphasis on individual sanctification and more on transforming the social order. One-third of the ministers surveyed agreed with this statement, which seems surprisingly low. This declaration is a rough measure of the concept of "social theology" (Guth et al. 1997), which taps the general orientation of clergy toward the traditional rationalist-fundamentalist split within Protestantism. Conventional wisdom would suggest that a majority of mainline clergy would agree that the church ought to emphasize transforming the social order, in light of mainline Protestantism's longstanding affinity for the social-justice mission (Niebuhr 1951; Wuthnow and Evans 2002). Yet a high percentage of Disciples clergy demonstrate a reluctance to weaken the importance of individual sanctification. Individual sanctification remains a key priority for them (and for other mainline clergy) despite more liberal views of the Bible.

Finally, Disciples clergy are split over three additional theological matters. Approximately half believe that Jesus was born of a virgin (53 percent) and that the devil actually exists (47 percent). Both issues separate theological conservatives and liberals, revealing more diversity within the Disciples of Christ than might be expected. Slightly fewer pastors agree that there is no way to salvation but through belief in Jesus Christ, which would be considered a standard response for an evangelical Protestant who believes that one must accept Christ as personal Savior. The denomination proclaims "no creed but Christ," and accepting Christ is a prerequisite for joining a Disciples congregation. Given this basic tenet, one would expect widespread agreement about the need to accept Christ among Disciples clergy. Yet the survey demonstrates no such unanimity. In fact, the percentage of Disciples pastors who agree to this statement is lower than that for colleagues in the United Methodist Church and the Evangelical Lutheran Church of America (see chapters 7 and 4 respectively).

Disciples of Christ belief statements show the tension the denomination attempts to hold between traditional beliefs and modern pluralism. The proclamations note that belief in Christ is essential for membership, baptism, and participation in communion, yet the statements also affirm that all persons are God's children and that Jesus offers saving grace to all. One must accept Christ to be a Disciple, but the doctrinal beliefs leave open the possibility that one may be recognized by God and receive saving grace in other ways.[16]

POLITICAL ENGAGEMENT
OF DISCIPLES OF CHRIST CLERGY

The theological diversity of Disciples clergy is consistent with the denomination's refusal to proclaim a specific written creed. In order to address how the religious variances translate into the realm of politics, we analyzed Disciples clergy in terms of three sets of questions related to political beliefs and practices. First, respondents were asked to rate the acceptability of various political activities by clergy. Second, their attitudes toward a series of charged policy issues were assessed and, finally, we examined the extent to which the survey participants undertook five specific political actions, along with their partisan identification and presidential vote choice in the 2000 general election.

Table 3.3

Political Norms of Disciples of Christ Clergy

	% Approving
Take a stand while preaching on some moral issue	87%
While preaching, take a stand on some political issue	44%
Publicly (not preaching) support a political candidate	48%
Contribute money to a candidate, party, or political-action committee	73%
Form an action group in one's church to accomplish a social or political goal	59%
Participate in a protest march	72%
Commit civil disobedience to protest some evil	55%

Table 3.3 shows the approval level expressed by Disciples ministers on seven specific types of potential political action. Clearly, differences of opinion exist within their ranks. On some matters, such as taking a stand on a moral issue while preaching, there is widespread agreement (87 percent approve), which is consistent with the Disciples' denominational commitment to preaching publicly about social justice and the need to fight against racism. It also runs parallel to the more generalized notion of free speech, which is a logical counterpart to the Disciples' tolerance of theological diversity. In contrast, fewer than half of the ministers believe it is acceptable to take a stand on a *political* (as opposed to a *moral*) issue while preaching.

Nearly three-quarters of the pastors approve of contributing money to a candidate, party, or political-action committee (73 percent). A nearly identical percentage (72 percent) approves of participating in a protest march, but only a bare majority (55 percent) endorses civil disobedience. These kinds of activities are significantly different: contributing money is a conventional means of participation in which ministers can take part as private citizens, whereas the latter two are highly public and unconventional tactics. It is reasonable to conclude that the clergy's approval of financial contributions flows from the right of each pastor to live his or her own life as a private citizen. Separately, the denomination's commitment to fighting injustice and racism may well be fueling their approval of public protest.

When one shifts to an examination of the political issues shown in Table 3.4, substantially more agreement is demonstrated among Disciples clergy on political than on theological matters. They reflect a great deal of tolerance and concern about individual rights, with 79 percent affirming the need for equal rights for homosexuals and 61 percent favoring affirmative action. (The latter is a substantial endorsement, in light of the growing disfavor with affirmative action among the American public at large.) Three-quarters of the pastors support public schools over religious alternatives, and 69 percent see a need for nationalized health care; both stances suggest a social-justice orientation consistent with the overall outward orientation of mainline Protestantism. Moreover, only 22 percent call for a constitutional amendment to stop abortion, which does not necessarily mean that the clergy are pro-choice, but does indicate (at a minimum) that many Disciples clergy are moderate on the issue. Nevertheless, Table 3.4 provides some evidence of a level of conservatism, or of political diversity, among Disciples ministers, since no policy position inspired more than 79 percent unanimity and more than half (58 percent) favored abstinence-based sex education in public high schools.

Table 3.4

Policy Positions of Disciples of Christ Clergy

	% Agreeing
The federal government should do more to solve social problems such as unemployment, poverty, and poor housing.	77%
Education policy should focus on improving public schools rather than encouraging alternatives such as private and religious schools.	75%
Sex-education programs included in the curricula of public high schools should be abstinence based.	58%
We need government-sponsored national health insurance so that everyone can get adequate medical care.	69%
African Americans and other minorities may need special governmental help in order to achieve an equal place in America.	61%
We need a constitutional amendment prohibiting all abortions unless to save the mother's life, or in cases of rape or incest.	22%
Homosexuals should have all the same rights and privileges as other American citizens.	79%
A lasting peace in the Middle East will require Israel to make greater concessions to the Palestinians.	57%

The data analyzed to this point indicate that a majority of Disciples clergy are political liberals. Table 3.5 summarizes the extent to which these ministers translated their political beliefs into action through involvement in the 2000 election campaigns. More than half of the ministers surveyed engaged in at least one political action *as a minister* during 2000. The most popular activity was urging church members to register and vote (57 percent), a noncontroversial path of involvement. Nearly as many clergy (54 percent) took a somewhat riskier step by praying publicly about an issue; only one in five ministers took a stand on an issue *from the pulpit*, despite evidence in Table 3.3 that nearly half approved of this activity in general. Preaching about issues from the pulpit can be fraught with danger for clergy, who are also charged with keeping members in the pews and money in the coffers during trying times for mainline Protestantism: ministers do not want to alienate laypeople from their congregations. Thirty percent of the clergy reported praying publicly for political candidates, though most ministers who pray publicly for candidates do so in a generic fashion rather than seeking God's blessing on one particular individual or political party.

Table 3.5

Political Activities of Disciples of Christ Clergy in the Election of 2000

	% Reporting
Urged their congregation to register and vote	57%
Contacted a public official about some issue	33%
Prayed publicly for political candidates	30%
Took a stand from the pulpit on some political issue	20%
Prayed publicly about an issue	54%
Party Identification	
Strong Democrat	38%
Weak Democrat	13%
Independent, lean Democrat	14%
Independent	8%
Independent, lean Republican	9%
Weak Republican	6%
Strong Republican	12%
Vote Choice in the 2000 Election	
Al Gore	64%
George W. Bush	29%
Pat Buchanan	*
Ralph Nader	4%
Other	*
Did not vote	3%

* = less than 1 percent

Finally, Table 3.5 reveals what most observers would have predicted: nearly two-thirds of the Disciples ministers report some affinity for the Democratic Party (65 percent), and roughly the same number (64 percent) cast their presidential votes for the Democrat candidate, Al Gore, in the election of 2000. Another 4 percent supported Ralph Nader. Clearly these data represent a solid level of support among Disciples clergy for Democrats and liberal causes. At the same time, a sizable minority (29 percent) voted for George W. Bush, and 27 percent identify to some degree with the Republican Party (12 percent report that they are strong Republicans). Political diversity clearly exists within the ranks of Disciples clergy. Yet, the level of political diversity does not match the higher level of *theological* diversity among these clergy. There are more theologically conservative Disciples clergy than there are politically conservative Disciples clergy. This suggests that a small core of Disciples ministers simultaneously hold conservative theological views and liberal political views. In fact, analysis of the survey data reveals that about 12 percent consider themselves politically liberal but also exhibit theological conservatism by agreeing that Jesus Christ is the only way to salvation.

The majoritarian voting processes by which official denominational political statements are set may reinforce limited political diversity among Disciples, whereas the strong noncreedal tradition may continue to sustain theological diversity. A review of recent General Assembly political statements by the Disciples of Christ reveals a strong liberal bent. So, while a theologically conservative pastor may feel affirmed because of the noncreedal traditions of the denomination, a politically conservative pastor would no doubt feel little support for his or her political views. Evidence of the possible demobilizing effects of this political disconnect shows up in analysis, revealing that politically conservative Disciples clergy appear less interested in politics and less likely to desire more political engagement for themselves or the denomination.

The fact that the church stresses freedom of belief combined with consistently liberal political statements implies that mobilizing conservative political action within the denomination would be particularly difficult. Noncreedal freedom of belief means that one does not have to fight for politically conservative denominational statements in order to be a faithful member of the denomination nor to continue to preach a faithful message. Meanwhile, efforts to get conservative political statements passed would seem unlikely given the strong hold that politically liberal views have among a majority of clergy in the denomination. However, this political disconnect may make conservative clergy more open to personal electoral mobilization by Republican elites and pro-life and "family values" groups who tap into political interests that do not match denominational emphases. A recent study found some evidence of this dynamic for politically conservative clergy in other mainline Protestant denominations (Djupe and Gilbert 2003). Analysis of electoral participation by Disciples clergy in the 2000 election shows no evidence that this has happened yet. Politically conservative clergy were not more mobilized than liberal clergy to campaign or to give money in the 2000 election cycle.

A closer look at the politically conservative clergy reveals that they are nearly all male (over 90 percent) and are relatively unlikely to work in large urban settings. Although one might guess that influxes of more women and more urban ministries would mean a trend toward enhanced political liberalism, no significant relationship exists between political liberalism and years in the ministry. Newer Disciples clergy are neither significantly more liberal nor significantly more conservative than Disciples who have been in the pulpit longer.

CONCLUSION

Pastors of different theological and political orientations coexist within the Christian Church (Disciples of Christ) beacause of its history of openness. The denomination retains the distinctive features of mainline Protestantism in its rejection of doctrinal orthodoxy, its emphasis on the image of Christ as a moral teacher, and its abiding concern for social justice. Yet it is more diverse than one might anticipate, playing host to an identifiable minority of theologically and politically conservative clergy. The Disciples of Christ is a denomination that weaves together theological and social threads from many other religious traditions, and it is therefore not surprising to find that its ministers do not espouse uniform views.

James Guth and colleagues acknowledge that the Disciples of Christ has had "a mixed experience with liberalism" (1997, 11). This potential for extremely different views within the church can be witnessed in two of the three members of the denomination elected to be president of the United States—Lyndon Johnson and Ronald Reagan—whose beliefs and policies were as divergent as their political affiliations.

The denomination has remained largely Midwestern and somewhat rural. Yet a significant number of Disciples clergy are educated at modernist seminaries. As such, "Since . . . 1968 . . . the Disciples have often exemplified advanced theological, social, and political liberalism" (Guth et al. 1997, 41). While conservative clergy are a small minority within the Disciples of Christ (Guth et al. 1997; see also Guth and Turner 1991), the evidence presented in this study reveals that a conservative minority is clearly present within the denomination—and should not be ignored. In this sense, the Disciples of Christ seemingly typifies today's Protestant denominations, revealing signs of the ideological split within and across denominations that Robert Wuthnow (1988) has identified as restructuring American religious life today.

Chapter 4

Evangelical Lutheran Church of America

Daniel Hofrenning, Janelle Sagness, and
L. DeAne Lagerquist

While many scholars have written about Lutheran theology, ethics, and church history, no social scientist since Lawrence Kersten (1970) has focused on the politics of either the Lutheran clergy or laity.[17] The Evangelical Lutheran Church of America (ELCA) is the largest Lutheran body in the United States. The denomination was forged in 1988, when three Lutheran bodies (the Lutheran Church in America, the American Lutheran Church, and the American Evangelical Lutheran Church) chose to merge their institutional resources. This merger resulted in a denomination that today is composed of 10,700 congregations; 17,670 clergy; 5,099,800 baptized members; and 2,460,500 communing and contributing members (Evangelical Lutheran Church of America).

While firmly ensconced among mainline Protestants, the distinctiveness of the ELCA tradition should not be underestimated. In fact, some observers have questioned the placement of the ELCA in the tradition of mainline Protestantism. In their earlier history, the predecessor churches of the ELCA had distinct immigrant identities and warily accepted some of the central tenets of modernist theology (particularly the historical criticism of biblical texts) that were hallmarks of mainline Protestantism. In fact, among mainline Protestants, the ELCA is the only denomination to describe itself as "evangelical." Though the ELCA Lutherans apply the term differently from its popular usage in the United States, their acceptance of the label distinguishes them from their sister denominations within mainline Protestantism. As a church founded on a radical, biblically-based challenge to medieval Catholicism, Lutherans profess the centrality of Scripture. Martin Luther's unique emphasis in this regard, *sola scriptura*, has endured in the contemporary church and distinguishes the ELCA from some mainline Protestant traditions that see the Bible in a less exalted place.

HISTORICAL BACKGROUND

The roots of the Evangelical Lutheran Church of America date back to the sixteenth century, when Martin Luther, an Augustinian monk, hoped to reform the Roman Catholic Church. His efforts resulted, however, in a dramatic break with the Catholics and the formation of a new church that was termed "Lutheran." His posting of the 95 Theses in 1517 marked the symbolic beginning of the Protestant Reformation and the formation of Lutheran churches. Initially, Luther directed his criticism at the practice of selling indulgences, a human method to pay sin's penalties. Always the reformer, he called the church to restore divine grace to its proper, central place in salvation as indicated by the slogan, "Faith alone; grace alone; Scripture alone." Luther's reading of Scripture, particularly the New Testament book of Romans, led him to proclaim that no human effort is sufficient to warrant salvation; rather, salvation comes only through God's gracious action. Faith alone—not indulgences or any human activity—is the sole requirement for salvation. In response to the pope's demand that Luther recant, Luther asserted that his conscience was captive to Scripture and made his famous confession: "Here I stand; I can do no otherwise. God help me. Amen!"

While he was a theological and ecclesiastical radical, Luther's politics are often termed conservative. He counseled obedience to temporal authorities in all but the most extreme cases. Disobedience to the state was justified only when the ruling authorities interfered with worship and the proclamation of the central gospel message. No doubt the most notorious expression of Luther's restraint was his negative response to the Peasants' Revolt. While initially expressing sympathy with the peasants' grievances, Luther subsequently concluded that the movement went too far. He urged the princes to subdue "the robbing, murdering hordes of peasants" in whatever way necessary (Kirshner 1972). For Luther, it seems that injustice was an insufficient cause for revolution; rebellion was justified only when the state interfered with the free exercise of religion. This reluctance to support the peasants' action reflected Luther's view that the proclamation of the gospel is the primary, ultimate value; politics is important, but secondary.

While the theological question of salvation was Luther's principle concern, he was also interested in worldly affairs. Luther argued that God's work of salvation takes place in two kingdoms: in the spiritual kingdom, humans receive the free gift of grace and salvation; in the temporal kingdom, humans work to order and sustain God's worldly creation. While the spiritual kingdom features the individual message of salvation, the temporal kingdom is the arena of politics and worldly affairs. Luther gave primacy to the spiritual kingdom, but he was attentive to the temporal kingdom. There, God's provision of daily bread and all that is needed for the life of believers and nonbelievers alike is carried out by human hands. Luther believed that nearly every earthly vocation is a mark of God and a means to care for God's creation.

Political leaders or rulers—no less than parents, shoemakers, and milkmaids—had a vocational obligation to carry out God's work in the temporal kingdom. Indeed, their authority came from God, even as did a priest's authority. While he rarely sought to overthrow or challenge the state, Luther sometimes lobbied rulers, arguing that the state should support public education and a community chest, while cautioning against the evils of usury. In the affairs of the state, Luther held that both believers and nonbelievers can carry out God's work of caring for creation. In the kingdom of temporal things, human reason—which is accessible to believer and nonbeliever alike—was necessary to sustain earthly communities. Even if he never stated it, the remark "Better to be ruled by a wise Turk than a stupid Christian" is consistent with his views.

Luther's willingness to continue an alliance between churchly and secular authority, in reduced scale, set him apart from more radical separatist groups such as Anabaptists. He shared this view with John Calvin, though the two movements developed the alliance in quite distinct ways. Calvin's Geneva and its Puritan descendents in New England moved further toward a theocracy than Luther's belief allowed. The Calvinists' covenantal theology fueled hopeful efforts to devise an earthly community directed by God's own rule. Evangelical Lutherans were less optimistic about both the church's capacity to discern God's will and the practical possibility of establishing God's rule on earth. While obedient to authority, they noted its failings and flaws and recognized that faithful people, when attentive to God's direction, often come to divergent views on political matters. This combination of skepticism and openness to personal conscience allowed Lutheranism to be adopted in a range of political situations, from German free cities to Scandinavian monarchies.

After Luther's death, the churches bearing his name moved through several phases of development. The initial dynamism of the reforming phase was followed by movements toward both orthodoxy and pietism. Seeking orthodoxy, church leaders attempted to make the reformer's often unruly theology more systematic. Responding to the perceived enervation of orthodoxy, pietism arose calling for warmer personal faith and deeper moral seriousness, which frequently resulted in works of charity and evangelism. Both of these currents flow within American Lutheranism, with pietism as the dominant stream in the colonial era and among nineteenth-century immigrants. Most Lutherans came to North America for economic or political, rather than religious, reasons. Each wave of immigrants was initially isolated from the surrounding American culture by language and by a tendency to be more concerned with the social needs of its own members than with larger political issues.

Lutheran avoidance of political activity was nourished by both an immigrant experience and a theological concern to divide salvation from earthly works properly.[18] During the American Revolution, for example, Lutherans determined their response to the war on an individual, not an ecclesiastical, basis. Historians conclude that Lutherans overwhelmingly supported the Patriot cause, but no Lutheran body took a corporate stance in favor of revolution. The Muhlenbergs, perhaps the leading Lutheran family in early America, were known for their support of the revolutionary cause. Peder Muhlenberg, son of the family patriarch, Henry Melchior Muhlenberg, once ended a sermon by removing his robe and revealing the uniform of a Virginia militiaman. He went on to become a general in the Continental army.

Similarly in the nineteenth century, Samuel Simon Schmucker was a leader in developing a distinct vision of American Lutheranism, helping to form ecclesiastical alliances and institutions. And, while Schmucker opposed slavery, his own church did not adopt his abolitionist views. Slavery was not a major issue among Lutherans, despite the location of a seminary in Gettysburg and the (Lutheran) Franckean Synod's abolitionist position. More than slavery, temperance was a topic of debate among Lutherans. Some, like Andrew Volstead, supported the cause and legislation; others, often Germans, opposed both. As individual citizens, German Lutherans generally came to identify with the Democratic Party, while Scandinavian Lutherans usually were Republicans.

Over time, the differences among Lutherans not only became more diluted, but their contact with other Americans increased. These factors all contributed to the Americanization of Lutheranism, moving its members and organizations out of ethnic enclaves and into the mainstream of American society. Beginning in the 1890s, Lutheran denominations in America reorganized in every generation. As a result, by the 1960s, three large bodies encompassed nearly all Lutherans. In broad strokes, they were: the liberal, more urban Lutheran Church in America; the pietist, more rural American Lutheran Church; and, the orthodox Lutheran Church–Missouri Synod. The first two denominations, along with the American Evangelical Lutheran Church, merged in 1988 to form the Evangelical Lutheran Church of America.

By the last third of the 1900s, both the Lutheran Church in America and the American Lutheran Church were urging individual members to be responsible citizens and offering them guidance through social-teaching statements. The ELCA has continued this practice, issuing statements on race, sexuality, economics, and numerous other social topics. These statements usually do not rigidly advocate a single position or action as the approved Lutheran stance. Rather, they offer instruction about the issue and point toward religious resources that might inform individual conscience. As was the case with Luther, the overriding principle is faithfulness to God rather than accomplishing God's reign; individual responsibility, more than corporate action, is the guiding principle. All members are urged to consider issues in light of biblical teaching and the church's doctrines, even as they make their own judgments.

The membership of the ELCA includes descendants of every immigrant Lutheran group as well as first-generation Lutherans. In addition to ethnicity, its diversity encompasses widely ranging opinions and practices regarding theology, piety, and worship styles, as well as political and social views. As a group, ELCA members are, nonetheless, largely middle-class, educated, and Euro-American. While the demographic similarities are striking, unresolved differences and internal variety account, in part, for opinions about the ELCA ranging from mainstream but moderate, all the way to being placed as a conservative denomination.

ELCA members can be arrayed along the entire political spectrum; for example, on the issue of abortion, membership opinions range from staunchly anti-abortion to adamantly pro-choice. On churchly matters ,a similar range of opinion exists, sometimes breaking out in sharp debate. However, among synodical and denominational leaders, as well as those officially involved in cooperative governmental-affairs programs, there is less variation. As with their mainline Protestant counterparts, these leaders hold more moderate or liberal views. The denomination is a member of the National Council of Churches and has established a lobbying office in Washington called the Lutheran Office of Governmental Affairs.

Despite some evidence of political activism, the most common belief is that Lutherans are quietistic. Many scholars charge that the Lutheran doctrine of the two kingdoms leads to political passivity (Troeltsch 1931; Niebuhr 1943; Wolin 1956). Some have even asserted that Lutheran theology was so apolitical that it led to a passive acceptance of Nazi Germany. While there is evidence to support the charge of quietism, there are also many instances of Lutheran activism. Dietrich Bonhoeffer, himself a Lutheran pastor in Germany, led a plot to murder Hitler. Some Lutheran churches, notably in Scandinavia, were part of the resistance to Nazism. Martin Luther, although he focused primarily on theological issues of the church, peppered his writings with exhortations on many political issues including usury, education, and care for the poor. With evidence of both passivity and activism, there are reasons to expect a uniquely Lutheran approach to politics; that is, that Lutheran clergy would likely continue to maintain the primacy of theology and the church while, at the same time, elements of the tradition should lead to political activism.

NATURE OF THE STUDY

Data for this study were obtained from responses to a questionnaire sent to a random sample of 1,492 Evangelical Lutheran Church of America pastors drawn from the ELCA clergy roster. Two waves of the survey were sent, as well as a postcard reminder. The first mailing was sent on February 20, 2001, and the second wave went out in mid-April. The two mailings produced 681 completed surveys for a response rate of 46 percent.

SOCIAL CHARACTERISTICS OF ELCA CLERGY

The most prominent characteristic of Evangelical Lutheran Church of America clergy is their high level of education, reflecting the Lutheran tradition's emphasis on biblical and theological studies. All their clergy are required to have a graduate degree, usually a master of divinity (M.Div.) or its equivalent. Most (two-thirds) of the surveyed ministers have attended a Lutheran seminary, most commonly Luther Seminary in St. Paul, Minnesota. Almost 30 percent completed postgraduate work for a D.Min., Th.D., or Ph.D., sometimes at secular universities.

ELCA clergy are overwhelmingly white, with less than 3 percent of the pastors being persons of color. In part, this lack of racial diversity is reflective of the denomination's origins among Scandinavian and German immigrants. Approximately 20 percent of the surveyed clergy are women, a high proportion in comparison to other Protestant churches. Three-quarters of the ministers are in their first marriage—14 percent have been divorced—and 80 percent of their spouses work outside the home.

Table 4.1

Social Characteristics of Evangelical Lutheran Church of America Clergy

	% of Clergy
Gender: Male	79%
Race: White	97%
Marital Status: Married, never divorced	75%
Education	
College Graduate	99%
Seminary Graduate	100%
Age	
Under 35 years of age	7%
Over 55 years of age	32%
Community Size	
Farm or small town	37%
Small or medium-sized cities	20%
Large cities	42%

The average ELCA pastor is fifty-one years old and has been ministering for twenty years. Half of the clergy are between the ages of forty and fifty-five; approximately one-third are older, and 14 percent are younger. Although most surveyed clergy are middle-aged (a finding consistent across mainline Protestant denominations), the ELCA has a slightly higher percentage of younger ministers than other mainline Protestant denominations.

ELCA clergy are quite mobile, as the mean years served in their present congregations is about four years. And although ELCA churches are concentrated in Pennsylvania and the Midwestern states, which are fairly rural, many of the responding ministers (42 percent) serve in metropolitan areas. A slightly smaller number of ELCA pastors (37 percent) work in rural and small town churches, with about 20 percent ministering within small and medium-sized cities. The size of their congregations varies greatly, from 25 to 4,500 adult members, with an average of 400. Weekly worship service attendance ranges from 4 to 2,200, averaging 180 parishioners.

THEOLOGICAL POSITIONS HELD BY ELCA CLERGY

Social scientists perceive a division between orthodox, traditionalist, and conservative clergy in one camp and modernist and liberal ministers in the other. Earlier studies by Hadden (1969) and Quinley (1974) have used this division, but more recently, Hunter (1991), Guth et. al. (1997), and Laymen (2001) have argued that the distinction extends to the mass public at large. The orthodox camp is decidedly literal in its approach to Scripture, and its members reject the pluralist ideas that there are several ways to salvation; indeed, only belief in Jesus Christ can save. Most churches in this tradition are deemed evangelical and/or theologically conservative. On the other side of the theological and political divide, modernists accept the historical-critical method of biblical criticism as a primary tenet of their theological identity. They reject the idea that biblical stories are literal renditions of historical acts, and they have a decidedly pluralistic approach to salvation, believing there are many ways to salvation (see Table 4.2).

The theological data show that Evangelical Lutheran Church of America pastors are at neither end of the famed orthodox-modernist divide on a consistent basis. ELCA ministers clearly identify with the modernist camp in some respects, but they draw from both traditions. More than four-fifths reject the idea that Adam and Eve were real people and that the Bible is the inerrant Word of God. However, large majorities of the clergy accept the orthodox notion that Jesus was born of a virgin and will return to earth some day. In addition, 70 percent conclude that the devil actually exists.

Table 4.2

Theological Views Held by Evangelical Lutheran Church of America Clergy

	% Agreeing
Jesus will return to earth one day.	86%
Jesus was born of a virgin.	72%
The devil actually exists.	70%
There is no other way to salvation but through belief in Jesus Christ.	63%
Adam and Eve were real people.	15%
The Bible is the inerrant Word of God, both in matters of faith and in historical, geographical, and other secular matters.	10%
The church should put less emphasis on individual sanctification and more on transforming the social order.	29%

The conservative theological tendencies of ELCA pastors are also revealed in their attitudes toward pluralism. Ten percent of responding ministers think that all great religions are equally good and true; 11 percent are unsure, and 79 percent disagree. Similarly, 63 percent of these pastors believe that the "only way to salvation [is] through belief in Jesus Christ." Only 23 percent of ELCA clergy disagree. These sentiments reveal attitudes not usually associated with mainline Protestant clergy. As with their more conservative and orthodox colleagues, ELCA pastors avoid theological relativism. Yet paradoxically, while they believe in the correctness of Christianity, they also believe (50 percent) that civil liberties are threatened by those imposing religion; only 30 percent disagree. This is an attitude more reflective of theological liberals, who accept a pluralism of belief and fear those who would impose their views. In part, the responding clergy appear to share their fears.

While the theological beliefs of ELCA ministers span the spectrum, their social theology is more consistently activist in nature. More than half see both social justice and liberation theology at the heart of the gospel (56 percent and 57 percent, respectively). Because the terms "social justice" and "liberation theology" are usually associated with left-ist politics, this is a surprising result given the conservative and moderate answers regarding pluralism and the status of the Bible. Without reference to ideology, only 10 percent think that "Christianity is clear about separating spiritual and secular realms," while 71 percent disagree with this statement. These data show that ELCA clergy do not have a theology that restrains their political activity; instead, they see politics as an integral part of faith.

Perhaps the views of human nature held by ELCA ministers help explain their mix of modernist and orthodox tendencies. Only 23 percent of the clergy believe that "human nature is basically good," corresponding to the Lutheran emphasis on sin. Lutherans see humans as sinners who are saved—not by anything they do—but only by the grace of God. This heavy emphasis on sin distinguishes Lutherans from some of their colleagues in mainline Protestantism and, in some ways, inclines them toward orthodox positions. Yet while they emphasize sin, they articulate a gospel message that can overcome evil. As redeemed sinners, Lutherans enter the political world. Yet because they view humanity as sinful, they enter with chastened expectations. While politics is important to maintaining God's creation, the theological message is more critical. Politics, for Lutherans, can be an important part of the Christian life, but politics is not salvation. True redemption comes only from beyond this world.

POLITICAL ENGAGEMENT OF ELCA CLERGY

Evangelical Lutheran Church of America ministers generally approve of clergy engagement in politics, but they do not approve of all activities. They vigorously affirm political action outside the congregational context, but are reticent about politics within their parishes. More than 80 percent of the surveyed pastors approve of the private, political activity of contributing money to a candidate, party, or political-action committee (see Table 4.3). Smaller percentages—but still a majority—of ELCA clergy support public-mobilizing political action such as protesting and committing civil disobedience. Agreement about appropriate political activities rebounds to 82 percent for taking a moral stand—not a political position—from the pulpit. The political norms of the ministers allow for pastoral involvement in political activity outside the church, but inside the church, only more indirect action is sanctioned.

Table 4.3

Political Norms of Evangelical Lutheran Church of America Clergy

	% Approving
Take a stand while preaching on some moral issue	82%
While preaching, take a stand on some political issue	38%
Publicly (not preaching) support a political candidate	44%
Contribute money to a candidate, party, or political-action committee	81%
Form an action group in one's church to accomplish a social or political goal	65%
Participate in a protest march	75%
Commit civil disobedience to protest some evil	57%

ELCA pastors avoid using their pulpit or ministerial office to provide political guidance to laity. Although 82 percent of clergy approve of preaching about a moral position from the pulpit, less than 40 percent believe it appropriate to take a stand on a political issue from the pulpit. Similarly, only 44 percent think that a pastor should publicly support a candidate. A majority of the ELCA respondents do not support pastoral political directives, despite broad clergy acceptance of engagement in politics. The clergy, then, believe that their position as religious authorities prevents them from providing political guidance to their laity.

When examining policy positions, ELCA clergy are consistently liberal. Nearly 80 percent of the ministers agree that the federal government should be more involved in the resolution of social problems (see Table 4.4). An even stronger majority asserts that homosexuals should receive equal rights, consistent with the liberal emphasis on civil rights. Support remains high, at approximately 70 percent, for focusing on improving public education and instituting national health insurance. Fifty-nine percent affirm that "African Americans and other minorities may need special governmental help in order to achieve an equal place in America." Furthermore, only one-fifth of ELCA clergy believe that abortion should be outlawed by a constitutional amendment, a position that is socially conservative. The only conservative policy position held by a majority (63 percent) of ELCA pastors is that high school sex-education programs should be abstinence based. Still, 37 percent of surveyed clergy disagree with the statement. In general then, the respondents clearly hold strongly liberal policy views.

Table 4.4

Policy Positions of Evangelical Lutheran Church of America Clergy

	% Agreeing
The federal government should do more to solve social problems such as unemployment, poverty, and poor housing.	79%
Education policy should focus on improving public schools rather than on encouraging alternatives such as private and religious schools.	70%
Sex-education programs included in the curricula of public high schools should be abstinence based.	63%
We need government-sponsored national health insurance so that everyone can get adequate medical care.	71%
African Americans and other minorities may need special governmental help in order to achieve an equal place in America.	59%
We need a constitutional amendment prohibiting all abortions unless to save the mother's life, or in cases of rape or incest.	20%
Homosexuals should have all the same rights and privileges as other American citizens.	85%
A lasting peace in the Middle East will require Israel to make greater concessions to the Palestinians.	70%

Given their liberal policy orientation, it should come as no surprise that the ELCA participants are strongly Democratic, especially in comparison with the general public (Burns et. al. 2000). Two-thirds of pastors identify themselves as Democrats (or as independents who are leaning Democratic), while only 50 percent of the broader electorate has a similar identification (see Table 4.5). In contrast, only 23 percent of ELCA ministers call themselves Republicans (or independents who are leaning Republican), while 38 percent of the general public identify with the Grand Old Party (GOP). (The remainder of the clergy, 11 percent, self-identified as true political independents.) ELCA pastors are Democratic not only in numbers, but in strength of identification: those who are Democrats tend to identify strongly with their party, while those claiming to be Republicans tend to hold a weaker tie to the GOP. Nearly half of the Democrats are strong Democrats, 13 percent are weak Democrats, and 24 percent are Independent, lean Democrat. Yet, the largest category (nearly half) of Republicans is Independent, lean Republican, and the smallest subsection—with approximately one-quarter of Republicans—is strongly Republican. The voting choices of ELCA clergy corroborate the party identification results: 67 percent voted for Al Gore, the Democratic candidate, and 26 percent chose

Republican George W. Bush. In addition, 5 percent of the Lutheran pastors selected Ralph Nader, the progressive Green Party candidate, while 2 percent did not vote. Party identification and 2000 vote choice both indicate that ELCA clergy are strongly Democratic.

Table 4.5

Political Activities of Evangelical Lutheran Church of America Clergy in the Election of 2000

	% Reporting
Urged their congregation to register and vote	50%
Contacted a public official about some issue	40%
Prayed publicly for political candidates	33%
Took a stand from the pulpit on some political issue	20%
Prayed publicly about an issue	56%
Party Identification	
Strong Democrat	29%
Weak Democrat	13%
Independent, lean Democrat	24%
Independent	11%
Independent, lean Republican	10%
Weak Republican	7%
Strong Republican	6%
Vote Choice in the 2000 Election	
Al Gore	67%
George W. Bush	26%
Pat Buchanan	*
Ralph Nader	5%
Other	*
Did not vote	2%

* = less than 1 percent

Despite their clear policy, party, and candidate preferences, the majority of ELCA clergy were not heavily engaged in political activity during 2000. Less than half—40 percent—acted in a private political manner by contacting a public official about some issue. Approximately half of ELCA pastors report having prayed publicly about an issue and urged their congregations to vote, activities that are usually nonpartisan and even nonprescriptive. Far fewer—20 percent—of ministers engaged in directive public action by taking a stand from the pulpit on a political issue. One-third of the respondents prayed publicly for political candidates, public action that is not necessarily prescriptive. Despite political norms among ELCA pastors who accept political activity (with the exception of public prescriptive action), they were not overwhelmingly politically active during election year 2000.

CONCLUSION

Evangelical Lutheran Church of America clergy have a distinctive place among mainline Protestants. Theologically, they can be termed modernist, but they disagree with some of the tenets of that movement. As with many modernists, they do not believe that the Bible is inerrant, yet they accept that Jesus was born of a virgin and that the devil actually exists. They reject the notion that most religions are equally valid, yet fear the intolerant behavior of some people of faith. Theologically, they can be termed moderate modernists.

Politically, ELCA clergy share the liberal orientation of many mainline Protestant colleagues. They overwhelmingly identify with the Democratic Party and voted two-to-one in favor of Al Gore in the 2000 presidential election. Five percent of them, five times the total of the general public, voted for Ralph Nader. Ideologically, most of these Lutheran pastors identify themselves as politically liberal. Examining their positions on a range of issues, one concludes that they favor a more active government role in the economy and in environmental protection.

While ELCA ministers are liberal politically, they resist politicizing their church. Survey participants strongly approve of political activity that takes place outside the church but are very reticent about politics within their parishes. They may make tangential reference to political issues from the pulpit; however, they rarely endorse particular positions or candidates. The pastors advocate for study groups but avoid actions in which the church must take a stand. In this sense, they can be viewed as descendants of the Lutheran tradition: Martin Luther was a theologian concerned with affairs of the church. His central question focused on what one must do to be saved. His answer: nothing. Believers, Luther said, were saved by the sheer grace of God; nothing they do can save them.

Politics, then, is cast in a distinctly second tier. It is important, but it has nothing to do with the central theological question of salvation. Luther himself spoke publicly on political issues, but only occasionally.

For Martin Luther, politics was important to maintain order and even to establish justice in God's creation. Yet proclaiming God's grace is the central task of the church. Hence, we can understand why Lutheran clergy avoid politicizing their churches. It is not that they are apolitical, as some critics have charged. They like politics and are very interested in candidates and issues. However, the central sphere of their churches is not the temporal kingdom. ELCA clergy may be active in politics in their private lives, but they will avoid partisan or prescriptive political activity in their churches. Should they lead their parishes to consider politics, it should be viewed as a secondary activity.

Chapter 5

Presbyterian Church (USA)

William (Beau) Weston

The Presbyterian Church (USA) has long been one of the most active denominations in the United States in the areas of politics and public life. Since the early 1700s, Presbyterians have played a major role in American religious, social, and political history. This engagement in social and political life stems from Reformed theology that arose largely out of the theological perspectives advanced by John Calvin, John Knox, and Ulrich Zwingli during the Reformation of the sixteenth century. This theology, which emphasizes the "Creation, Fall, Redemption" narrative, calls Christians not to withdraw from a fallen world, but to engage the culture of which they are a part in the knowledge that God is at work redeeming his fallen creation and that Christians can bring Christ's renewing influence to bear on public life.

Over the past several decades, different segments of the PCUSA have exhibited different theological and political tendencies. The members of the church have tended to be traditional both theologically and politically, while the ruling elders of the church, its lay leaders, generally have been even more traditional in their theological and political views. By contrast, the specialized clergy (those ordained ministers who do not serve in congregations but serve instead as teachers, chaplains, church bureaucrats, and the like) have been much more liberal in their theological and political views than either church members or the ruling elders.

This study examines those leaders between the laity and these specialized clergy—namely, those clergy of the PCUSA that serve as ministers within the life of Presbyterian congregations. Most of these pastors are centrists, loyal to the church and to the institutions of American society (Weston 2003). While the clergy in the church bureaucracy and in specialized ministries sometimes make headlines for liberal causes, PCUSA pastors take a less polarizing role in political action.

HISTORICAL BACKGROUND

The PCUSA is a large, national, mainline Protestant denomination that traces its roots back to John Calvin's church in Geneva. Historically, the denomination owes much to the Church of Scotland, especially the form of Scottish Presbyterianism brought to this country from Ulster in Ireland. The Presbyterian Church was one of the "big three" colonial denominations, along with the Congregational and Episcopal churches. That influential position, coupled with Scottish Presbyterianism's history as the established church of Scotland, gave Presbyterians in the United States an early and active role in shaping American political institutions and culture.

Presbyterian polity centers on the presbytery, a regional body composed of clergy (teaching elders) and an equal number of lay elders (ruling elders) chosen by the congregations. The presbyteries send commissioners (representatives) to synods and to a national general assembly. In these "higher judicatories," the principle of the equal representation of clergy and laity is maintained. All congregational pastors and specialized clergy are members of the presbytery, not of a local church. Clergy are entitled to a vote in presbytery, and all their official relations with the church come through the presbytery. Lay elders and regular church members, by contrast, are members through local congregations.

The denomination is governed by a written constitution. Modifying the constitution requires a vote of the general assembly, which must then be ratified by a majority of the presbyteries. The judicatories have a series of permanent judicial commissions arranged as a hierarchy of appeals courts. These courts review the constitutionality of actions of the judicatories.

The parallel between these structures and that of the federal government of the United States is not coincidental. Presbyterians have always been disproportionately represented among elected officials of the United States. The only clergyman to sign the Declaration of Independence, John Witherspoon, was a Presbyterian. To emphasize the continuing vitality of this example of Presbyterian ministers involved in political life, the new headquarters of the PCUSA in Louisville, Kentucky, was given the address "100 Witherspoon Street."

Theologically, Presbyterians have emphasized God's sovereignty over all aspects of creation. Human beings are stewards of all creation on behalf of the sovereign God. Presbyterians have interpreted this stewardship responsibility to include taking an active role in creating and administering the institutions that govern human societies. In common with other Protestants, Presbyterians have emphasized the "priesthood of all believers," which has led to a strong emphasis on Bible reading. However, extending beyond most other Protestant denominations, Presbyterians have also insisted that their clergy be able to read the Bible in its original languages. Putting these elements together, it is not surprising that the denomination has been especially concerned with education and was instrumental in creating common and public schools wherever the church has been planted. Even today, Presbyterians are disproportionately represented among public school teachers and supporters.

The Presbyterian Church has long had a conservative wing that emphasizes strict subscription to its constitutional doctrines and a liberal wing that is less insistent on doctrinal conformity and more interested in moral and ethical action (Weston 1997). This tension, when coupled with other issues, has led to a series of schisms. The most significant of these breaks separated northern and southern Presbyterians from the time of the Civil War until 1983, when the merger creating the current Presbyterian Church (USA) was completed.

In the twentieth century there were a number of conservative movements that broke off from the main body. In the 1930s, a segment of the denomination left the northern Presbyterian body as a result of the fundamentalist-modernist conflict and formed the Orthodox Presbyterian Church. And in the 1970s the Presbyterian Church in America was created by conservative elements withdrawing from the southern Presbyterian Church. With the departure of the more conservative elements from the southern Presbyterian church, the remaining southern Presbyterians (the Presbyterian Church in the U.S.) were then free to reunite with the northern Presbyterians (the United Presbyterian

Church in the U.S.A.), and they did so in 1983. As a consequence of these earlier departures of its most conservative elements, there exists no significant fundamentalist party within the denomination, as few biblical inerrantists, young-earth creationists, or rapture-ready premillennialists are to be found within its ranks.

Since the 1950s, women have been ordained to all offices in the PCUSA. However, for the past generation, the church has been, and continues to be, torn by a sustained controversy over ordaining practicing homosexuals, a conflict that reflects, in part, a competition between the liberal and conservative wings of the church for the "loyalist center" (Weston 1998). Most recently, this liberal-conservative controversy has turned on whether Jesus is the only way to salvation as well as on an older, more long-running, dispute related to the authority of Scripture. In fact, this conflict has grown so intense that a blue-ribbon denominational Task Force on the Peace, Unity, and Purity of the Church was created in 2001 and given a six-year mandate to resolve these issues.

Finally, it should be noted that, in common with most mainline denominations, the PCUSA has been losing membership among American Christians. The pattern began in the late 1960s and has continued to the present. Currently, the denomination's membership is just under 2.5 million, including about 20,000 clergy.

NATURE OF THE STUDY

As part of the Cooperative Clergy Study Project, clergy from the PCUSA were surveyed. The sample was drawn from the annual directory of clergy that is published by the PCUSA as part of the *Minutes of the General Assembly.* Of the approximately 20,000 ministers listed, about one-third are noted as retired. Within the active clergy group, about 8,700 are congregational pastors, while more than 4,000 are specialized (noncongregational) clergy.

A random sample of 1,000 congregational ministers was drawn from the 8,700 pastors listed in the directory. Those selected to be part of the sample were mailed a survey one week after the 2000 election. Those clergy who did not respond were then sent a second survey in the spring of 2001. Completed questionnaires were obtained from 406 pastors, for a response rate of approximately 41 percent. (An additional survey of specialized clergy is not included in the results reported here, but the results are available from the author via e-mail at weston@centre.edu.)

SOCIAL CHARACTERISTICS
OF PRESBYTERIAN CHURCH (USA) CLERGY

Overall, clergy of the Presbyterian Church (USA) tend to be largely male, overwhelmingly white, and highly educated. As shown in Table 5.1, nearly four out of five (78 percent) pastors surveyed are males, while only one out of twenty (5 percent) list themselves as non-Caucasian. Given its emphasis on educated clergy, the denomination requires, except in rare circumstances, that its candidates for ministry be college and seminary graduates. Therefore, it is hardly surprising that all of the pastors responding are college and seminary graduates. In fact, nearly half (46 percent) of the pastors surveyed indicated they had advanced seminary training beyond the normal requirement, and nearly two-thirds (64 percent) reported having received some advanced nonseminary training.

Table 5.1

Social Characteristics of Presbyterian Church (USA) Clergy

	% of Clergy
Gender: Male	78%
Race: White	95%
Marital Status: Married, never divorced	73%
Education	
College Graduate	99%
Seminary Graduate	99%
Age	
Under 35 years of age	3%
Over 55 years of age	30%
Community Size	
Farm or small town	37%
Small or medium-sized cities	28%
Large cities	35%

Overall, PCUSA clergy tend to be relatively advanced in age. Only a small percentage (3 percent) reported being below 35 years of age, while nearly one-third of the pastors (30 percent) indicated they were over 55 years of age. The vast majority (73 percent) stated they are still in their first marriage, though more than one in ten (12 percent) have experienced divorce.

Given the age of PCUSA clergy, they are, as a whole, quite experienced in terms of their ministry, with a mean time spent in the ministry of 19.5 years. On the other hand, they tend to be rather mobile in terms of their place of service, as the average reported length of time with their present congregation was eight years, with the median being six years.

Most PCUSA clergy serve congregations located outside major metropolitan centers. More than one-third (37 percent) reported that their churches were located in a rural or small-town setting, while another quarter (28 percent) indicated that they worked in a small- or medium-sized city. On the other hand, PCUSA pastors tend to serve relatively sizable congregations, as half of the pastors reported that their congregations had more than 250 members.

THEOLOGICAL POSITIONS HELD
BY PRESBYTERIAN CHURCH (USA) CLERGY

With the earlier departure of its more conservative elements, it is not surprising that Presbyterian Church (USA) pastors tend, as a group, to be somewhat liberal in their theological views. This relative liberalism can be seen in Table 5.2, which examines the theological positions expressed by PCUSA clergy. On the one hand, responding ministers tend to embrace some historic tenets of the Christian faith. For example, more than four in five (81 percent) indicated their belief that Jesus will return to earth again one day.

Table 5.2

Theological Views Held by Presbyterian Church (USA) Clergy

	% Agreeing
Jesus will return to earth one day.	81%
Jesus was born of a virgin.	66%
The devil actually exists.	59%
There is no other way to salvation but through belief in Jesus Christ.	57%
Adam and Eve were real people.	29%
The Bible is the inerrant Word of God, both in matters of faith and in historical, geographical, and other secular matters.	24%
The church should put less emphasis on individual sanctification and more on transforming the social order.	29%

There is far less adherence to certain other historic understandings. Only two out of three PCUSA clergy (66 percent) stated that they believe Jesus was born of a virgin, and less than three out of five (59 percent) reported belief in the actual existence of the devil. As noted earlier, one contemporary controversy within the denomination has turned on whether Jesus is the only way to salvation, and less than three out of five PCUSA clergy (57 percent) reported agreement with the statement that "there is no other way to salvation but through belief in Jesus Christ."

PCUSA clergy are neither biblical inerrantists nor biblical literalists. Less than one-quarter of the pastors surveyed reported agreement with the assertion that "the Bible is the inerrant Word of God," while only a little more than a quarter of the respondents agreed that Adam and Eve were real people. Finally, while responding clergy would not soft-peddle individual sanctification, a relatively sizable segment assert that "the church should put less emphasis on individual sanctification and more on transforming the social order."

This tendency toward more theologically liberal interpretations of the Christian faith is reflected, in part, in the ideological self-classification reported by PCUSA clergy. When asked to place themselves ideologically on a seven-point scale ranging from "extremely liberal" to "extremely conservative," these clergy tend to fall on the more liberal side of the mid-point of the ideological scale. Few pastors placed themselves at the ideological extremes (only 3 percent classified themselves as "extremely liberal," and 1 percent self-identified as "extremely conservative"). More than two-thirds placed themselves toward the middle of the spectrum (with 20 percent choosing the "moderate" mid-point option, and another 28 percent selecting "somewhat liberal" and another 20 percent marking the "somewhat conservative" category). Finally, 17 percent identified themselves as "very liberal," while 11 percent chose the "very conservative" category.

Every theological item in the survey was significantly correlated with the ideological scale, and always in the expected direction. The strongest correlation with ideological self-classification was with the statement that "All clergy positions should be open to practicing homosexuals," with a correlation of a negative .775 (that is, the more conservative, the less likely a pastor was to agree with the statement). The second theological position most highly correlated with ideological self-classification was: "There is no other way to salvation but through belief in Jesus Christ," which had a correlation of .699 (the more conservative, the more likely a pastor was to express agreement). As noted earlier, these two statements epitomize the most currently divisive issues within the denomination. While the standard demographic variables did confirm some corresponding trends with theological positions, all such correlations are far weaker than those between theological positions and ideology. Thus, the differences among Presbyterian pastors owe more to their convictions than to their sociological backgrounds.

POLITICAL ENGAGEMENT
OF PRESBYTERIAN CHURCH (USA) CLERGY

Presbyterian Church (USA) pastors are generally supportive of political action on the part of clergy. As can be seen in Table 5.3, when asked whether or not they approved of clergy undertaking a variety of political activities, a majority of PCUSA clergy tended to express approval. Of all the possible actions analyzed in the table, respondents were most prone to support taking a stand while preaching on some moral issue (91 percent expressing approval). However, they were far less likely to assert that clergy could appropriately take a stand on some political issue while preaching, though even in this instance a majority of the ministers (54 percent) surveyed expressed approval.

Table 5.3

Political Norms of Presbyterian Church (USA) Clergy

	% Approving
Take a stand while preaching on some moral issue	91%
While preaching, take a stand on some political issue	54%
Publicly (not preaching) support a political candidate	43%
Contribute money to a candidate, party, or political-action committee	77%
Form an action group in one's church to accomplish a social or political goal	63%
Participate in a protest march	75%
Commit civil disobedience to protest some evil	59%

When the focus shifts to more individual, campaign-related, activities, PCUSA clergy tend to favor those activities that are more private than public in nature. Those surveyed were strongly supportive of pastors contributing money to support a candidate or party (77 percent expressing approval). But they were far more hesitant to have ministers become public in their support for particular candidates, as only about two in five (43 percent) voiced approval for clergy to do so.

And, finally, PCUSA clergy are generally supportive of using in-church activities to address political concerns, as well as of engaging in protest and civil disobedience activities to address some moral wrong. Nearly two out of every three pastors surveyed (63 percent) indicate they approve of forming action groups in one's church to achieve some social or political goal. PCUSA ministers are also strongly supportive of protest and civil disobedience activities, as three out of four clergy (75 percent) voiced approval for pastors participating in protest activities and nearly three out of five (59 percent) express support for engagement in civil disobedience as a means to protest some evil they may seek to address.

Table 5.4

Policy Positions of Presbyterian Church (USA) Clergy

	% Agreeing
The federal government should do more to solve social problems such as unemployment, poverty, and poor housing.	71%
Education policy should focus on improving public schools rather than on encouraging alternatives such as private and religious schools.	62%
Sex-education programs included in the curricula of public high schools should be abstinence based.	66%
We need government-sponsored national health insurance so that everyone can get adequate medical care.	59%
African Americans and other minorities may need special governmental help in order to achieve an equal place in America.	59%
We need a constitutional amendment prohibiting all abortions unless to save the mother's life, or in cases of rape or incest.	30%
Homosexuals should have all the same rights and privileges as other American citizens.	76%
A lasting peace in the Middle East will require Israel to make greater concessions to the Palestinians.	61%

Not only do PCUSA pastors generally approve of clergy being engaged politically, they generally tend to favor state-based efforts to solve social problems, as can be seen in Table 5.4, which analyzes the policy preferences reported by these ministers. First of all, when asked whether or not they thought that "the federal government should do more to solve social problems" in terms of addressing poverty or providing better housing, the vast majority (71 percent) of the Presbyterian clergy surveyed reported agreement with the statement. This same preference for a more activist government was evident in their responses to health insurance, as nearly three out of five PCUSA pastors (59 percent) reported agreement with the statement that there was a need for "government-sponsored national health insurance so that everyone can get adequate medical care." Finally, the strong state orientation of PCUSA clergy is further evident when it comes to choosing between state involvement and the action of private, possibly even Christian, institutions; when asked if "education policy should focus on improving public schools rather than encouraging alternatives such as private and religious schools," more than three out of five of the clergy surveyed (62 percent) expressed agreement that the emphasis should be placed on improving public schools.

Second, PCUSA pastors tend to be supportive of governmental actions to protect or extend the rights of social groups generally thought to be socially, economically, or politically disadvantaged. More than three out of four respondents (76 percent) assert that "homosexuals should have all the same rights and privileges as other American citizens." In the same fashion, nearly three out of five ministers surveyed (59 percent) note their agreement with the belief that "African Americans and other minorities may need special government help" in order to achieve equality within the American setting. PCUSA pastors are hesitant to place limitations on the ability of women to obtain abortions, as less than one out of three voiced agreement (30 percent) that there was a need for a constitutional amendment prohibiting abortions except under exceptional circumstances. In fact, even the foreign-policy stance of PCUSA ministers in relationship to the conflict in the Middle East can be viewed in such a fashion, as more than three of five responding pastors (61 percent) believe that Israel will need to make greater concessions to the Palestinians before a lasting peace can be achieved in the region.

When the focus shifts from the policy positions of PCUSA clergy to their actual behavior during the course of the 2000 election, one finds, as shown in Table 5.5, that the activity levels reported tend to fall short of the levels of approval generally expressed for such activities. Certainly gaps between approval and actual behavior, by themselves, are not surprising. One's time and energy are limited, and while one may approve of certain activities, one may not necessarily have the time, energy, or perhaps even the opportunity to engage in those behaviors. Rather, what is somewhat surprising is that, while PCUSA pastors generally express higher levels of approval than other mainline Protestant ministers for various forms of clergy political activity, they nevertheless tend to exhibit lower levels of actual activism than most other mainline Protestant clergy within the specific behaviors examined.

Table 5.5

Political Activities of Presbyterian Church (USA) Clergy in the Election of 2000

	% Reporting
Urged their congregation to register and vote	46%
Contacted a public official about some issue	33%
Prayed publicly for political candidates	33%
Took a stand from the pulpit on some political issue	21%
Prayed publicly about an issue	55%
Party Identification	
Strong Democrat	27%
Weak Democrat	13%
Independent, lean Democrat	5%
Independent	9%
Independent, lean Republican	9%
Weak Republican	13%
Strong Republican	14%
Vote Choice in the 2000 Election	
Al Gore	52%
George W. Bush	42%
Pat Buchanan	*
Ralph Nader	4%
Other	*
Did not vote	2%

* = less than 1 percent

As seen in Table 5.5, PCUSA clergy are not prone to politicize their congregants. Slightly more than half (55 percent) reported that they had prayed publicly about an issue during the election year, and less than half (46 percent) had urged their congregation to register and vote in the 2000 election campaign. Only one-third (33 percent) prayed for candidates seeking public office, whether it be in terms of health, safety, or their seeking spiritual direction for thoughts and actions. And, while a majority of the ministers surveyed (54 percent) agreed that it is proper for a pastor to take a stand on a political issue from the pulpit, only one in five (21 percent) actually did so.

However, PCUSA pastors themselves were highly politicized, as nearly all of them (98 percent) voted in the 2000 election. Given their general inclination to an activist form of government, it is not surprising that they tilt toward the Democratic side in terms of partisan identifications. More than a quarter of PCUSA clergy (27 percent) expressed that they are strong Democrats—nearly double the percentage reporting to be strong Republicans (14 percent). Given this tilt toward the Democratic Party, it is hardly surprising, therefore, that PCUSA pastors noted having voted for Al Gore by a solid margin over George Bush (52 percent versus 42 percent, respectively, with 4 percent casting their ballots for Ralph Nader). This tilt toward the Democratic Party stands in contrast to the general Republican tendencies evident among most PCUSA laypeople (Weston 2001).

CONCLUSION

Presbyterian Church (USA) clergy tend, at the turn of the millennium, to be theological and political liberals. Theologically, they are less prone than other mainline Protestant pastors to express adherence to certain historic understandings of the Christian faith, including whether Jesus is the only way to salvation. Politically, PCUSA clergy are supportive of all kinds of political action, and the pastors lean toward a liberal, state-oriented approach to solving social problems. These characteristics, combined with the well-established historical Presbyterian commitment to organizing society, make any turn toward political quietism unlikely in the near future.

On the other hand, what may well happen is an increasing political mobilization on the part of the conservative wing of the church. Such a movement could challenge the entrenched liberal position within the PCUSA as the only way for the church to be involved in politics. Despite the fact that over the course of the past century, different conservative elements have left to form separate, conservative Presbyterian denominations (the Orthodox Presbyterian Church and the Presbyterian Church in America), the PCUSA continues to be divided between liberal and conservative wings that are trying to win over the moderate center of the church (Rogers 1995; Kirkpatrick and Hopper 1997; Haberer 2001; Weston 2003). This competition is part of a larger movement in which almost all mainline churches are being torn by left-right divisions. American religion seems to be restructuring itself along this new cleavage, cutting across the old divides that created the denominations now in existence (Wuthnow 1988; Hunter 1992). Only time will tell whether the PCUSA holds together under this restructuring and continues its political action in traditional ways.

Chapter 6

Reformed Church in America

Corwin E. Smidt

The Reformed Church in America (RCA) is the direct outgrowth of the immigration of Dutch colonists to the United States over a span of more than three hundred years. Despite its long history on American soil, the RCA remains relatively small, having long tied its outreach primarily to individuals of Dutch descent. Yet, in contrast to this ethnic distinctiveness, RCA clergy tend to fall in the moderate or middle range on religious orthodoxy indices when studied in relation to pastors in other denominations (Guth et al. 1997).

Theologically, the RCA stands in the Calvinistic tradition of the broader, historic Christian faith. Accordingly, it subscribes to three Calvinistic confessions (the Heidelberg Catechism, the Belgic Confession, and the Canons of Dort) and three longstanding ecumenical creeds of the Christian faith (the Apostles Creed, the Nicene Creed, and the Athanasian Creed).

Calvinistic doctrine is frequently summarized by the TULIP acronym: total depravity, unconditional election, limited atonement, irresistible grace, and perseverance of the saints (as outlined in the Canons of Dort). However, the theological theme that dominates the Reformed perspective is that of "Creation, Fall, Redemption." Reformed thinking emphasizes the goodness of creation (in that God created all

71

things good), but that all of creation (both culture and the natural world) has been corrupted by evil. As a result, the whole cosmos must be, and is in the process of being, redeemed through Jesus Christ. For Reformed people, all of life (including art, education, music, government, and so forth) belongs to God the Creator and is therefore "sacred" in that "the whole of it stands under the blessing, judgment, and redeeming purposes of God" (Plantinga 2002, xvi). Accordingly, from the Reformed perspective, Christians have a cultural mandate they must pursue: they are called to engage in the redeeming or transformational purposes of God, restoring and reclaiming that which is fallen and corrupted through the corrosive power of sin. This emphasis—that all of life is corrupted by sin and in need of redemption, including the political realm—moves members of the Reformed tradition into the political world.

HISTORICAL BACKGROUND

The Reformed Church in America is a denomination whose roots can be traced to the theological thought of John Calvin, in the manner found in Dutch society and the Dutch Reformed Church. With the establishment of the New World colony of New Amsterdam (New York City), the RCA's American roots go back to the establishment of a Dutch Reformed congregation in that city in 1628. Though the British eventually took control of the Dutch colony in 1664, the Dutch Reformed congregations were permitted to continue their existence; as a result, the RCA marked its 375th year of continual presence on American soil in 2003. Accordingly, the RCA can rightfully claim to be the oldest, continually present denomination within the United States.

Throughout history, a particular emphasis of the RCA has been on the importance of an educated clergy. In order to interpret the biblical text properly, mastery of Greek and Hebrew has been deemed necessary for proclamation of the Word from the pulpit. From the Reformed perspective, the mere possession of certain gifts for the ministry is insufficient for being an ordained pastor; these gifts must be supplemented with particular skills that are acquired through educational training.

Over the centuries, the RCA has transformed itself into a mainline *American* denomination. As historians of the RCA point out (e.g., Corwin 1894; Eenigenberg 1959; Brown 1928), this change occurred neither quickly nor easily. Throughout the nineteenth century, the denomination struggled to find its identity as members battled internally over issues related to church policy, style of worship, and Americanization in general (Japinga 1992). Waves of Dutch immigrants arriving in America during the nineteenth century increased the size of the denomination, but did little to reduce tension over issues of Americanization. In a notable symbolic gesture, however, the Dutch Reformed Church was officially renamed the Reformed Church in America in 1869, "signaling (perhaps prematurely) its transformation into an American denomination" (Guth et al. 1997, 33).

Today, the RCA claims 201,000 confirmed members in about 960 congregations throughout Canada and the United States. These are grouped into forty-six classes, which are organized into eight regional synods. Classes send delegates to the annual general synod, the governing body of the denomination; each individual class is is given a significant amount of power and independence, but all the classes are bound under a formal constitution. The RCA's membership is concentrated on the east coast of the United States (particularly New York and New Jersey) and in the Midwest (spanning from western Michigan through northern Illinois, Wisconsin, southern Minnesota, and Iowa to the eastern half of South Dakota); heavy concentrations are found in Arizona and California as well.

Studies of the RCA indicate marked differences between older, historic congregations found in the East and those in the Midwest and West in terms of religiosity, orthodoxy, and ethnicity. Churches outside the East exhibit higher levels of membership attendance, greater adherence to traditional norms of Christian orthodoxy, and are more concentrated among persons with Dutch ancestry (Luidens and Nemeth 1987). Over the years, these differences have produced considerable theological conflict within the denomination.

The RCA has a long history of cooperative efforts related to the mission, temperance, and antislavery campaigns of the nineteenth century, and it readily joined most twentieth-century ecumenical movements. The RCA was a charter member of the Federal Council of Churches, the National Council of Churches (NCC), and the World Council of Churches (WCC); and RCA executives have held leadership posts in both the NCC and the WCC.

Membership in such organizations has come, however, at the price of internal dissension over the perceived drift toward liberalism within the denomination (Luidens 1993). Many of the liberal policies and positions of other mainline churches have been officially adopted by the general synod of the RCA, despite sharp debate from conservatives. However, some of the more conservative pastors (about 20% of all RCA clergy) have joined the National Association of Evangelicals on their own. Moreover, the RCA also has a significant number of members who do not even identify themselves with the denomination, as their loyalties do not go beyond their local congregation (Meeter 1993).

Controversy and dissension are not, however, new to the RCA; throughout its history, the denomination has experienced theological conflict and diversity. The Reverend Theodorus Jacobus Frelinghuysen (1692–1747) was an early controversial figure in the RCA who settled in the Raritan Valley area of New Jersey in 1720 and quickly caused an uproar with his pietism, his "howling prayers," and his criticism of "dead orthodoxy." Frequently viewed as a leading figure in the First Great Awakening, there is some historical debate over the extent to which his preaching actually produced religious revival. Nevertheless, whether or not Frelinghuysen was successful as an evangelist, his influence contributed to an important strand of pietism that has been evident historically within the life of the RCA (Japinga 1992).

More contemporary RCA figures who have generated religious controversy within the denomination are the Rev. Norman Vincent Peale and the Rev. Robert Schuller. Peale, pastor of the Marble Collegiate Reformed Church in New York City, was the initial exponent of the "power of positive thinking," while Schuller, a disciple of Peale, is best known as a televangelist. Schuller's *Hour of Power* is carried on many television stations, and his Crystal Cathedral is the showcase of his ministry. This emphasis on "positive thinking" is viewed differently by different segments within the denomination. For some, it is a message that is foreign to the gospel and stands outside of, if not inconsistent with, the gospel message, while for others it is a tool by which nonbelievers may be drawn into the church.

NATURE OF THE STUDY

As part of a cooperative research effort to study the role of clergy in American politics generally and in the election of 2000 more specifically, pastors in the Reformed Church in America were sent a questionnaire composed of a common core of questions used across all of the denominations. The focus of the cooperative study was on pastors who serve their congregations, in part, by preaching from the pulpit with some regularity.

Given the small size of the RCA, all pastors within the denomination who preach from the pulpit with some regularity were initially sent the survey. Additionally, because the study focused on the role of clergy in American politics, RCA clergy serving churches outside the United States were removed from the sample. As a result, 683 surveys were mailed in mid-January of 2001, and a second wave of questionnaires was mailed in late February, 2001. In the end, a total of 372 completed surveys were returned, for a response rate of 55 percent.

SOCIAL CHARACTERISTICS OF RCA CLERGY

In many respects, pastors in the Reformed Church in America are fairly homogeneous in terms of their social characteristics. More than nine out of ten pastors are white (96 percent) and male (93 percent), with nearly six out of seven (85 percent) being married, having never been divorced or widowed. The age of the pastors ranged from twenty-seven to seventy-four years of age; 53 percent were fifty years of age or younger (mean age = 49.8 years).

Virtually all RCA pastors are seminary graduates, with 30 percent having done some postseminary work. Only four of the responding clergy reported having been ordained as a pastor in the RCA without completing seminary training (a rare, but permissible, provision that can be used under special circumstances).

Table 6.1

Social Characteristics of Reformed Church in America Clergy

	% of Clergy
Gender: Male	93%
Race: White	96%
Marital Status: Married, never divorced	85%
Education	
College Graduate	99%
Seminary Graduate	99%
Age	
Under 35 years of age	26%
Over 55 years of age	27%
Community Size	
Farm or small town	23%
Small or medium-sized cities	24%
Large cities	53%

The RCA pastors who returned the survey were drawn from both relatively new and experienced pastors alike. One-third (34 percent) of the clergy surveyed had served fourteen years or less in the ministry, while another one-third (34 percent) had worked as pastors for twenty-four years or more (mean = 20.1 years). RCA pastors appear to be fairly mobile: fully half of the respondents reported six years or less of service in their present congregations; one-fifth (21 percent) had been with their present congregation twelve years or more (mean = 8.4 years).

THEOLOGICAL POSITIONS HELD BY RCA CLERGY

Previous studies have revealed that the theological stances of Reformed Church in America clergy tend to fall in the middle of the spectrum—neither as liberal as clergy in many other mainline Protestant denominations nor as conservative as those in evangelical denominations (Guth et al. 1997). RCA clergy tend to hold rather orthodox positions on historical matters of the Christian faith but do not necessarily subscribe to positions of biblical inerrancy or adopt stances tied to premillennial dispensationalism, given the historic amillennial stance of the denomination in terms of eschatology.

As seen in Table 6.2, these general patterns continue to be evident among RCA clergy at the turn of the millennium. On questions related to the nature and ministry of Jesus, there is nearly unanimous agreement that Jesus will return to earth again one day (90 percent), that Jesus was born of a virgin (89 percent), and that salvation is obtained only through belief in Jesus Christ (84 percent). In addition, a high percentage of RCA clergy (86 percent) believe that the devil actually exists.

Table 6.2

Theological Views Held by Reformed Church in America Clergy

	% Agreeing
Jesus will return to earth one day.	90%
Jesus was born of a virgin.	89%
The devil actually exists.	86%
There is no other way to salvation but through belief in Jesus Christ.	84%
Adam and Eve were real people.	58%
The Bible is the inerrant Word of God, both in matters of faith and in historical, geographical, and other secular matters.	45%
The church should put less emphasis on individual sanctification and more on transforming the social order.	14%

However, when one shifts from the nature and ministry of Jesus to other issues, there tends to be less theological agreement among RCA clergy. Only a little more than half of the respondents (58 percent) report that they believe Adam and Eve were real people. Likewise, somewhat less than half of the surveyed clergy (45 percent) state they subscribe to the position of biblical inerrancy.

However, while the RCA is a mainline Protestant denomination, it is clear that its clergy today place much greater emphasis on working toward individual sanctification than they do on transformation of the social order. Only 14 percent of the RCA clergy surveyed agreed that "the church should put less emphasis on individual sanctification and more on transforming the social order," while over two-thirds (68 percent) disagreed with this assertion. Whether this stance results from some relative assessment (e.g., in terms of the social condition of contemporary American society generally or in terms of the current emphasis found within either the denomination specifically or the broader Christian church generally) or from some particular standard of theological emphasis, is not clear. Whatever the reason, RCA clergy clearly do not believe there should be less emphasis placed upon the need for individual sanctification.

POLITICAL ENGAGEMENT OF RCA CLERGY

For Reformed Church in America pastors, the engagement of clergy in politics is a controversial matter. Differences of opinion prevail with regard to both the kinds of political activity in which clergy should engage and the levels of clerical involvement within any approved activities.

In addition, there may be certain forms of political activity that are legal and rightful for citizens of the United States (e.g., voting) that are relatively private in nature and which are not deemed problematic for members of the clergy, while other forms of political activity, though lawful in nature, may be controversial given one's public role as a pastor.

Table 6.3 addresses the norms of political engagement in terms of the level to which RCA clergy approve of pastoral engagement in activity in and away from the pulpit. RCA pastors consider themselves to be ministers of God's Word, and one of their most important responsibilities in the Reformed tradition is the proclamation of the Word. In that role, it is necessary to exposit the meaning and implications of biblical passages and exhort one's congregants to heed and obey its instructions. And yet, as a minister of the Word, one is bound by the biblical text; as a result, one should not substitute personal opinion or viewpoint for the biblical truth.

Table 6.3

Political Norms of Reformed Church in America Clergy

	% Approving
Take a stand while preaching on some moral issue	92%
While preaching, take a stand on some political issue	46%
Publicly (not preaching) support a political candidate	45%
Contribute money to a candidate, party, or political-action committee	68%
Form an action group in one's church to accomplish a social or political goal	58%
Participate in a protest march	65%
Commit civil disobedience to protest some evil	43%

Given this Reformed understanding of the role of clergy, it is not surprising that almost all RCA clergy (92 percent) approve of pastors taking a stand on a moral issue while preaching from the pulpit. In fact, what might be viewed as unusual is that there is not unanimous agreement on the matter. Perhaps when answering the question, ministers had different scenarios in mind in which the moral issues addressed were tied (or not so closely tied) to the biblical text on which they were preaching.

On the other hand, there appears to be a greater difference of opinion among RCA clergy regarding when it is appropriate for pastors to take a stand on a political issue while preaching. Obviously, not all RCA clergy believe that moral issues necessarily (or perhaps even occasionally) constitute political issues. While almost all respondents approve of taking a stand while preaching on some moral issue, less than half (46 percent) hold the same opinion about addressing a political issue from the pulpit.

The approval expressed by RCA clergy for different forms of political activity appears to be related to whether: (a) the action falls within the domain of their legal rights as citizens, (b) the extent to which the action is relatively public in nature, and (c) the perceived appropriateness of a particular activity as related to the pulpit from which the Word is proclaimed. When it comes to engaging in political activity that is relatively invisible to others, the clergy demonstrate greater support for the activity. For example, a full two-thirds of RCA ministers (68 percent) approve of pastors contributing money to a candidate, a party, or a political-action committee (a rather private or invisible act). On the other hand, even when the pastor is off the pulpit and is no longer assuming the mantel of religious authority, there are concerns about clergy becoming too public in terms of their political inclinations; only 45 percent of RCA respondents approve of ministers publicly supporting a candidate (e.g., placing candidate signs in one's yard or wearing a pin in support of a candidate), even if one does so when not preaching the Word.

Consistent with historic patterns in mainline Protestant denominations (Guth et al. 1997), RCA clergy generally approve of ministers seeking to accomplish some social or political goal through the formation of an action group within the church (58 percent approving). Moreover, given the history of clergy engagement in social action, particularly related to the civil-rights movement, it is not surprising that most RCA pastors (68 percent) approve of ministers participating in protest marches, while nearly half (43 percent) believe that a minister may participate in civil disobedience as a means to protest a particular evil.

As one moves from the norms governing clergy political engagement to the specific positions that pastors adopt on major policy issues of the day, one finds RCA ministers tending to adopt rather moderate policy positions. Table 6.4 presents the responses given by RCA clergy to questions regarding current issues. Perhaps not surprisingly, most agree (80 percent) that sex-education programs included in public high school curricula should be based on the encouragement of sexual abstinence. However, such a stance cannot be viewed in terms of some political liberalism-conservatism dimension, because RCA ministers are far from being conservatives in their public-policy positions. For example, three-fifths of survey respondents (61 percent) agree that "the federal government should do more to solve social problems such as unemployment, poverty, and poor housing"—which is generally viewed to be a more liberal political stance.

On certain issues, RCA clergy appear to be fairly divided in terms of their policy stances. Basically half of responding pastors (51 percent) express agreement that there is a need for a constitutional amendment "prohibiting all abortions unless to save the mother's life, or in cases of rape or incest." Likewise, half of surveyed RCA ministers (48 percent) assert that there is a need for "government-sponsored national health insurance so that everyone can get adequate medical care." Forty-nine percent believe "African Americans and other minorities may need special governmental help in order to achieve an equal place" in American society, and half (49 percent) also state that "education policy should focus on improving public schools rather than encouraging alternatives."

Table 6.4

Policy Positions of Reformed Church in America Clergy

	% Agreeing
The federal government should do more to solve social problems such as unemployment, poverty, and poor housing.	61%
Education policy should focus on improving public schools rather than on encouraging alternatives such as private and religious schools.	49%
Sex-education programs included in the curricula of public high schools should be abstinence based.	80%
We need government-sponsored national health insurance so that everyone can get adequate medical care.	48%
African Americans and other minorities may need special governmental help in order to achieve an equal place in America.	49%
We need a constitutional amendment prohibiting all abortions unless to save the mother's life, or in cases of rape or incest.	51%
Homosexuals should have all the same rights and privileges as other American citizens.	65%
A lasting peace in the Middle East will require Israel to make greater concessions to the Palestinians.	62%

When assessing levels of support for certain groups that have experienced discrimination and/or suffering within contemporary political life, RCA clergy tend to be generally positive about extending the rights of those individuals. Nearly two-thirds of the pastors (65 percent) agree that "homosexuals should have all the same rights and privileges as other American citizens," and more than three out of five survey participants assert that "a lasting peace in the Middle East will require Israel to make greater concessions to the Palestinians."

While RCA clergy tend to express relatively moderate views on public policy, their partisan loyalties tend in the Republican direction. As seen from Table 6.5, the ministers were more likely to adopt Republican partisan identifications than Democratic leanings: 43 percent reported either strong or weak Republican identifications, compared to only 14 percent who listed strong or weak Democratic identifications. Given these patterns, it is not surprising that RCA clergy reported having supported George W. Bush over Al Gore in the presidential election of 2000 (64 percent to 29 percent respectively).

Table 6.5

Political Activities of Reformed Church in America Clergy in the Election of 2000

	% Reporting
Urged their congregation to register and vote	59%
Contacted a public official about some issue	40%
Prayed publicly for political candidates	51%
Took a stand from the pulpit on some political issue	27%
Prayed publicly about an issue	68%
Party Identification	
Strong Democrat	8%
Weak Democrat	6%
Independent, lean Democrat	17%
Independent	12%
Independent, lean Republican	14%
Weak Republican	22%
Strong Republican	21%
Vote Choice in the 2000 Election	
Al Gore	29%
George W. Bush	64%
Pat Buchanan	0%
Ralph Nader	3%
Other	*
Did not vote	4%

* = less than 1 percent

RCA pastors are relatively active in political endeavors; only 4 percent of the surveyed ministers reported not having voted in the 2000 election. Nearly two-thirds (65 percent) had urged their congregation to register and vote, half (47 percent) had contacted a public official about some issue, and nearly one-third (32 percent) had actually taken a stand on some political issue from the pulpit. In addition, they report having prayed publicly both for political candidates (41 percent) and for some political issue (27 percent).

CONCLUSION

The Reformed Church in America has a long history in the United States. Rooted in Dutch ancestry, it continues to retain an ethnic distinctiveness despite its efforts to break out of the past ethnic base.

Though relatively small, the RCA is a noteworthy denomination given its historic continuity on the American scene and its bridge across different theological divides.

The theological views of RCA clergy generally fall in the middle of the theological spectrum. Although the denomination is a member of the National Council of Churches, the theological positions of pastors in the RCA are not as liberal as many clergy in other mainline Protestant denominations. RCA pastors articulate rather orthodox positions on historic matters of the Christian faith, though not to the same extent as those clergy found in evangelical Protestant denominations.

Politically, the issue positions articulated by RCA clergy also tend to fall in the middle of the political spectrum, at least when examined in relation to the public-policy stances articulated overall by clergy examined in this volume. And, when questioned about political engagement, many pastors appeared to make a definitive distinction between public activity and more private actions. Still, overall, RCA ministers tend to express approval for political-action groups, government involvement in social issues, and the responsibility of clergy to speak out on moral issues—which tends slightly toward the more liberal end of the political spectrum, despite the group's Republican leanings. In conclusion, RCA pastors carry their historic belief about the Calvinist's responsibility to transform all of creation with them into the political arena, where they exhibit a relatively high level of commitment and activity in political endeavors.

Chapter 7

United Methodist Church

John C. Green

The United Methodist Church (UMC) is the largest mainline Protestant denomination and the third largest religious body in the United States. Of some two dozen churches within the Methodist-Pietist denominational family, it has the greatest number of members. All these churches originated in the Methodist revival begun by John Wesley in 1729, which found its fullest development in the United States, where Methodist congregations began to flourish at about the time of the American Revolution. Since that time, American Methodism has been transformed from a religious movement into a number of different institutional churches. Based on its history, size, diversity, and geographic dispersion, the UMC comes close to the status of a "national church" in the American religious landscape (Mead 1990c, 154).

Unlike members of other religious movements in American Protestantism, Methodists have never been adverse to engagement in civic and political affairs. This openness to civic engagement stems from Methodist belief and practice and results in all the major political divisions in the country often being found within the UMC. Dubbed the church of the "golden mean" and the "large standard deviation," Methodists are found across the entire political spectrum (Green and

Guth 1998), as illustrated by two of the UMC's most prominent daughters: U.S. senators Hillary Rodham Clinton (D-NY) and Elizabeth Hanford Dole (R-NC), the spouses of the 1996 Democratic and Republican presidential candidates, respectively.

HISTORICAL BACKGROUND

The United Methodist Church was founded in 1968 with the merger of two denominations, the Methodist Church and the Evangelical United Brethren. In turn, each of these bodies was the product of earlier mergers.[19] The Methodist Church was created in 1939 when the Methodist Episcopal Church, the Methodist Episcopal Church-South, and the Methodist Protestant Church became one denomination. The Evangelical United Brethren dated to 1946, when the Evangelical Church merged with the United Brethren in Christ. However, numerous other denominations in the Methodist family still remain separate, including the black Methodist churches (such as the African Methodist Episcopal, African Methodist Episcopal Zion, and Christian Methodist Episcopal) and Holiness churches (such as the Wesleyan Church, the Free Methodists, and the Salvation Army).

Methodism began in 1729 at Oxford University in Great Britain, where John Wesley, his brother Charles, and other students belonged to a group called the Holy Club, dedicated to rigorous religious observance. From this personal discipline came the term "methodist," originally a term of derision. Armed with "methods" of personal discipline and a commitment to holiness, the members of the Holy Club set out to evangelize the masses in Great Britain. A series of private experiences molded Wesley's approach to this task, including service as a missionary in colonial Georgia in 1736 and his famous "heart warming" conversion experience on Aldersgate Street in 1738. Shortly thereafter, Wesley and his associates launched a series of dramatic revivals to, in his words, "reform the nation and especially the church, and spread Scriptural holiness over the land" (UMC 2002d).

Wesley's intention was to reform the Church of England, not found a new church (Heitzenrater 1995), but the revivals quickly developed their own specialized structure and methodology: outdoor preaching, itinerant ministers, classes and bands, lay leaders, and annual conferences. The revival movement soon spread beyond Great Britain to Ireland and the British colonies in North America. This success led

Wesley to sanction new organizational departures. For example, after the American Revolution, Wesley appointed Thomas Coke and Francis Asbury as "superintendents" of the American Methodists. They organized the Methodist Episcopal Church in 1784 and adopted the title of "bishop." In short order, a new American denomination was born, independent of both England and the Church of England.

Methodism was successful in America because its beliefs and practices were well suited to the diverse and rapidly growing nation. It offered converts a "breathtaking message of individual freedom, autonomy, responsibility and achievement" (Hatch 1989, 177), and the Methodist circuit riders spread that message across the country during the Second Great Awakening in the first part of the nineteenth century. As a result, the Methodist Episcopal Church grew rapidly, and other Methodist denominations also developed. For example, in the early nineteenth century Jacob Albright, William Otterbein, and Martin Boehm organized churches among German immigrants based on Methodist principles that would eventually become part of the UMC. Black Methodists formed their own independent churches during this period as well. Organizational splits also occurred: the Methodist Protestant Church broke away in 1830, the Free Methodists left in 1860, and the most serious division occurred in 1844 over slavery, producing the Methodist Episcopal Church-South and the Methodist Episcopal Church (in the North). Various other religious movements continued to agitate Methodism, the most notable of which was the Holiness movement of the late nineteenth century, which produced another new set of denominations. In fact, the tendency to adapt ideas from new movements continues to survive in attenuated form within Methodism to this day.

By the beginning of the twentieth century, Methodists had fully developed a variety of denominations, with extensive agencies and a wide range of allied institutions, from colleges to hospitals. The Methodist Episcopal Church, the largest such denomination, had become central to the cultural life of the nation and to the emerging religious tradition of mainline Protestantism. As part of this structural development, Methodists turned to organizational consolidation, including the mergers mentioned above, but also to the formation of ecumenical structures. Methodists were among the founders of the Federal Council of Churches (1908), the World Council of Churches (1948), the National Council of Churches (1950), and the World Methodist Conference (1951). By mid-century, however, Methodists, along with other mainline Protestants, were losing their preeminent position in American society. Membership decline, financial woes, and challenges from other religious traditions combined to make the last third of the twentieth century an anxious time for the newly formed United Methodist Church.

In 2000, the UMC was the third largest denomination in the United States, with 10.3 million adherents (8.4 million adult members) and some 37,000 congregations found in every state and nearly every county. The church polity centers on an updated version of Wesley's structure: a compromise between the hierarchy of the original Church of England and the lay participation of the revivals. Methodists have a "connectional" system of mutual responsiveness, accountability, and fellowship. The clergy are the backbone of this connection, appointed to local churches by a bishop; the bishops, clergy, and laity are all linked together by a series of regular conferences (Heitzenrater 1995).

Local congregations are managed by a yearly "charge conference" and send an elected lay delegate to the annual conference in a geographic area, which includes all the local clergy. All of the seventy-two annual conferences participate in one of five jurisdictional conferences, organized by region. A national general conference is held every four years with one thousand delegates, evenly divided between clergy and laity, and elected on a proportional basis from the annual conferences. The general conference sets broad policy for the annual conferences and participates in the appointment of bishops (one for each annual conference). The Council of Bishops and an array of quasi-independent commissions, boards, and agencies assist in the work of the conferences, clergy, and local churches. This connectional system is a reflection of Methodist belief and practice.

Methodist theology is Arminian, emphasizing the agency of the individual in accepting salvation, as well as pietistic, focusing on a personal relationship between the individual and God (Mead 1990c, 155–60). John Wesley made a distinctive contribution to these perspectives, which has had a wide influence even outside of Methodism, especially in the Holiness and Pentecostal churches. However, Wesley regarded himself as squarely within the Christian tradition. As he put it, Methodism was "the old religion, the religion of the Bible, the religion . . . of the whole church in the purest ages" (UMC 2002d). In this regard, Methodists accept the historic tenets of Christianity as interpreted by the Protestant Reformation. What sets Methodism apart from other Protestant denominations is not its fundamental doctrine, but its focus on the process of becoming and being a disciple of Jesus Christ.

Indeed, Wesley was fond of describing his perspective as "practical theology" (Maddox 1999).

Such practicality can produce a tendency toward theological eclecticism. Indeed, theological pluralism, modernist and traditionalist religious movements, and doctrinal squabbles have been consistently seen within Methodism and the UMC (Guth et al. 1997). Wesley was well aware of this possibility, but believed there was a core of truth in Christianity to which all Methodists would adhere. He advocated four sources for discovering this truth: Scripture, tradition, experience, and reason. As one commentator described it, "This living core . . . stands revealed in Scripture, illumined by tradition, vivified in personal and corporate experience, and confirmed by reason" (UMC 2002d). Beyond the core truths of "the old religion," Wesley further counseled tolerance of diverse opinions, noting "In essentials, unity; in non-essentials, liberty; and in all things, charity" (UMC 2002d). Wesley strongly endorsed a catholic spirit among Christians who hold differing perspectives, a view that has historically tempered the sectarian spirit among Methodists.

The Wesleyan perspective is rooted in a special understanding of God's grace, the Holy Spirit, and discipleship. A critical concept is "prevenient grace," the belief that God's divine love surrounds all humanity and prompts individuals to seek reconciliation with Him. Prompted by such grace and encouraged by faith communities, individuals can experience spiritual rebirth, a "decisive change in the human heart," and repent of their sins. God responds to such repentance with "justifying grace," that is, "through faith, we are forgiven our sin and restored to God's favor." Believers can expect, according to Wesley, assurance from God that they have been justified. Indeed, "feeling saved" is central to Methodism, giving believers the confidence to become disciples of Christ within the world, rather than to separate from it.

After having been born again, discipleship leads believers to a sanctifying grace by the Word and Spirit in the context of the faith community. Sanctification means the individual is "cleansed from sin in their thoughts, words and acts, and is enabled to live in accordance with God's will, and to strive for holiness without which no one will see the Lord." Sanctification allows believers to move on toward perfection, enjoying an increasingly full relationship with God in this life and into eternity. Thus, holiness is both a means and an end within the Christian life of individual disciples.

The community of believers provides the setting that fosters disciple-ship and enhances the journey from the first dim awareness of God's love through the process of conversion, justification, and sanctification. Social relationships were critical to Wesley's practical theology. One commentator noted: "For Wesley there is no religion but social religion, no holiness but social holiness" (UMC 2002d). Thus, the central task for the people called Methodists is to nurture the appropriate relation-ships with one another, with the broader society, and indeed with the entire world. Accordingly, the UMC defines its mission as follows:

> The mission of the Church is to make disciples of Jesus Christ by pro-claiming the good news of God's grace and thus seeking the fulfillment of God's reign and realm in the world. The fulfillment of God's reign and realm in the world is the vision Scripture holds before us. . . . Jesus' words in Matthew 28:19–20 provide the Church with our mission: "Go there-fore and make disciples of all nations, baptizing them in the name of the Father and of the Son and of the Holy Spirit, and teaching them to obey everything that I have commanded you." (UMC 2002a)

Thus, discipleship is the method by which the world is reconciled to God. One pastor captured this sense of discipleship when he described the UMC this way:

> It's a church that touches our hearts and stretches our minds. It's a church that accepts us as we are and yet challenges us to be better. And it's a church that gathers us to worship and then sends us out to serve in the name and spirit of Jesus Christ. (Moore 2002, 1)

Hence Methodism has a special worldly focus in the service of other-worldly ends. This synthesis motivates evangelism, service to individuals and communities, and efforts to reform society, including political involvement. Yet, given the nature of Methodist beliefs and structure, such political activity often occurs in a multifaceted and contradictory fashion. Wesley himself is a good example of this characteristic. He strongly endorsed the abolition of slavery, an issue that divided Methodists in the United States, but he also strongly opposed the American Revolution, a cause endorsed by many converts in North America. Indeed, Methodists have a long tradition of expressing their diverse opinions on political matters, from the struggle for prohibition to the civil-rights movement.

In its annual and general conferences, UMC members routinely adopt resolutions on a wide variety of topics. The UMC has been described as the caucus church because of its penchant for internal organizing around issues (Bellah et al. 1991). Progressive social activists have been especially prominent in this regard, but traditional evangelicals are active as well. However, in contrast to some other denominations, these resolutions are not regarded as binding on individual church members—each individual is encouraged to develop and express one's own views.

Perhaps the best example of such position taking is the Methodist Social Creed, first adopted in 1908, and updated since. In 2002, the Creed stated:

> Grateful for God's forgiving love, in which we live and by which we are judged, and affirming our belief in the inestimable worth of each individual, we renew our commitment to become faithful witnesses to the gospel, not alone to the ends of earth, but also to the depths of our common life and work. (UMC 2002c)

The Creed further directs individual believers toward six topics: the Natural World, the Nurturing Community, the Social Community, the Economic Community, the Political Community, and the World Community. With regard to the political community, the Creed states:

> While our allegiance to God takes precedence over our allegiance to any state, we acknowledge the vital function of government as a principal vehicle for the ordering of society. Because we know ourselves to be responsible to God for social and political life, we declare the following. . . .
>
> On political responsibility: The strength of a political system depends upon the full and willing participation of its citizens. We believe that the state should not attempt to control the church, nor should the church seek to dominate the state. Separation of church and state means no organic union of the two, but it does permit interaction. The church should continually exert a strong ethical influence upon the state, supporting policies and programs deemed to be just and opposing policies and programs that are unjust.

This call for civic engagement is widely accepted among Methodists, even when they vigorously debate the ends and means of such involvement. On the latter score, the UMC has been sharply divided on a variety of political questions, with the denominational leadership tending toward liberal perspectives and the laity leaning toward conservatism (Green and Guth 1998). The parish clergy operate within this context, often experiencing numerous cross-pressures.

NATURE OF THE STUDY

As part of a cooperative research effort to study the role of clergy in American politics, a mail survey of UMC pastors serving local churches was conducted at the University of Akron. A random sample of 1,000 pastors and a special oversample of 500 female clergy were drawn from the official lists of ministers, which were generously provided by UMC denominational officials. The surveys were mailed in the spring of 2001, and pastors in the selected sample were contacted four times. These efforts produced 453 usable returns for the main sample, providing a response rate of 50.3 percent; the female oversample generated 199 usable returns for a return rate of 44.2 percent. This level of participation is similar to the surveys of clergy in other mainline denominations, but lower than the response rate for a 1988 survey of UMC clergy (Guth et al. 1997). The length of the questionnaire appears to have contributed to a lower response rate in 2001.

The responses were carefully inspected for response bias, but none was detected. A comparison with the 1988 survey of UMC clergy revealed few differences, except of a modestly larger number of women. For purposes of the analysis found in this chapter, the two samples were weighted together to produce 652 cases.

SOCIAL CHARACTERISTICS
OF UNITED METHODIST CLERGY

Table 7.1 describes the social characteristics of the United Methodist Church clergy. As is the case in many Protestant churches, the pastorate is somewhat less diverse than the laity. Despite a concerted effort to recruit more women and minorities, the UMC clergy is still largely male (79 percent) and white (89 percent). Two-thirds are married and never divorced, and some 70 percent reported that their spouses work outside the home. The clergy are middle-aged, with a mean age of fifty-one years. More than one-third of the sample is over the age of fifty-five and less than one-tenth is under thirty-five years old.

Although the UMC is national in scope, more than two-fifths of the clergy reside in the South and nearly one-third in the Midwest; only about one-sixth are found in the Northeast and one-tenth in the West. About half of the UMC pastors live in farm communities or small towns, with roughly one-quarter residing in small cities and another quarter in major cities. The UMC clergy largely serve predominately white congregations, with just one-eighth in minority or mixed churches. These congregations vary more by socio-economic status than by race, with about one-fifth of the sample serving working-class groups, and some two-fifths each in mixed and middle-class churches. These congregations also vary in size, with about one-quarter serving either churches with 120 or fewer adult members and another quarter working in churches with 500 or more adult members.

Table 7.1

Social Characteristics of United Methodist Clergy

	% of Clergy
Gender: Male	79%
Race: White	89%
Marital Status: Married, never divorced	66%
Education	
College Graduate	90%
Seminary Graduate	82%
Age	
Under 35 years of age	7%
Over 55 years of age	36%
Community Size	
Farm or small town	51%
Small or medium-sized cities	23%
Large cities	26%

The UMC clergy are well educated: more than 90 percent report having a four-year college degree and in excess of four-fifths are seminary graduates. In addition, postgraduate work of some kind has been done by another one-quarter of the respondents. The largest number of pastors attended Methodist seminaries, but a substantial proportion went to ecumenical seminaries, including many of the most prestigious in the country. The UMC sample reflects professional ministers at mid-career, with a mean number of years in the ministry of 18.6. As one might expect, given the Methodist tradition of regularly moving ministers between congregations, the average amount of time in the present church was 5.2 years.

THEOLOGICAL POSITIONS HELD
BY UNITED METHODIST CLERGY

Table 7.2 presents six tenets of Protestant orthodoxy along with the percentage of the United Methodist clergy agreeing with each statement: these data present something of a mixed picture. On the one hand, there was widespread agreement with many of these doctrines, as four-fifths of the UMC pastors agreed that "Jesus will return to earth one day," and more than two-thirds asserted that "Jesus was born of a virgin." In addition, just about three-fifths affirmed that "the devil actually exists" and that "there is no other way to salvation but through belief in Jesus Christ." These figures reveal a remarkable degree of agreement among these highly educated religious professionals, suggesting some warrant for Wesley's faith that the core of Christian truth would be discerned.

On the other hand, considerable diversity of opinion is also revealed, even on matters that Wesley (and the official posture of the UMC) regarded as essential to the Christian faith. For instance, the fact that some two-fifths of the UMC clergy are either undecided or disagree with the notion that salvation comes only by belief in Jesus Christ may be extending the catholic spirit a bit farther than Wesley himself would have accepted.

Table 7.2

Theological Views Held by United Methodist Clergy

	% Agreeing
Jesus will return to earth one day.	80%
Jesus was born of a virgin.	69%
The devil actually exists.	62%
There is no other way to salvation but through belief in Jesus Christ.	59%
Adam and Eve were real people.	34%
The Bible is the inerrant Word of God, both in matters of faith and in historical, geographical, and other secular matters.	35%
The church should put less emphasis on individual sanctification and more on transforming the social order.	15%

The orthodox views of these ministers do not extend to biblical inerrancy, as only about one-third agree that the "Bible is the inerrant Word of God" and that "Adam and Eve were real people." These figures are not surprising given the high rate of seminary education of these ministers, but they also fit well with the Wesleyan quadrilateral, in which Scripture is not the sole source of religious authority. Given the denominational emphasis on multiple sources of authority, the basic agreement on the first several items in Table 7.2 are all the more impressive.

The final query in Table 7.2 addresses a central concern of Methodism: individual sanctification. Only about one-sixth of clergy agreed that "less emphasis should be placed on individual sanctification and more on transforming the social order." Most UMC pastors (two-thirds to be precise) supported the traditional Methodist focus on individual sanctification. This question is sometimes posed as a means of differentiating theological modernists from traditionalists; however, individual sanctification and the social order are closely connected for Methodists, so that the former is critical to the latter. Thus, even modernist Methodist ministers are likely to regard individual sanctification as critically important.

Beyond these seven questions, the survey reveals considerable theological diversity among the UMC clergy. This can be seen in the religious labels that the ministers applied to themselves, in which they were free to choose multiple items (with instructions to include all the descriptions they thought appropriate for themselves). Some 63 percent of UMC ministers chose "mainline" as a label that described them, but 51 percent claimed the "evangelical" brand, while 49 percent willingly called themselves "ecumenical." These patterns are consistent with the importance of both evangelical renewal movements (McKinney and Finke 2002) and progressive social activists (Bellah et al. 1991) within the UMC.

POLITICAL ENGAGEMENT OF UNITED METHODIST CLERGY

United Methodist clergy approve of pastoral involvement in a wide variety of political activities, both inside and outside the church. As can be seen in Table 7.3, almost all (91 percent) of the ministers approve of taking "a stand while preaching on some moral issue," though there was less support for taking a stand on a political issue while preaching (50 percent) or publicly supporting a political candidate (45 percent). These data suggest a standard distinction between moral questions, which are a special province of the clergy, and strictly political matters, on which ministers may lack authority.

Table 7.3

Political Norms of United Methodist Clergy

	% Approving
Take a stand while preaching on some moral issue	91%
While preaching, take a stand on some political issue	50%
Publicly (not preaching) support a political candidate	45%
Contribute money to a candidate, party, or political-action committee	71%
Form an action group in one's church to accomplish a social or political goal	62%
Participate in a protest march	71%
Commit civil disobedience to protest some evil	42%

UMC pastors also approve of clergy making a financial contribution to a candidate, party, or political-action committee (71 percent), participating in a protest march (71 percent), and forming an action group within their congregations (62 percent). Fewer respondents support civil disobedience (52 percent), but this figure is substantial as well. These responses reveal another commonly noted distinction between the activities of clergy as private citizens and as religious professionals and leaders of local institutions and are certainly consistent with the Methodist perspective regarding civic engagement.

The issue positions of UMC ministers are included in Table 7.4, which presents the percentage of surveyed clergy who agree with statements covering a variety of policy questions. Overall, strong support exists for federal welfare programs, with 69 percent of respondents agreeing that "the federal government should do more to solve problems such as unemployment, poverty, and poor housing" and a slightly smaller 62 percent asserting the need for government-sponsored health insurance. Both positions are consistent with the denomination's resolutions, but do not necessarily reflect the views of the laity.

Other policy issues present a more nuanced picture. The UMC clergy tend to take liberal positions on several of the more controversial topics, as less than two-fifths favor a constitutional amendment that would ban abortions, except to save the mother's life or in cases of rape or incest. Similarly, more than two-thirds of the respondents assert that "homosexuals should have all the same rights and privileges as other American citizens." Considerable disagreement exists among United Methodist leaders and laity on these issues (Green and Guth 1998), with the pastors' positions appearing to reflect a concern for individual rights, an area where the denomination has been quite vocal. It is thus surprising that only a bare majority of the ministers express support for affirmative action, one of the most controversial rights issues. Similarly, on a policy that is often regarded as a human-rights issue, not quite half (48 percent) agreed that Israel will need to make greater concessions to the Palestinians in order to achieve peace in the Middle East.

Table 7.4

Policy Positions of United Methodist Clergy

	% Agreeing
The federal government should do more to solve social problems such as unemployment, poverty, and poor housing.	69%
Education policy should focus on improving public schools rather than on encouraging alternatives such as private and religious schools.	56%
Sex-education programs included in the curricula of public high schools should be abstinence based.	69%
We need government-sponsored national health insurance so that everyone can get adequate medical care.	62%
African Americans and other minorities may need special governmental help in order to achieve an equal place in America.	51%
We need a constitutional amendment prohibiting all abortions unless to save the mother's life, or in cases of rape or incest.	38%
Homosexuals should have all the same rights and privileges as other American citizens.	68%
A lasting peace in the Middle East will require Israel to make greater concessions to the Palestinians.	48%

Responses to other policy issues suggest some concern for traditional values. More than two-thirds of the sample agree, for example, that "sex-education programs included in the curricula of public high schools should be abstinence based." And only a bare majority (56 percent) support the statement that "education policy should be focused on improving public schools rather than encouraging alternatives such as private and religious schools." Quite likely this figure reveals a measure of skepticism about public education along with some support for school vouchers.

UMC clergy behavior in the 2000 election is reported in Table 7.5. When examining actual political activities, almost half of the UMC ministers reported having urged their congregations to register and vote, and the same proportion indicated they had prayed publicly about an issue. However, other activities were less commonly engaged in. Just two-fifths had contacted a public official about an issue in 2000, and less than one-third had either taken a stand on a political issue from the pulpit or prayed publicly for a political candidate during that year. While far more active than the general public, these figures are lower than might have been expected given the strong support for political activity reported in Table 7.3. It is possible that disapproval by the congregation inhibits political activity by many of these clergy (Guth et al. 1997).

Table 7.5

Political Activities of United Methodist Clergy in the Election of 2000

	% Reporting
Urged their congregation to register and vote	49%
Contacted a public official about some issue	39%
Prayed publicly for political candidates	29%
Took a stand from the pulpit on some political issue	30%
Prayed publicly about an issue	49%
Party Identification	
Strong Democrat	23%
Weak Democrat	11%
Independent, lean Democrat	14%
Independent	12%
Independent, lean Republican	15%
Weak Republican	12%
Strong Republican	14%
Vote Choice in the 2000 Election	
Al Gore	46%
George W. Bush	46%
Pat Buchanan	0%
Ralph Nader	4%
Other	*
Did not vote	4%

* = less than 1 percent

The UMC ministers were divided in terms of partisanship. The largest single group labeled themselves as strong Democrats, with about one-quarter of the sample. Taking all the self-identified partisans along with those who lean in a partisan direction together, Democrats outnumber Republicans 48 to 41 percent (with the balance being independents). When these data are compared to the 1988 survey of UMC clergy, the results suggest that there has been some partisan polarization over the past decade, as the number of pastors who leaned Democrat or Republican have been replaced by stronger party identifiers. In addition, it appears that this polarization has slightly widened the Democratic tendency of the UMC clergy.

The partisan divisions are brought into sharp relief with the 2000 presidential vote: 46 percent of the UMC clergy reported having voted for Democrat Al Gore and 46 percent cast their ballots for Republican George W. Bush. In this regard, the respondents closely mirrored the actual results of the election, with Gore collecting a handful more votes. From the perspective of the two-party tally, these numbers resemble the 1988 election, where the pastors split evenly between Democrat Michael Dukakis and former president George H. Bush (Guth et al. 1997). The 4 percent who reported voting for Ralph Nader, the Green Party candidate, was a bit higher than the national total, but there was no support among UMC ministers for Pat Buchanan, the Reform Party nominee.

CONCLUSION

United Methodist clergy tend to be middle-aged, white males, who are very well educated and concentrated in the South and Midwest. Like other mainline Protestant clergy, they are generally mid-career religious professionals, and their ranks are slowly including more women and minorities. On theological matters, they are quite orthodox on some basic Christian doctrines, while exhibiting more diversity on others, and with considerable Methodist distinctiveness on still other matters. Thus, within this basic pattern of unity, these ministers also exercise considerable "liberty."

The UMC clergy believe that a wide variety of political activity is appropriate for ministers to undertake, both within and outside the church. The greatest approval focuses on action involving moral issues and those that involve pastors as private citizens. In terms of political issues, UMC pastors tend to hold liberal views on public social-welfare programs, but a more complex pattern appears when examining other policies. They are sharply divided on party identification, where there is a slight edge for the Democrats. However, in the 2000 election, they split their presidential ballots evenly between the major party candidates, similar to patterns evident among UMC clergy in the 1988 election.

In conclusion, United Methodist clergy encompass much of the range and division that exists in American politics. It is therefore unlikely that they will present a distinctive voice in political debate; instead, this large, dispersed, and diverse denomination is likely itself to be a forum for debating the pressing issues of the day—as befits a church that includes both Hillary Rodham Clinton and Elizabeth Hanford Dole. For a denomination that comes close to being a "national church," this can be a useful civic role.

Part 3

Politics of Evangelical Protestant Clergy

Chapter 8

Southern Baptist Convention

James L. Guth

Over the past twenty years, the Southern Baptist Convention (SBC) has undergone a remarkable theological, organizational, and political transformation. Throughout the 1980s, theological conservatives mounted a sustained and ultimately successful campaign to "take back" the SBC from the hands of denominational bureaucrats and theological moderates. As a result, conservative militants not only came to dominate elected offices, but denominational seminaries and agencies were "purged" of those unwilling to adopt the fundamentalist theological standards imposed by the new regime (Ammerman 1990). By the mid-1990s, the SBC's organizational transformation was complete. These changes had enormous social and political ramifications. The new SBC elites were both theological traditionalists and political conservatives. The newly established leadership not only cut organizational ties with their old Baptist lobbying allies, but also created a new set of denominational structures to advance conservative values. As part of that effort, the new Baptist leadership encouraged pastors and laity to be politically active—a campaign that had considerable effect. Not only did many Southern Baptist clergy set aside old reservations about political involvement, but Baptist laity emerged as prominent leaders of the new

Republican Right, from the state level to the United States House of Representatives.

HISTORICAL BACKGROUND

The Southern Baptist Convention is not only part of the biggest "family" of American Protestants—Baptists—but is also the nation's largest Protestant body, with more than 17 million members in 40,000 congregations. In most of the South, the SBC is considered the "established church" because, as the ancient witticism puts it, "there are more Baptists than people." Despite its name, the SBC is not a regional body, but a national group; migration and evangelism have taken its churches to every state in the Union.

This success has been remarkable, given the Baptists' origin as religious outcasts. Emerging from the Reformation's radical wing, colonial Baptists faced persecution, not only in Puritan New England but also in Anglican Virginia. Ardent friends of the American Revolution, Baptists later joined Madison and Jefferson in the fight for separation of church and state. Their tenets about believer's baptism (adult, rather than infant), individual interpretation of Scripture, congregational autonomy, and a called (rather than professional) clergy were shaped by, and in turn, fostered democratic culture. In one sense, however, the SBC itself began in a less democratic vein as Southern Baptists abandoned their Yankee brethren in 1845, following a quarrel over slaveholding. This split was a harbinger of the Civil War, and unlike later schisms among Presbyterians and Methodists, the rupture has never been overcome.

During the post-Civil War period of Reconstruction, Southern Baptists began a steady expansion that accelerated after World War I. The SBC centralized in the 1920s, replacing a multitude of semi-autonomous agencies with one Cooperative Program in which churches merged their funds for mission agencies, seminaries, and other institutions. The Program not only strengthened mission capabilities, but fostered institutional loyalty as well, encouraging Baptists to ignore minor theological differences and work toward denominational success. The new SBC agencies planted churches, trained thousands of religious workers (by 1981, four of the five largest American seminaries were run by the SBC), and produced materials for almost every church function. Indeed, the Program's success eliminated any need to cooperate with other denominations, and with few exceptions, the SBC strenuously avoided such entanglements, even with like-minded conservative Protestants.

During this era, Southern Baptist politics combined varying proportions of church-state separationism, premillennialist passivity, and activism on issues involving moral standards such as prohibition, gambling, and the teaching of evolution. On the whole, Southern Baptist ideology was deeply conservative, accepting the social and political status quo, a posture clearly evident in Baptist resistance to the 1960s civil-rights movement. Nevertheless, by the 1970s there was evidence of change. The SBC leadership was inching toward the left on issues ranging from abortion and civil rights to the emerging environmental and women's movements, a tendency epitomized by a Baptist Sunday-school teacher named Jimmy Carter.

This shift toward the center was soon challenged, however. In the 1980s the SBC was torn internally by bitter factional warfare. After sidestepping theological quagmires for decades, the SBC faced a campaign by conservatives to eject the moderate leaders, who had supposedly allowed infiltration by theological and political liberals. After fifteen years of massive mobilization, countermobilization, strident confrontations, and tightly contested annual elections, the two-party competition ended with a conservative triumph. The victorious conservatives quickly purged the denominational officials with suspect theologies or, sometimes, those who simply exhibited too much sympathy for the losers. They also moved the SBC into greater cooperation with other orthodox groups, as several new SBC leaders joined groups such as the National Association of Evangelicals.

The conservative triumph had enormous political implications. Its leaders were at least sympathetic to, if not actively involved in, the Christian Right movement. They worked to place the SBC behind a staunchly conservative political agenda, often drawn up in close cooperation with Republican officials. Indeed, throughout the 1980s, political debates often garnered as much attention at SBC meetings as theological battles, but the 1991 denominational convention symbolically ratified the conservative victory. Attended by more than 23,000 "messengers" from local churches, the meeting looked like a "God and Country" rally. Southern Baptists heard pleas for political action from Lt. Colonel Oliver North, SBC leaders, and figures from the Christian Right, as well as from their keynote speaker, President George Bush.

The new SBC leadership also reorganized the social and political agencies of the church. They removed funding for the old Baptist Joint Committee on Public Affairs (BJC), the SBC's long-time voice on religious-liberty issues and a staunch defender of church-state separation. Then they transformed the Christian Life Commission (once the SBC's liberal social conscience) into the Ethics and Religious Liberty Commission (ERLC). The Commission was given a well-staffed Washington office, led by its new chief, Dr. Richard Land. Land took the ERLC into a vigorous political role, sometimes on the liberal side, as on racial bias and hunger, but most frequently in alliance with the Christian Right on abortion, gay rights, and other moral issues. During the presidential elections of the 1990s, the ERLC voter guides were decidedly favorable to GOP candidates for office. As if reflecting these developments, growing numbers of Southern Baptist members of Congress were found on the GOP side, including House Speaker, Newt Gingrich; House Majority Leader, Tom Delay; and Senate Republican leader, Trent Lott.

During most of the 1990s, Land and other SBC leaders concentrated their fire on fellow Southern Baptists Bill Clinton and Al Gore. Although denomination leaders initially pledged their cooperation with the new administration, Clinton's early actions reversing Reagan-Bush abortion limitations, his proposals on gays in the military, along with other policy positions, quickly soured relations with the SBC. At the 1993 SBC meeting, almost half of the forty measures introduced were critical of Clinton administration policies; they were finally combined in a single resolution admonishing Clinton and Gore to "affirm biblical morality in exercising public office." An abortive attempt was even made to "withdraw fellowship" from both men, and messengers from Immanuel Baptist, Clinton's home church in Little Rock, were required to state their personal opposition to homosexuality to the credentials committee before being seated. When the Lewinsky scandal broke, SBC leaders loudly called for Clinton's resignation and, failing that, his impeachment. Southern Baptists in Congress were among the most adamant supporters of his impeachment. In the years leading up to the presidential election of 2000, Richard Land became a close political adviser of George W. Bush, organizing prominent SBC and state leaders in support of the Texan's candidacy. The Democratic ticket of Al Gore and Joe Lieberman, on the other hand, elicited no visible support from any Southern Baptist source. It was in this denominational and political setting that the 2000 Southern Baptist Clergy survey was conducted.

NATURE OF THE STUDY

This survey is the sixth in a quadrennial series undertaken by the author in each presidential election year since 1980. The survey for the 2000 election was ten pages in length, and it was sent to 1,500 Southern Baptist clergy chosen randomly from the listing of pastors in the *Southern Baptist Convention Annual 2000*. This source is publicly available, but is, unfortunately, at least six months out-of-date by the time it is published each year. Given the tendency for rather frequent movement by Southern Baptist clergy, the original sample contained a fairly high number of obsolete addresses. The survey was mailed out in early 2001, and after three mailings, the questionnaire elicited 455 responses from ministers at 1,271 currently valid addresses, for a response rate of 36 percent. To check for possible response biases, respondents were compared to an official profile of Southern Baptist clergy produced by the denomination. Survey respondents were slightly better educated than the overall clergy group, but did not differ substantially in other demographic ways, with the possible exception of underrepresenting the growing number of minority pastors.

To check whether our respondents might be more interested and involved in politics than nonrespondents, and therefore reflect an unrepresentative sample, we included a variable to assess the rapidity with which respondents returned their questionnaires. This variable turned out not to predict general activism—suggesting that ministers responding quickly to the first letter were no more politically active than those responding tardily to the third letter requesting their participation. Nor did early responders exhibit any greater level of political interest (in fact, the correlation runs very weakly in the other direction). Thus, despite the relatively low response rate (at least in terms of previous mail surveys of Southern Baptist clergy), it is unlikely that nonrespondents would be markedly different from participants.

SOCIAL CHARACTERISTICS
OF SOUTHERN BAPTIST CLERGY

While the survey respondents in 2001 reflect many of the changes that have taken place in the Southern Baptist clergy over the past few decades, they also reveal some denominational continuity. The biggest changes have come in education of pastors. Unlike the patterns associated with the "called ministry" of the past, most Southern Baptist ministers today are college-educated, with only 10 percent reporting no undergraduate training at all and 76 percent holding a college degree. Only 10 percent report having had no theological training, though another 10 percent have had Bible-college education only. However, two-thirds of the SBC clergy (67 percent) are seminary graduates, while nearly one-third (31 percent) report additional postgraduate theological education.

Table 8.1

Social Characteristics of Southern Baptist Clergy

	% of Clergy
Gender: Male	99%
Race: White	93%
Marital Status: Married, never divorced	87%
Education	
College Graduate	76%
Seminary Graduate	67%
Age	
Under 35 years of age	5%
Over 55 years of age	35%
Community Size	
Farm or small town	58%
Small or medium-sized cities	18%
Large cities	24%

The respondents are virtually all men (only 1 percent female) and nearly all white (93 percent). The mean age for survey respondents is fifty-two years, having been in the ministry an average of twenty-two years and serving their current church for about eight years. Very few of the respondents were single, divorced, or widowed; in fact, 87 percent reported being married only once, to their current spouses. Lest they be seen as too traditionalist, note that over 60 percent of the spouses work outside the home, with teachers (22 percent) and clerical workers (14 percent) the most frequently listed occupations.

The pastors' place of residence reflects the historic rural and small-town dominance of the denomination. Despite burgeoning metropolitan growth in the South, by raw numbers SBC pastors still tend to serve in farm or rural areas (31 percent), small towns (26 percent), or small to medium-sized cities (18 percent), with the remainder residing in larger metropolitan areas. They preach to congregations that range from a handful of members to those with more than 4,000 people on the rolls, but the average membership is 273, with an average Sunday worship attendance of 202 individuals.

THEOLOGICAL POSITIONS HELD
BY SOUTHERN BAPTIST CLERGY

As might be expected, given both the historic theological stances of the denomination and its recent "purges," Southern Baptist ministers are relentlessly orthodox in their doctrinal affirmations. As Table 8.2 shows, nearly all agree that Jesus was born of a virgin (98 percent); the devil exists (98 percent); there is no other way to salvation but through belief in Jesus Christ (97 percent); and Adam and Eve were real people (93 percent). In affirmation of the Apostles' Creed, Baptist ministers agree that Jesus will return to this world one day (98 percent). In addition, SBC pastors assert a very literal view of Scripture, agreeing that the Bible is authoritative not just on issues of faith and practice, but also for history, geography, and other secular matters (87 percent). The respondents also insist that the primary task of the church is to save and sanctify individuals, not to transform the social order, with only one in twenty-five (4 percent) agreeing that "the church should put less emphasis on individual sanctification and more on transforming the social order."

Table 8.2

Theological Views Held by Southern Baptist Clergy

	% Agreeing
Jesus will return to earth one day.	98%
Jesus was born of a virgin.	99%
The devil actually exists.	98%
There is no other way to salvation but through belief in Jesus Christ.	97%
Adam and Eve were real people.	93%
The Bible is the inerrant Word of God, both in matters of faith and in historical, geographical, and other secular matters.	87%
The church should put less emphasis on individual sanctification and more on transforming the social order.	4%

Other survey questions, which are not reported in the table, reveal that particular theological attitudes have relevance for contemporary social and political controversies. More than two-thirds (68 percent) see the present-day state of Israel as a nation specially blessed by God (and therefore, as a later question reveals, it deserves support by true Christians). Fifty-seven percent agree with a six-day theory of creation, perhaps explaining their strong support for teaching creationism an equal amount of time as evolution theory in public school curricula.

There is virtually no sympathy for any contemporary political interpretations of Christian faith, such as liberation or feminist theology. Only 20 percent think the ordained ministry should be open to women, and only 2 percent feel the same about gays. And yet, few SBC pastors label themselves as fundamentalists: using traditional SBC labels, only 14 percent consider themselves "fundamentalist," while 83 percent labeled themselves as "conservative" and 15 percent as "moderate" (only 1 percent chose to call themselves "liberal"). There are relatively few obvious theological fault lines remaining in the SBC, although there is some evidence that the recent incursions of self-conscious Calvinist or Reformed clergy may soon create a new cleavage within the denomination.

POLITICAL ENGAGEMENT
OF SOUTHERN BAPTIST CLERGY

As shown in earlier work (Guth 1996; Guth et al. 1997), Southern Baptist clergy have become increasingly supportive of political engagement in recent decades, but still have some distinct preferences about the preferred mechanisms of that engagement. As Table 8.3 suggests, they are quite supportive of pulpit pronouncements on contemporary political issues, especially those that fall into the category of moral issues, a rubric with broader scope among these clergy than would prevail among, for example, CBS news executives. Virtually all (99 percent) approve of taking a stand on a moral issue while preaching from the pulpit, and two-thirds (66 percent) support taking a stand, while preaching, on a political issue. A majority (55 percent) even approve of undertaking direct engagement in electoral politics, such as endorsing candidates and contributing money, though such activities are obviously still controversial.

More radical political activity receives less support from the survey participants. Only a little more than two-fifths (43 percent) approve of participating in a protest march, only one-third (35 percent) believe it appropriate for clergy to form an action committee within one's congregation, and less than one-quarter (23 percent) assert that clergy may engage in civil disobedience. Least acceptable of the fifteen actions listed in the survey was endorsing a candidate from the pulpit, with only 11 percent of the respondents approving.

Table 8.3

Political Norms of Southern Baptist Clergy

	% Approving
Take a stand while preaching on some moral issue	99%
While preaching, take a stand on some political issue	66%
Publicly (not preaching) support a political candidate	56%
Contribute money to a candidate, party, or political-action committee	55%
Form an action group in one's church to accomplish a social or political goal	35%
Participate in a protest march	43%
Commit civil disobedience to protest some evil	23%

The policy preferences of SBC clergy remain very consistent with earlier surveys. Table 8.4 reports the extent of agreement with a representative sample of the statements offered in the 2001 survey. Southern Baptist ministers are fairly conservative, especially on contemporary moral controversies, but they hold a more liberal stance on a number of social-welfare issues. Large majorities favor abstinence-based sex education (95 percent) as well as an antiabortion amendment to the Constitution (83 percent). Few favor improving public schools at the expense of encouraging alternative forms of education (32 percent), advocating gay rights (33 percent), or offering special governmental help to advance racial equality in America (21 percent). As noted before, most are quite supportive of Israel in the Middle East conflict.[20] Only on questions about national health insurance and the need for more government action to solve various social problems does a substantial liberal minority appear, but even this may be more limited than the initial response statistics would appear to show. For example, on a more in-depth question, when asked whether welfare laws—currently under attack by many religious groups—are too harsh in their effects on children, only 11 percent agree.

Table 8.4

Policy Positions of Southern Baptist Clergy

	% Agreeing
The federal government should do more to solve social problems such as unemployment, poverty, and poor housing.	37%
Education policy should focus on improving public schools rather than on encouraging alternatives such as private and religious schools.	32%
Sex-education programs included in the curricula of public high schools should be abstinence-based.	95%
We need government-sponsored national health insurance so that everyone can get adequate medical care.	48%
African Americans and other minorities may need special governmental help in order to achieve an equal place in America.	21%
We need a constitutional amendment prohibiting all abortions unless to save the mother's life, or in cases of rape or incest.	83%
Homosexuals should have all the same rights and privileges as other American citizens.	33%
A lasting peace in the Middle East will require Israel to make greater concessions to the Palestinians.	22%

The largely positive attitudes about participation and conservatism on issues were found to translate into political activism by the surveyed clergy. As Table 8.5 shows, SBC clergy demonstrated significant political activism in the 2000 election in a variety of ways, with a solid majority urging their congregations to vote, and substantial minorities undertaking other kinds of activities. Caution should be exercised here, however, because different kinds of ministers tend to "specialize" in a variety of political actions.[21]

The likely partisan beneficiaries of political involvement by SBC ministers can be ascertained from pastors' responses to the standard National Election Studies party identification scale. Half (50 percent) of SBC clergy say that they are strong Republican partisans, with another one-third (31 percent) reporting themselves to be weak identifiers or Republican "leaners." Only 13 percent have *any* kind of Democratic attachment. Among younger SBC clergy, Republicans have an even larger advantage. And not unexpectedly, they voted overwhelmingly for Republican George W. Bush over "fellow" Southern Baptist Al Gore. Third-party candidates, including conservative Pat Buchanan, received virtually no votes from SBC ministers. Moreover, Bush loyalists demonstrated more tangible support for their candidate through campaign activities than did those who favored Gore, as nearly two-thirds of Bush voters (62 percent) reported some degree of "active" work on behalf of their candidate, compared with only one-third (33 percent) of the minimal Gore contingent.

Table 8.5

Political Activities of Southern Baptist Clergy in the Election of 2000

	% Reporting
Urged their congregation to register and vote	59%
Contacted a public official about some issue	35%
Prayed publicly for political candidates	38%
Took a stand from the pulpit on some political issue	32%
Prayed publicly about an issue	39%
Party Identification	
Strong Democrat	5%
Weak Democrat	5%
Independent, lean Democrat	3%
Independent	6%
Independent, lean Republican	18%
Weak Republican	13%
Strong Republican	50%
Vote Choice in the 2000 Election	
Al Gore	11%
George W. Bush	86%
Pat Buchanan	*
Ralph Nader	*
Other	*
Did not vote	3%

* = less than 1 percent

CONCLUSION

Our year 2000 survey of Southern Baptist clergy provides solid confirmation that the political trends present within the denomination for the past two decades have finally come to full fruition. Baptist ministers have been transformed from a predominantly Democratic-identifying and Democratic-voting contingent into solid Southern (Baptist) Republicans. Indeed, it is difficult to envision the pastors of such a large national denomination collectively leaning any further in the direction of conservative ideology and Republican electoral choices.

Furthermore, it appears that SBC clergy have reached a (relatively high) plateau in their level of political activity, which grew consistently from 1980 through 1992 and has remained relatively constant in the years since (Guth 1996, 2001). Although the absolute level of their involvement may well fluctuate with the shifting national political agenda, with the attractiveness of Republican candidates and the efficacy of various mobilization efforts directed at them, SBC ministers have become an important Republican constituency and are likely to play a continuing electoral role. In addition, their voices on issues ranging from charitable choice to the Middle East crisies are likely to be heard by Republican policymakers.

Chapter 9

Churches of Christ

Mel Hailey and Timothy C. Coburn

The Churches of Christ is an offspring of the largest church group whose origins are strictly American. Historically, the Churches of Christ traces its roots to a primitive back-to-the-Bible revivalist movement of the early part of the nineteenth century.[22] Leaders of what is today known as the Restoration Movement included three ex-Presbyterian ministers: Alexander Campbell, Thomas Campbell, and Barton W. Stone.

Their followers (known as Campbellites, Reformers, Disciples, or Christians) have grown from a single congregation of thirty members at Brush Run, Pennsylvania, into what constitutes three sizable religious bodies: the Christian Church (Disciples of Christ), the Christian Church, and the Churches of Christ. Today, some four million Americans are part of this religious heritage based on the practice of primitive Christianity as found in the biblical text.

The principle enunciated by Thomas Campbell, "Where the Scriptures speak, we speak; and where the Scriptures are silent, we are silent," captures the originally unsophisticated and uncomplicated nature of the movement (Walker 1959, 512). Assessing the personality of Campbellism, Martin Marty writes:

No one better formulated the concept of simplicity than did Alexander Campbell and his fellow Disciples of Christ or members of the Churches of Christ. Formed out of a number of schismatic groups after 1809, these primitive movements wanted to contribute to the American concept of community. They rejected complexity and religious development. Men would find God and be found in him if they could overlap nineteen centuries of the Fallen Church and restore first-generation biblical Christianity. (1970, 86–87)

HISTORICAL BACKGROUND

Today, the Churches of Christ consists of independent churches that do not consider themselves as a denomination per se. Unlike most other communities of faith, there are no central headquarters, national governing body, common missionary societies, or administrative hierarchies for the Churches of Christ. The denomination does not hold annual authoritative conventions of congregational representatives, and there are no "official" membership records of adherents or even congregations.

Despite this long tradition of separatism from other congregations (and certainly from other religious groups), there is an "unofficial" but very well developed network of Churches of Christ congregations and ministers. This is primarily established through various meetings and lectureships that have been arranged by universities and colleges associated with the Churches of Christ. And, while congregations of the Churches of Christ are located throughout the United States, they tend to be concentrated in the South and Southwest. Since there is no central headquarters, there are no official statistics, but according to an unofficial directory, there were 9,806 mainstream congregations of the Churches of Christ in 2000, representing around 1.4 million adherents (Lynn 2000).

Because the principle is to speak where the Bible speaks and to be silent where the Bible is silent, the Bible is seen to be the vehicle through which God-fearing people achieve spiritual unity in terms of faith and morals. Accordingly, members of the Churches of Christ do not recognize any other written creed or confession of faith. The governing statement is "No creed but Christ."

In addition to its practice of local congregational autonomy, the Churches of Christ is further distinguished from other denominations by its observance of the Lord's Supper every Sunday and its lack of any instruments of music in the worship service.[23] Given the restorationist desire to return to the life and practice of the New Testament church and its emphasis on the Bible as the foundation for faith and practice, this opposition to the use of instrumental music within the worship service is based on the fact that it was neither evident in the early church nor authorized in the New Testament.

The most visible person in a local congregation of the Churches of Christ is the pulpit minister. Ministers are ordained by the local congregations rather than licensed by a denomination, and pastors remain in their pulpits by mutual agreement with the local elders of the congregations they serve. The governance of the church is vested in its elders rather than through the pastor. Members within the Churches of Christ do not become part of a particular congregation on the basis of some vote of acceptance. Rather, once they have confessed Jesus as the Son of God and have been subsequently baptized by immersion, they are accepted as equals in the brotherhood of believers.

In recent years, there has been a loosening of church boundaries, and some have maintained that the Churches of Christ is moving into the evangelical orbit. Certainly, the denomination fits into what Richard Quebedeaux would describe as the evangelical center and right (1978, 7–51). Richard Hughes, a leading Churches of Christ historian, would reject the evangelical label for the Churches of Christ as it developed in the nineteenth century, though even he admits that more and more preachers seem to be drawn into the "evangelical spectrum" (1991, 61). So does Ed Myers, a Bible professor at the Churches of Christ-related Harding Graduate School of Religion, who writes, "I conclude confidently that Churches of Christ are well within the evangelical camp. In short, yes, we are evangelical" (2002, 67).

NATURE OF THE STUDY

Historically, any effort to survey ministers of the Churches of Christ has proven to be a difficult task, as there is no comprehensive list of clergy within the denomination. The best current source for locating pastors is through an "unofficial" list compiled by Mac Lynn, a professor at David Lipscomb University. His compilation is as definitive a list of all Churches of Christ congregations as exists, but even this listing contains no names of the pastors for these different churches. Hence, congregations rather than pastors served as the sampling frame.

In deciding how to draw the survey sample, a decision was made to select congregations with more than fifty members. Many of the very small congregations within the Churches of Christ do not have a full-time minister on staff, as the preaching and teaching duties are simply shared by the male members on a volunteer basis. In fact, in some congregations, preaching is still not done on a regular basis; instead, Sunday services are a time of Bible study, singing, praying, and the taking of communion (Lord's Supper), which is the focal point of every Sunday morning service.

Once congregations of less than fifty members were eliminated, the remaining population of eligible churches numbered 5,826. A random sample of these remaining congregations was conducted, with every fourth congregation being selected to be part of the sample. And because there are no names of clergy listed with these congregations, the survey that was mailed was simply addressed to "Pulpit Minister" at the named church.

The first mailing of 1,500 surveys was completed on November 6, 2000. Several weeks later, the questionnaire was sent again. After two mailings, 358 responses were received. Not surprisingly, 116 surveys were also returned as undeliverable by the post office, likely due to the relocating, merger, or closing of a congretation. Among respondents who completed the entire instrument, there were frequent complaints along the lines of what one preacher wrote, "This form is very long. It wouldn't surprise me if that hindered your return rate." However, many others were complimentary of the detail included in the survey and included words of encouragement similar to "Good survey. I hope you got a good response from ministers." In all, the final response rate was 25.6 percent, which is consistent with other national surveys of Churches of Christ clergy. The returned surveys were checked against the total population of congregations in terms of their size and geographic location; the resulting surveys revealed no major biases in terms of such representation.

SOCIAL CHARACTERISTICS
OF CHURCHES OF CHRIST CLERGY

Churches of Christ ministers are, as seen in Table 9.1, overwhelmingly male, white, and married. These findings largely reinforce previous studies of Churches of Christ pastors, particularly regarding gender. Almost all respondents (99 percent) were male, which is hardly surprising when 93 percent of the Churches of Christ survey participants disagreed with the statement, "All clergy positions should be open to women." It is also not surprising to find very few female respondents in our sample.[24] If there is any movement toward greater gender inclusiveness, one slight indicator may be that not as many preachers wrote specific comments about the role of women in the church as were found in earlier surveys. One respondent noted, "On the question of women in ministry, we believe all Christians are ministers, but women are not to usurp authority over men," but there were very few other actual notations on the issue. Nearly nine of ten ministers are white, while 5 percent are African American. Finally, over 92 percent of the ministers are married, having never divorced; only 2 percent have never married.

Table 9.1

Social Characteristics of Churches of Christ Clergy

	% of Clergy
Gender: Male	99%
Race: White	89%
Marital Status: Married, never divorced	92%
Education	
College Graduate	82%
Seminary Graduate	12%
Age	
Under 35 years of age	8%
Over 55 years of age	33%
Community Size	
Farm or small town	40%
Small or medium-sized cities	31%
Large cities	29%

With each new survey of Churches of Christ pastors, one finds that the educational level of the preachers continues to climb.[25] Today, Churches of Christ ministers are fairly well educated, with around 82 percent holding an undergraduate college degree, and 54 percent reporting some graduate work or a graduate degree. The two schools with the highest number of ministers doing graduate work are Abilene Christian University's Graduate School of Theology and Harding University Graduate School of Religion. However, taken together the schools account for only around 15 percent of clergy doing graduate work.

The "typical" preacher has been in the ministry for a little more than twenty-three years and is fifty-one years of age. He has served his current congregation for the past eight years. Historically, the Churches of Christ has been described as a predominately southern religious movement (Harrell 2002), so it comes as no surprise that 67 percent of the respondents are located in the South, with Texas and Tennessee having the largest number of pastors.

THEOLOGICAL POSITIONS HELD
BY CHURCHES OF CHRIST CLERGY

Churches of Christ ministers are not a diverse group theologically, as continues to be confirmed in survey after survey. While some denominations are more inclusive of different theological beliefs, it can be said that Churches of Christ ministers show a high degree of solidarity in their conservative theological leanings.

As shown in Table 9.2, all of the respondents agreed that Jesus was born of a virgin and nearly all (99 percent) answered in the affirmative that the devil actually exists. The overwhelming response to both questions was the "strongly agree" option. There is no gray area in these matters for Churches of Christ clergy, as these questions touch the core of Churches of Christ doctrine. Any minister who strays from these beliefs does not stay hired for long in the typical Churches of Christ congregation.

Table 9.2

Theological Views Held by Churches of Christ Clergy

	% Agreeing
Jesus will return to earth one day.	71%
Jesus was born of a virgin.	100%
The devil actually exists.	99%
There is no other way to salvation but through belief in Jesus Christ.	98%
Adam and Eve were real people.	95%
The Bible is the inerrant Word of God, both in matters of faith and in historical, geographical, and other secular matters.	95%
The church should put less emphasis on individual sanctification and more on transforming the social order.	4%

Most Churches of Christ pastors (95 percent) view the Bible as the inerrant Word of God that should be taken literally, having little patience with other views or interpretations of Scripture. Thus, given this particular stance, it is not surprising that virtually all (95 percent) of the pastors surveyed reported that they believe Adam and Eve were real people. By the same token, Churches of Christ clergy exhibit near unanimity in their opposition to the theory of evolution as accounting for the origins of life on earth, as 96 percent expressed disagreement with its accounts and only 1 percent supported it.

Churches of Christ clergy are not pluralists when it comes to the matter of religious truth. Nearly 99 percent of respondents either strongly disagree (80 percent) or disagree (18 percent) with the statement, "All the great religions of the world are equally good and true." One minister commented sharply, "This is largely irrelevant as it says nearly nothing about the concerns and methods of the New Testament church, which is NOT merely a community of faith among communities of faith. It is the church among thousands of counterfeits. . . ." Another wrote, "I cannot believe that the Apostle Paul nor any of the other early preachers would want to be included in a survey of ministers from fifteen different religious faiths of their day. Instead, these men worked diligently to teach Christ and destroy false doctrines rather than be surveyed with them." As seen from these comments, Churches of Christ clergy contend that correct religious principles must be defended without compromise. This proclivity can also be seen with regard to the realm of politics, where only one in five ministers felt that it is better in politics to compromise and achieve something than to stick to one's principles at the risk of achieving little.

The common survey instrument used in the Cooperative Clergy Study Project sought to include questions that were universally understandable to clergy from very diverse religious groups. It seems likely that, for the most part, the survey instrument did successfully minimize denominational bias. However, one question regarding theology did not communicate nearly as well for Churches of Christ ministers as it might have for clergy in other denominations. When Churches of Christ clergy were asked whether "Jesus will return to earth one day," one might have expected, based on their responses to other questions on theology, nearly uniform agreement with regard to his return. However, less than three of four Churches of Christ clergy (71 percent) indicated agreement, while more than a quarter (28 percent) disagreed. The disparity might best be explained by the comment one minister made, "Do you mean 'Return for the saints who have fallen asleep in Christ and those still living and waiting?' or do you mean 'Returning to establish His kingdom here on earth upon his return?' I believe in the former statement, not the latter." In other words, the question could be viewed as a determination of a person's view on premillennialism, and other studies of Churches of Christ ministers have shown that they clearly reject a premillennial understanding of history (Foster, Hailey, and Winter 2000).

When asked about salvation, there was virtually unanimous agreement (98 percent) with the statement, "There is no other way to salvation but through belief in Jesus Christ." For the typical minister, this is the heart of the matter. Social justice may be important, but it must always take a secondary position to bringing individuals into a "right relationship with Jesus Christ." As will be shown later in this chapter, ministers are not opposed to political participation and involvement. But when asked to choose between transforming the social order or emphasizing individual sanctification, there was an overwhelming rejection of the former, with a support level of only 4 percent. Once again, this is consistent with the traditional Churches of Christ rejection of the "social gospel." In recent years, there has been more interest among preachers in social justice, but over half (57 percent) still disagreed with the survey statement that "Social justice is at the heart of the gospel," though more than a third (35 percent) did register agreement with the social-justice statement (with the remainder not sure).

POLITICAL ENGAGEMENT
OF CHURCHES OF CHRIST CLERGY

By now it should be clear that Churches of Christ ministers are theologically conservative. This theological conservatism of the clergy translates into a political conservatism as well. Nearly all of the respondents (85 percent) classified themselves as political conservatives, with 51 percent calling themselves either "very" or "extremely" conservative. More ministers opted for the extremely conservative option (5 percent) than those who identified with any of the liberal responses. Political liberals are clearly an endangered species among the ranks of Churches of Christ pastors, with only three out of one hundred preachers claiming to be either "very" or "somewhat" liberal in their self-identification. More than seven of ten ministers voiced agreement with the statement, "It would be hard to be a true Christian and a political liberal."

Churches of Christ ministers express a desire for greater civic engagement, but still show reluctance to become involved beyond minimal acts of participation. As one preacher penned, "Christians need to become more vocal when it comes to moral issues in politics. We can serve people informally as they have need without establishing an unneeded, perpetuating program."

By and large, as seen in Table 9.3, Churches of Christ ministers insulate the pulpit from their political pronouncements. When asked if it would be appropriate to take a stand while preaching on some moral issue, 98 percent of the pastors approved. But when asked about taking a stand on some political issue while preaching, less than half agreed. One minister likely expressed the majority's opinion by writing, "I believe that ministers and congregations should take a strong stand on moral, ethical, and social issues. If it referred to a political issue, I would answer 'strongly disagree.'"

Table 9.3

Political Norms of Churches of Christ Clergy

	% Approving
Take a stand while preaching on some moral issue	98%
While preaching, take a stand on some political issue	46%
Publicly (not preaching) support a political candidate	99%
Contribute money to a candidate, party, or political-action committee	68%
Form an action group in one's church to accomplish a social or political goal	23%
Participate in a protest march	31%
Commit civil disobedience to protest some evil	13%

The reluctance to take a public role is consistent across several fronts. Nearly all the preachers agree that it is permissible for them when off the pulpit to support a political candidate publicly, though more than nine out of ten respondents also added that they have never endorsed a candidate from the pulpit. One wrote, "Ministers should be aware of political conditions in the U.S. but never use the pulpit as a political tool. The pulpit should be used to 'preach' the gospel of Christ." Alson, pastors do not believe it appropriate for ministers to form an action group in church to accomplish a social or political goal. Less than one in four Churches of Christ pastors (23 percent) expressed some level of approval for the creation of such a group within one's congregation (though it is worth noting that, on this particular question, nearly one-third of the ministers were unsure of their opinion).

Table 9.4 examines the issue positions expressed by Churches of Christ pastors. As noted earlier, these pastors overwhelmingly classify themselves as conservatives ideologically. Therefore, it should come as no surprise that only a little more that one third of the ministers surveyed (37 percent) indicate that the federal government should do more to solve social problems. This generally conservative stance was also evident in the fact that Churches of Christ ministers overwhelmingly approve of a constitutional amendment prohibiting abortion (82 percent approving), favor abstinence-based sex education programs in public high schools (97 percent approving), and oppose affirmative action (20 percent approving).

Table 9.4

Policy Positions of Churches of Christ Clergy

	% Agreeing
The federal government should do more to solve social problems such as unemployment, poverty, and poor housing.	37%
Education policy should focus on improving public schools rather than on encouraging alternatives such as private and religious schools.	36%
Sex-education programs included in the curricula of public high schools should be abstinence based.	97%
We need government-sponsored national health insurance so that everyone can get adequate medical care.	24%
African Americans and other minorities may need special governmental help in order to achieve an equal place in America.	20%
We need a constitutional amendment prohibiting all abortions unless to save the mother's life, or in cases of rape or incest.	82%
Homosexuals should have all the same rights and privileges as other American citizens.	31%
A lasting peace in the Middle East will require Israel to make greater concessions to the Palestinians.	34%

Nor are Churches of Christ pastors particularly strong advocates of public education or national health insurance. Only about one-third (36 percent) indicate that they believe education policy should focus more on improving public schools than fostering alternatives to them, while less than one-quarter (24 percent) express agreement that there is a need for government-sponsored national health insurance. It would appear that opposition to these policies was not primarily a function of the expenditure of money, as 62 percent of the clergy agreed that the United States should spend more money on the military and defense. And, while Churches of Christ pastors approve of capital punishment (87 percent), relatively few (20 percent) support gun control.

One hot issue for Churches of Christ clergy was that of homosexuality—though this was more apparent through written comments than in responses to the survey question itself. Slightly more than three out of ten responding pastors (31 percent) agreed with the statement, "Homosexuals should have all the same rights and privileges as other American citizens." However, many respondents were quick to add notations next to the question similar to the following comment, "I believe homosexuals should have *most* of the rights extended to others. However, all rights and privileges would include marriage, which biblically is limited to a man and a woman."

Table 9.5

Political Activities of Churches of Christ Clergy in the Election of 2000

	% Reporting
Urged their congregation to register and vote	47%
Contacted a public official about some issue	31%
Prayed publicly for political candidates	35%
Took a stand from the pulpit on some political issue	25%
Prayed publicly about an issue	48%
Party Identification	
Strong Democrat	4%
Weak Democrat	2%
Independent, lean Democrat	3%
Independent	10%
Independent, lean Republican	23%
Weak Republican	17%
Strong Republican	42%
Vote Choice in the 2000 Election	
Al Gore	7%
George W. Bush	89%
Pat Buchanan	*
Ralph Nader	*
Other	*
Did not vote	4%

* = less than 1 percent

When one moves from stands on political issues to engagement in political activities, one finds that Churches of Christ clergy are not very engaged politically—at least in terms of their role as pastors of their congregations. As shown in Table 9.5, less than half (47 percent) of the pastors surveyed reported that they had engaged in the fairly innocuous endeavor of having urged their congregation to register and vote. Likewise, less than half (48 percent) reported that they had even prayed publicly about an issue, and only one quarter (25 percent) reported that they had taken a stand from the pulpit on some political issue. On the other hand, as a citizen within American political life, the overwhelming majority (96 percent) reported having voted in the 2000 presidential election.

When asked about their partisan identifications, it was not surprising that most of the ministers surveyed classified themselves as Republicans. Nearly six in ten Churches of Christ ministers (59 percent) clearly identified as either a weak or strong Republican. And, when one adds those respondents who chose to label themselves as "independent, lean Republican," more than eight of every ten Churches of Christ pastors (82 percent) called themselves Republicans. Yet, even with this Republican Party hegemony among the preachers, one commented, "The greater wisdom is for the church to avoid political identity." Still, as members of the Republican army, Churches of Christ pastors gave the party what it needed most—their votes. Nearly nine in ten of the pastors surveyed (89 percent) reported that they had cast their ballot for George W. Bush in the 2000 presidential election contest, while only about one in fourteen pastors (7 percent) stated they had voted for Al Gore.

CONCLUSION

If some denominational studies result in a political mosaic of many different hues, the canvas of Churches of Christ ministers is monochromatic in both theological beliefs and political identification. There is some movement, and perhaps slight diversity, in their issue orientation, but not much. In the election of 2000, the character issue surfaced, in part as a retrospective judgment on the Clinton years. For Churches of Christ pastors, the culture wars are real, and George W. Bush was, disproportionately, the recipient of the votes of the preachers. When asked to identify the biggest problem facing the United States today, minister after minister wrote about the common theme of the breakdown of morality.[26] On the other hand, the economy—or the economic disparity between the haves and have nots—was listed as the number one problem by less than 1 percent of the ministers.

The Churches of Christ has been a separatist movement with tightly drawn borders. Preachers do not belong to local ministerial alliances, and they do not join other conservative evangelical organizations. Generally speaking, Churches of Christ ministers talk to other Churches of Christ ministers. They talk theology with other ministers; they talk politics with other ministers; they talk issues with other ministers; and at the end of the day, the survey results would seem to indicate that they reach common agreement.

Chapter 10

Lutheran Church–Missouri Synod

Jeff Walz and Steve Montreal

> The monstrous attacks on New York City and Washington, D.C., are an astounding example of mankind's fall into sin and the forces of evil at work in this world. . . . To deal with such sin and evil in the civil world, God has given us civil authorities—President Bush and our government—to promote peace, order and to provide protection for the American people.
>
> Rev. Dr. Gerald B. Kieschnick, President,
> LCMS, 11 September 2001

Dr. Kieschnick's words in the wake of the September 11 attacks are consistent with evangelical Protestant theology: human sin spawned the attacks; governments work to protect their citizens. At a deeper level, however, the statement in its entirety is a textbook example of the Lutheran philosophy of two kingdoms—both in theory and practice. Recognizing the totality of sin in the world, Lutherans are hesitant to try and remake the world in their image. Instead, they focus on spreading the gospel in a world protected and sustained by government. More so than many other traditions, Lutherans believe they are to be in the world but not of it (John 17:14-18).

In their post-September 11 sermons, as well as in the 2000 political arena, LCMS pastors followed the two-kingdom theory of separating the spiritual and earthly realms. They take a "bottom-up" approach to addressing the world's problems, emphasizing a gospel message that can change individual lives and improve societal conditions. The church, conversely, should speak on public issues rarely and only when a clear biblical mandate exists.

HISTORICAL BACKGROUND

Founded on April 26, 1847, by twelve pastors representing fifteen congregations, "The German Evangelical Lutheran Synod of Missouri, Ohio, and Other States" was the forerunner to today's Lutheran Church–Missouri Synod (LCMS). Established by German immigrants in the American Midwest, the church wished to preserve its Lutheran faith in the face of government encroachment in Europe. The original group (which became the LCMS in 1947) was protective of its theology and cultural vision and ethos, and feared the secularizing effects of mainstream American life. The original constitution was written in German, which remained the language used in most synod churches until World War I. To keep its distance from secular society and to bring the good news of Jesus Christ to others, particularly its young people, the LCMS established and continues to maintain a thriving parochial school system (Nafzger 1994).

The LCMS today has 2.6 million members in 6,145 congregations concentrated in the Midwest. Theologically, the LCMS is conservative and evangelical with a focus on bringing the gospel to the nation and world while maintaining strict adherence to the church's theological underpinnings. The denomination strongly upholds its "confessional" nature, as pastors and congregations together affirm specific "confessions of faith" delineating the beliefs, teachings, and practices of the church. The basis for these confessions is *The Book of Concord* (formulated in 1580), which includes the fundamental teachings of the Lutheran Church (Nafzger 1994). The LCMS is theologically comparable to the Wisconsin Evangelical Lutheran Synod, and both oppose female ordination. The LCMS is more conservative than the larger Evangelical Lutheran Church of America (ELCA), which has been receptive to female ordination, practices open Holy Communion (not limited to its own members), and is more ecumenical.

The LCMS was split by a schism between conservatives and liberals in the early 1970s, and since then, the denomination has tried to maintain its doctrinal strictness while expanding its evangelistic appeals. The synod is dealing with at least three controversies as it moves beyond its 150th anniversary. First, the church has struggled with incorporating contemporary worship formats in an effort to broaden its "market share" while maintaining its doctrinal purity. While most within the synod agree this can be done, those on the ideological edges would either like to see these services end or, for individuals at the other extreme, become a more central part of the LCMS worship experience. Second, varying interpretations of the synod's closed Holy Communion policy are held among the congregations. In theory, the LCMS ordinarily communes only those who have been instructed in the teachings of the LCMS church and who have specifically and publicly confessed their faith in these teachings. In practice, however, some churches interpret this much more liberally, creating a trend that is anathema to the denomination's hard-line conservatives. Third, the Church is struggling with the role of the pastor and the scope of his ministry, as a shortage of pastors becomes a more looming concern. Whether out of choice or by necessity, lay members have begun to take more active roles in some congregations, leading to concern on the part of some of the old guard.

Following the death of synod president Alvin L. Barry in March 2001, only four months prior to the triennial convention, delegates elected the Rev. Dr. Gerald B. Kieschnick (president of the LCMS Texas District) to a three-year term as LCMS president. Moderate candidate Kieschnick defeated his conservative challenger by a handful of votes, mirroring the theological split between the Church's conservative and moderate wings. In his July 18, 2001, convention remarks accepting the synod presidency, Kieschnick said that fulfilling the Great Commission of Jesus Christ is first in a list of six "matters of importance" facing the Missouri Synod. Other important issues specified by Kieschnick include: recruiting and training pastors, teachers, and other church workers; using the gifts of lay people; improving relationships among the national church body, its thirty-five districts, and 6,100-plus congregations; emphasizing the grace of God; and building solidarity within the synod under Scripture and the Lutheran Confessions (LCMS July 2001).

Render Unto Caesar . . . and Unto God: A Lutheran View of Church and State provides insight into the LCMS two-kingdom theory. Published by the LCMS in 1995, this ninety-two-page manuscript contains a historical and contemporary model of church-state relations in the American context.[27] The anonymous authors of *Render Unto Caesar*, subtitled "A Report of the Commission on Theology and Church Relations of the LCMS," claim this model "best preserves and safeguards the Biblical tension" (33). They continue that the two-kingdom theory's greatest weakness, however, is in its "persistent passivity toward government," since government does not perform any gospel-based functions (33).

Indeed, the great struggle for all Lutherans has been to square the two-kingdom theory with its application over time: the theory is much better developed than the application. In theory, "Christians are simultaneously in the kingdom of the left hand, which includes the Law and secular reason, and the kingdom of the right hand, governed by grace and the Gospel" (Menuge 2001, 3). The challenge is to separate spiritual righteousness from civil righteousness. Civil government, blessed by God, can be an effective tool in creating and maintaining good and just societies. Christians can and should occupy civil offices and use them for society's good.

The problem, historically, has been application. Afraid of being too sure of God's intent in a fallen world, LCMS pastors and parishioners have tended largely to abdicate civil society to others. Mark Noll (1992) notes that Lutherans continue to be underrepresented on the national political scene. No Lutheran has ever been president, and the highest national office filled by a Lutheran has been that of Chief Justice of the U.S. Supreme Court (William Rehnquist, 1986–present). There are twenty-three Lutherans in the 108th Congress, but only three of those are Missouri Synod Lutherans (Representatives John Shimkus, R-IL and Doug Bereuter, R-NE; and Senator Conrad Burns, R-MT). Some of this office quietism may stem from a denomination that has gone to great lengths to preserve its German theology and heritage, especially in the first half of the twentieth century. A larger piece of the puzzle, however, goes back to social theology.

The LCMS, like other denominations, tries to avoid the continuum extremes of political apathy or overinvolvement—tending to err on the passive side. Former LCMS President Dr. A. L. Barry released a series of pamphlets on important issues to the church. In "What About . . . Pastors," Barry makes no mention of a public-affairs component to clergy duties. "We must never allow other things to take priority over . . . key pastoral duties and activities" (2001). The Church sees its impact through individual Christians pursuing their vocations with indirect and unintentional influence on the world around them, letting the Word speak for itself. The expectation is that individual Christians, in turn, will have "a transforming effect upon the society in which they live" (*Render Unto Caesar*, 74).

NATURE OF THE STUDY

With the collaboration of others in the field of pastors and politics, and under the direction of Corwin E. Smidt, Executive Director of the Henry Institute for the Study of Christianity and Politics at Calvin College, we surveyed parish pastors in the Lutheran Church–Missouri Synod.[28] The synod was very helpful in facilitating the project and granted us permission to do the study along with providing an electronic address list of all current parish pastors at a minimal cost. We used a random sample to send the survey to one of every four parish pastors, with a sample size of approximately 1,500. The survey was mailed first in mid-January 2001 and again in mid-February 2001. A response rate of about 44 percent was achieved, with 652 surveys returned. Given the general antipathy toward politics and government exhibited in some segments of the LCMS, a larger initial sample size was used, fearing response rate challenges.

SOCIAL CHARACTERISTICS OF LCMS CLERGY

The social characteristics of Lutheran Church–Missouri Synod clergy, as shown in Table 10.1, suggest a relatively homogeneous membership that is concentrated in the Midwest. The LCMS ordains only men. Almost all respondents are white (97 percent), with only nineteen respondents defining themselves as Asian, Black or African American, Hispanic or Latino, Native American, or of mixed race.

Virtually all pastors have postgraduate education; most are seminary graduates. A little more than half (52 percent) the respondents attended the St. Louis Seminary, about one-quarter (27 percent) went to Fort Wayne, and 16 percent attended the Springfield, Illinois seminary, which closed in the mid-1970s. A very high percentage of LCMS pastors are married and have never been divorced, and a minority of respondents' wives are employed outside the home.

Table 10.1

Social Characteristics of Lutheran Church-Missouri Synod Clergy

	% of Clergy
Gender: Male	100%
Race: White	97%
Marital Status: Married, never divorced	88%
Education	
College Graduate	99%
Seminary Graduate	99%
Age	
Under 35 years of age	10%
Over 55 years of age	27%
Community Size	
Farm or small town	42%
Small or medium-sized cities	25%
Large cities	33%

Most LCMS clergy are experienced in pastoral ministry and relatively stable in service to their congregation. The typical LCMS pastor has been in the ministry for more than 18 years (the mean is 18.6 years) and has served at his church for almost eight years (the mean is 7.97 years). The average LCMS minister might be described as 49 years old, serving a small-to-medium-sized city, in a church with 509 members and averaging weekly Sunday morning attendance of 273, and preaching six times a month.

THEOLOGICAL POSITIONS HELD BY LCMS CLERGY

The theological views of the Lutheran Church–Missouri Synod clergy are strongly conservative and rooted in a literal interpretation of the Bible. This can be seen in Table 10.2. Fully 97 percent of responding clergy agree that Jesus Christ will return to earth one day as he promised; 99 percent give credence to the account of the virgin birth. A near unanimous 98 percent say the devil actually exists. This is a striking uniformity of position, more so than that of most other denominations participating in this project, and it illustrates a strong willingness to believe in the supernatural and the reality of the miraculous. While this apparent monolithic opinion is somewhat striking to the outside observer, some of those within the LCMS who have looked at the data expressed mild surprise that there were dissenters among the flock.

Table 10.2

Theological Views Held by Lutheran Church–Missouri Synod Clergy

	% Agreeing
Jesus will return to earth one day.	97%
Jesus was born of a virgin.	99%
The devil actually exists.	98%
There is no other way to salvation but through belief in Jesus Christ.	98%
Adam and Eve were real people.	94%
The Bible is the inerrant Word of God, both in matters of faith and in historical, geographical, and other secular matters.	86%
The church should put less emphasis on individual sanctification and more on transforming the social order.	3%

To LCMS pastors there is no way to salvation but through belief in Jesus Christ—98 percent agree with that sentiment, taking a strongly literalist stand on what the Bible says and, in effect, ruling out the possibility of salvation for all non-Christians. The survey indicates that 94 percent of the respondents believe Adam and Eve to be actual historical figures. The positions are consistent with what the LCMS believes and what is taught in its seminaries; as an organization that seeks to ensure that its pastors, and through the pastors its laypeople, adhere to the organization's doctrine, the denomination is very successful. This is a remarkable degree of consistency of opinion among well-educated individuals and is likely due to the efforts of the seminaries to inculcate theological uniformity among their students (as well as possible self-selection biases among the men who choose to enter the seminary).

Given the striking literalness of biblical interpretation exhibited in the answers to the first five questions in Table 10.2, it is somewhat surprising that only 86 percent of LCMS pastors assert that the Bible is the inerrant Word of God, both in matters of faith and in historic, geographical, and other secular matters. This constitutes a significant majority believing in the accuracy of a very old document, but it is a smaller majority than the other questions exhibit. The inclusion of the areas of history, geography, and other secular matters in the statement may account for some of the lack of agreement. It might be easier to accept the biblical precepts and admonitions on matters of faith, like the first five questions, than to believe in all of the historical accounts, descriptions of geography, and other non-faith based matters. But even given this caveat, there remains a high percentage who agree with the concept of biblical inerrancy.

The last response in Table 10.2 is a clear affirmation of the primacy the LCMS places on preaching the gospel and the proper role for the church in society. Only 3 percent of pastors agree that the church should concentrate more on changing society and put less emphasis on individual sanctification. The two-kingdom doctrine is obviously in practice here: the focus is on preaching Christ, and there should be little involvement with the affairs of government in an attempt to change society. Efforts to transform the social order through church involvement, either through the secular means of authority or not, run the risk of contaminating the church, of replacing the church's primary mission—preaching the gospel—with an emphasis on a social gospel. According to Menuge (1999, 45), an "emphasis on transforming [the] culture has the danger of becoming the whole reason for the church's existence."

The theological views of LCMS pastors are quite conservative and literalist. These views are taught in the seminaries and preached from the pulpits. Are these orientations impacting the political beliefs and activities of the pastors?

POLITICAL ENGAGEMENT OF LCMS CLERGY

Table 10.3 presents responses to questions relating to the political norms of Lutheran Church–Missouri Synod clergy. The pastors overwhelmingly approve of taking a stand on a moral issue from the pulpit, but disapprove by a large majority of addressing a political issue while preaching. Again, the strong desire to maintain the separation between church and state is apparent: while preaching, secular political issues are not taken up. Of course many moral issues may also be political matters, and so the distinction is not as cleanly drawn as presented, and much can depend upon an individual pastor's definition of a particular question. While issues such as abortion can be easily classified, whether to build a new prison or raise sales taxes is not as easily classified.

Table 10.3

Political Norms of Lutheran Church–Missouri Synod Clergy

	% Approving
Take a stand while preaching on some moral issue	91%
While preaching, take a stand on some political issue	29%
Publicly (not preaching) support a political candidate	38%
Contribute money to a candidate, party, or political-action committee	76%
Form an action group in one's church to accomplish a social or political goal	30%
Participate in a protest march	43%
Commit civil disobedience to protest some evil	17%

Only 38 percent of pastors approve of taking a public stand in favor of a candidate even when away from the pulpit, suggesting that a majority of ministers view themselves as representing the church even when not in the pulpit and therefore are reluctant to get involved in politics. This sentiment changes when pastors can take action in private: more than three-quarters of pastors approve of giving money to a political cause or entity. It would appear that when action can be taken away from public view, when there is no explicit or apparent connection between the church and politics, pastors are more likely to participate in political activity.

Further evidence of the impact of the two-kingdom doctrine is the finding that only 30 percent of respondents approve of forming an action group in church to achieve a social or political goal; this might be seen as an endorsement of a political issue by the church and therefore should be avoided. This is a striking application of the doctrine, given the strong church opposition to abortion: only three in ten would approve of organizing a group to further the church's position. And only 17 percent approve of committing civil disobedience to protest evil. Breaking the law—disobeying the rulers that St. Paul admonished Christians to obey—is overwhelmingly disapproved. But in an interesting deviation from the rest of the data in this table, 43 percent approve of participating in a protest march. It is not clear from the survey question whether the protest is against the government or against a private-sector interest; still, a significant number indicate acceptance of a pastor who would lend his personal support to a protest action.

The policy positions of LCMS clergy are generally conservative, as indicated in Table 10.4. A minority of pastors state that the federal government should be more involved in solving social problems (33 percent), that government-sponsored national health insurance is necessary (21 percent), and that affirmative action is a desired public program (21 percent). A larger number, but still a minority, (37 percent) agree that homosexuals should be accorded the same rights and privileges as other citizens. On the other side, nearly three-quarters of the pastors believe the Constitution needs to be amended to prohibit all abortions unless to save the mother's life, or in cases of rape or incest, and 92 percent assert that abstinence should be included in the sex-education curricula of public high schools.

Table 10.4

Policy Positions of Lutheran Church–Missouri Synod Clergy

	% Agreeing
The federal government should do more to solve social problems such as unemployment, poverty, and poor housing.	33%
Education policy should focus on improving public schools rather than on encouraging alternatives such as private and religious schools.	18%
Sex-education programs included in the curricula of public high schools should be abstinence based.	92%
We need government-sponsored national health insurance so that everyone can get adequate medical care.	21%
African Americans and other minorities may need special governmental help in order to achieve an equal place in America.	21%
We need a constitutional amendment prohibiting all abortions unless to save the mother's life, or in cases of rape or incest.	74%
Homosexuals should have all the same rights and privileges as other American citizens.	37%
A lasting peace in the Middle East will require Israel to make greater concessions to the Palestinians.	39%

Nearly four out of ten, however, believe that Israel will need to make greater concessions to the Palestinians to achieve peace. This differs from the traditional conservative position that tends to back Israel more strongly; the variance is perhaps best explained by the LCMS theological belief that Israel has no special significance as a state. The LCMS position stands in contrast to many other conservative Protestant denominations who view the current nation of Israel as having biblical importance.

Table 10.5 presents some of the political activities engaged in by LCMS clergy during the 2000 election. A little over half said they urged their congregation to register and vote; one-third contacted a public official about an issue. So while the number who encouraged participating in the political process by voting is less than might be expected, a higher percentage than anticipated engaged in a political act of higher magnitude and political efficacy. Almost one-third prayed publicly for political candidates, though we don't know if these prayers were offered for specific candidates or for all candidates in general (given the two-kingdom doctrine, it is probably the latter). A small number, only one-fifth, said they took a position on a political issue from the pulpit, and almost half prayed publicly about an issue.

Table 10.5

Political Activities of Lutheran Church–Missouri Synod Clergy in the Election of 2000

	% Reporting
Urged their congregation to register and vote	52%
Contacted a public official about some issue	33%
Prayed publicly for political candidates	32%
Took a stand from the pulpit on some political issue	21%
Prayed publicly about an issue	49%
Party Identification	
Strong Democrat	4%
Weak Democrat	2%
Independent, lean Democrat	3%
Independent	6%
Independent, lean Republican	18%
Weak Republican	18%
Strong Republican	47%
Vote Choice in the 2000 Election	
Al Gore	8%
George W. Bush	87%
Pat Buchanan	*
Ralph Nader	1%
Other	1%
Did not vote	3%

* = less than 1 percent

The partisan orientations of LCMS pastors are tilted heavily toward the Republican side. More than 80 percent of survey participants identify themselves as some type of Republican, with a full 47 percent calling themselves strong Republicans. Not even one in ten considers himself to be connected with the Democratic Party. The reasons for this overwhelming support for one party are unknown, but may be based on specific issue positions (i.e., abortion, homosexual rights, taxes) or result from upbringing or psychological factors. Given the party-affiliation numbers, the figures regarding candidate vote choice in the last presidential election are not surprising. Eighty-seven percent voted for Bush while only 8 percent cast their ballot for Gore. No other candidate received more than 1 percent. Certainly in terms of the national election, LCMS pastors mirrored their partisan leanings and gave solid support to the Republican candidate.

Based on the responses to survey issue positions and the reported party identification, LCMS pastors can be described as conservative and heavily Republican. The two-kingdom doctrine, however, keeps them from overt actions in the political arena in support of these beliefs. With emphasis placed on preaching the gospel and reaching individuals for Christ, the pastors are less concerned with changing society and the means through which that may be achieved; such activity is left to the laity. To do otherwise runs the risk of diluting the church's true mission.

CONCLUSION

What emerges from this study of the political attitudes and activities of Lutheran Church–Missouri Synod clergy is consistent with the strongly held two-kingdom theory of church and state. In *Temporal Authority: To What Extent It Should Be Obeyed*, Martin Luther made a distinction between the spiritual and secular realms. The spiritual realm focuses on church, the gospel, and the Word of God. Christians live simultaneously in a civil realm premised on reason and justice. However, the two realms are far from equal, at least in the eyes of the church. While we are called to do good works in the civil realm, "the church must not become preoccupied with transforming the civil order" (*Render Unto Caesar*, 39). Nothing must impede or distract Missouri Synod Lutherans from proclaiming the gospel message.

As leaders in the church, LCMS pastors carry the banner for a theological purity largely unencumbered by activity in the affairs of this world. Theologically, ministers are biblical literalists who believe that greater emphasis should be placed on individual sanctification than on transforming the social order. This is consistent with the LCMS's bottom-up approach to social ills: individual believers can, through their vocations, have a transforming effect on society. Pastors believe they should play a role in encouraging parishioners to fulfill their citizenship roles, but only on issues they consider moral, not political. The church should not be a hotbed for political discussion or dissent. Only 30 percent of LCMS pastors agree that church action groups are an appropriate way to accomplish social or political goals; less than half have prayed publicly about an issue; only one in five pastors has taken a stand from the pulpit on some specific political issue; and barely a majority (52 percent) have urged their congregation to register and vote in political elections.

As private citizens outside of their pastoral roles, however, LCMS pastors are more politically inclined. Many approve of contributing money to a candidate, party, or political-action committee, almost half accept the value of participating in a protest march, and one-third have contacted a public official about some issue. These responses, also, are consistent with the two-kingdom model. While the church as an institution, including its clergy, should enter the political realm with the utmost caution and care, individuals are urged to be active citizens for the good of society and world, a role that at least a significant minority of LCMS pastors appears to relish. However, a key question these ministers may need to ask themselves is whether they are providing sufficient cues to their parishioners to do the same: to be thoughtful and active contributors in an increasingly secular public square.

Chapter 11

Presbyterian Church in America

Brent F. Nelsen and Beverly A. Gaddy

The Presbyterian Church in America (PCA) is neither large nor old, but it is increasingly visible among American evangelical churches. The denomination began in 1973 with 260 churches and 40,000 members concentrated primarily in the states of the Old South. It now includes more than 1,300 congregations comprising more than 300,000 members located in 47 states.

Such strong growth has come primarily through well-organized church planting that has dotted the rural southern landscape with PCA churches and has, more importantly, changed the face of evangelicalism in southern urban centers such as Atlanta, Georgia (through the large network of Perimeter churches); Dallas, Texas; and Miami, Florida. Moreover, Mission to North America, the church-planting arm of the PCA, has increasingly targeted nonsouthern cities including New York, Chicago, and Salt Lake City.

Some PCA pastors and congregants have assumed fairly visible political roles, such as Dr. D. James Kennedy, a Florida PCA pastor, who is a prominent televangelist and author of the widely used program *Evangelism Explosion*. Kennedy is also known as a spiritual advisor to presidents and a conservative political activist. As for political office holders, seven recent or current members of the United States House of

Representatives are affiliated with the PCA. Additionally, three Republicans on the House Judiciary Committee during the Clinton impeachment debate—Ed Bryant, Charles Canady, and Bob Inglis—were PCA members. And while South Carolina's Bob Inglis left the House in 1998 because of a term-limit pledge, he was replaced by Jim DeMint, a PCA elder.

Scholars who study evangelical churches in America have largely ignored the PCA thus far. The increasing prominence of the denomination in American religious and political life, however, merits increased scholarly attention.

HISTORICAL BACKGROUND

The Presbyterian Church of America was born out of theological and social conflicts that ravaged the Presbyterian Church in the United States—commonly known as the Southern Presbyterian church—during the 1960s. Beginning in the 1950s a growing number of conservative church leaders were disturbed by the theological liberalism creeping into the denomination. Seminary professors and clergy were openly questioning the inerrancy and authority of the Bible and arguing for a loosening of traditional Presbyterian adherence to the doctrinal standards of the Reformed faith as set down in the *Westminster Confession of Faith and Catechisms*. In the view of most conservatives, this new liberalism led to a raft of unholy practices: a failure to address heresy in the church courts; support for the liberal ecumenism of the World Council of Churches; the development of new forms of worship that employed modern music, dance, and drama; approval of women's ordination; and the teaching of evolution (Smith 1999).

Furthermore, theological liberalism led to social and political liberalism. As early as the 1930s, the church had begun to speak out on national issues, thus abandoning its doctrine of the "spirituality of the church"—first articulated during the slavery controversies of the early nineteenth century—that prohibited the church from taking positions on public affairs (Hudson 1981; Sweet 1939). The denomination's emphasis on the social gospel in missions, opposition to the Vietnam War, and support for abortion rights angered many clergy and parishioners (Smith 1999). Moreover, the church's action on behalf of the civil-rights movement clearly dissatisfied many conservatives, though the exact role played by race in the dispute is still a matter of debate (Alvis 1994).

The conservative-versus-liberal struggle finally came to a head in the early 1970s, with conservatives forming a Continuing Presbyterian Church movement in 1971. Members of this movement eventually broke with the Southern Presbyterian Church in 1973, and the new denomination took the name Presbyterian Church in America in 1974.

The young denomination stood wholly unified against liberalism and in favor of the infallibility of Scripture and Reformed theology as outlined in the Westminster Standards. Independence, however, revealed a difficult truth: the PCA, for all its talk of unity, was a marriage of convenience. Two groups of Reformed Protestants had joined forces to resist liberalism in the South. One group had its roots deep in southern Old School Presbyterianism with its adherence to a "strict subscription" to the Westminster Standards (Smith 1999). These Old School traditionalists, in the relatively sheltered confines of the rural South, preserved their Reformed beliefs and practices and resented any attempt to alter the status quo. Allied with these traditionalists, however, was a second group of theological conservatives who were just as committed to the inerrancy of Scripture, but more willing to loosen adherence to the Westminster Standards as southern society changed. These Presbyterians were more urban and cosmopolitan, more broadly connected to the American evangelical movement, and more deeply committed to evangelizing an increasingly secular culture using nontraditional means. Thus, in one new church two conservative movements existed. One was Old South, staunchly Reformed, and committed to practice only what conformed to a strict interpretation of the Standards. The other was New South, broadly evangelical, and more pragmatic than principled in the application of the Standards. These factions continue to divide the denomination today.

The past twenty years have seen remarkable church growth that has, in some ways, further exacerbated factional tension. Worship practice in the PCA has become very diverse with the evangelical wing adopting a range of "worship styles" from the radically contemporary, to the "blended" (contemporary and traditional), to the highly liturgical. Traditionalists decry the erosion of Reformed worship and call for renewed adherence to the "regulative principle" (whatever is not commanded in Scripture is forbidden) while also developing a variety of styles that range from the austere (psalm singing; no instruments), to the traditional Presbyterian (hymns and creeds), to the Baptistic (three hymns and a sermon). The battles over worship also extend to the role of women, with evangelical churches having gradually extended the right to teach Scripture and lead worship to women as long as they refrain from doing so from the pulpit. Traditional churches see this as creeping theological liberalism and have used the church courts to try, with some success, to reverse the practice. Finally, the PCA factions have clashed over the "days of creation" with the traditionalists arguing that a literal interpretation of Genesis 1 is the only acceptable view, while evangelicals argue (successfully so far) for an acceptance of a plurality of views on the method of creation.

From the beginning, the broadly evangelical faction of the PCA has held the upper hand in denominational controversies. Today, evangelicals hold a commanding majority, bolstered by PCA growth in the boom cities of the South and in regions beyond Dixie. More than three-fifths (62 percent) of PCA pastors say the term "evangelical" fits them "very well," while only one-fifth (21 percent) say the same of "truly reformed," the label used by most traditionalists (Smith 1999, 552). Ironically, the traditionalists have almost no hope of reversing the evangelical trend due to their own insistence—in reaction to their experiences in the 1960s—that the new denomination give great authority to churches and local presbyteries. Such grassroots governance makes it impossible for a minority to capture the machinery of the denomination and enforce its will on the majority. The only option for the traditionalists would be to withdraw once again to form a new denomination. But, while the traditionalists are not happy, few believe a split is imminent.

NATURE OF THE STUDY

As part of the Cooperative Clergy Study Project, the questionnaire that was mailed to PCA clergy included the standard questions common to all the clergy surveys.[29] Our survey, however, also contained several additional queries designed to explore specific PCA issues. The first surveys were mailed in November of 2000 to 1,361 senior or solo pastors in the PCA—the entire population of pastors listed in the September 2000 denomination directory. A second mailing followed in March/April 2001, and a third in August 2001. Four hundred sixty-four surveys were completed and returned; 69 surveys proved undeliverable. Despite the three mailings, the resulting response rate was 36 percent. Apparently Presbyterian guilt was not enough to motivate most busy pastors to complete this very long survey.

The relatively low response rate raises concerns about the representative nature of our sample. To test the sample, we compared it to known characteristics of the PCA. Specifically, we compared the geographic distribution of our sample against the known regional distribution of PCA churches, and we also examined the average size of a church in our sample with that of a PCA church calculated from denominational statistics. In both cases, our sample was found to be quite representative of the denomination as a whole. In the PCA, 65 percent of the churches are located in the South, 13 percent in the Northeast, 12 percent in the Midwest, and 9 percent in the West. Our sample slightly overrepresents the South (67 percent)—perhaps due to the fact that the survey originated at a southern university—while underrepresenting the West (5 percent). As for the size of PCA churches, according to denominational figures the average church has 210 communing and noncommuning members (*PCA Yearbook 2000*). Our sample yields an average number of adult members of 198 and an average weekly attendance of 212. Thus our sample seems representative of the PCA as a whole.

SOCIAL CHARACTERISTICS OF PCA CLERGY

The clergy of the Presbyterian Church in America are socially homogeneous from almost every possible viewpoint. The denomination restricts ordination and Bible teaching responsibilities to men, so it is no surprise that the clergy is 100 percent male. As can be seen from Table 11.1, only three of the 464 pastors were not currently married and only fifteen of the respondents (3 percent) in this socially conservative denomination had ever been divorced. Forty-three percent of the pastors' wives work outside the home.

Less than one in twenty (4 percent) are nonwhites, with Asians (mainly Koreans) making up the largest racial minority. The mean age of the pastors surveyed was forty-nine years, although almost a quarter of the clergy were thirty something. The average pastor has over eighteen years of ministry experience and has served his current church almost eight years.

The denomination is committed to an educated clergy, which is reflected in the backgrounds of the respondents. Almost all (97 percent) of the clergy hold seminary degrees, though a smaller percentage (94 percent) report being college graduates. This seeming incongruity is due to the policy of some seminaries that allow admission to individuals who may have completed a Bible-college degree or only some portion of a bachelors degree. Almost half of PCA pastors have gone either to Covenant Seminary, the denomination's seminary in St. Louis, or one of the three campuses of Reformed Theological Seminary. Substantial numbers (14 percent) have also graduated from traditional evangelical seminaries (e.g., Fuller, Trinity), while fewer than 2 percent of the respondents have attended a prestige seminary such as Harvard or Princeton. Over 40 percent have also received some postseminary training.

Table 11.1

Social Characteristics of Presbyterian Church in America Clergy

	% of Clergy
Gender: Male	100%
Race: White	94%
Marital Status: Married, never divorced	95%
Education	
College Graduate	94%
Seminary Graduate	97%
Age	
Under 35 years of age	8%
Over 55 years of age	22%
Community Size	
Farm or small town	27%
Small or medium-sized cities	25%
Large cities	33%

THEOLOGICAL POSITIONS HELD BY PCA CLERGY

Table 11.2 demonstrates that the theological conservatism of the Presbyterian Church in America clergy is so uniform that we can speak of the "accepted position" rather than "central tendencies."

PCA pastors are thoroughly biblical in their understanding of the tenets of the Christian faith. Given the history of the denomination, it is not surprising that pastors accept the Bible as wholly trustworthy. Moreover, a plain reading of the biblical text teaches the virgin birth of Jesus, salvation through faith in Christ alone, and the future return of the Messiah to earth. Adam and Eve and the devil also figure as real beings in the biblical text. PCA pastors, therefore, express few doubts that these doctrines of the faith are true. Their biblicism is also evident when one examines their views on the origins of life and the universe. While the denomination has given pastors some freedom to interpret the Bible's account of creation, 96 percent of the clergy reject evolution as an explanation for the origins of life, with 65 percent believing that God created the world in six twenty-four-hour days. The General Assembly, therefore, may sanction pluralism, but the clergy clearly prefer a conservative view of creation.

Table 11.2

Theological Views Held by Presbyterian Church in America Clergy

	% Agreeing
Jesus will return to earth one day.	99%
Jesus was born of a virgin.	100%
The devil actually exists.	100%
There is no other way to salvation but through belief in Jesus Christ.	100%
Adam and Eve were real people.	99%
The Bible is the inerrant Word of God, both in matters of faith and in historical, geographical, and other secular matters.	97%
The church should put less emphasis on individual sanctification and more on transforming the social order.	6%

Reformed doctrine and history seem to support a transformative role for the church in the world (Van Til 1959). PCA pastors, however, are trained to detect hints of theological liberalism, so when asked to choose between "individual sanctification" and "transforming the social order," the respondents reject social transformation as sounding too much like the social gospel of the mainline churches. But the rejection is not absolute; some respondents, in their marginal comments on the survey, questioned the implication that individual sanctification and social transformation were mutually exclusive. As a group, however, they proved unwilling to back a more prominent role for the church as an agent of social transformation. For similar reasons respondents also rejected liberation theology (87 percent) and feminist theology (93 percent). Furthermore, their theology and their biblicism does not allow them to accept women (97 percent disagree) or practicing homosexuals (99 percent disagree) for ordination, despite the growing importance of women in less visible leadership roles.

POLITICAL ENGAGEMENT OF PCA CLERGY

In general, Presbyterian Church in America clergy take a positive approach to personal political activity. Almost without exception, this activity is aimed at furthering conservative political objectives.

Table 11.3 demonstrates some variation in political norms among PCA pastors: respondents were nearly unanimous in their support for preaching on moral issues, but only 60 percent approved of taking a stand in the pulpit on political issues, and many qualified this by writing in the margin of the survey "if moral." A narrow majority of pastors asserted that ministers could appropriately take a public stand in favor of a particular candidate, but only 6 percent would approve of endorsing a candidate from the pulpit. Large majorities of the respondents approved of contributing money to political causes and participating in legal protest marches, but just over one-third supported organizing a political-action group in the church and even fewer approved of participating in extralegal protest. In sum, PCA pastors see little wrong with clergy involvement in politics as long as it remains personal or involves the pastor in his role as social and cultural critic. They do object, as did their forefathers in the 1960s, to clergy involvement in politics if it is illegal or strongly identifies their church with a particular political cause. One respondent summed it up this way: "I believe strongly in personal activity in politics, but not ecclesiastical activity. . . . This is an important distinction for me." Thus, for many PCA pastors, the "spirituality of the church" remains an important doctrine.

Table 11.3

Political Norms of Presbyterian Church in America Clergy

	% Approving
Take a stand while preaching on some moral issue	96%
While preaching, take a stand on some political issue	60%
Publicly (not preaching) support a political candidate	51%
Contribute money to a candidate, party, or political-action committee	75%
Form an action group in one's church to accomplish a social or political goal	35%
Participate in a protest march	62%
Commit civil disobedience to protest some evil	29%

Ideologically the PCA clergy are almost uniformly conservative. Ninety-six percent identify themselves as "conservative," with 78 percent choosing the label of either "very conservative" or "extremely conservative." This stance is reflected in the policy positions favored by PCA pastors as shown in Table 11.4. Respondents strongly supported traditional conservative causes including abstinence based sex education (94 percent) and a constitutional amendment prohibiting abortions (83 percent). Support for an abortion amendment may actually have been higher if the question had not qualified the prohibition of abortion with the words "unless to save the mother's life, or in cases of rape or incest." Many respondents, in fact, crossed out these words before agreeing with the statement.

Table 11.4

Policy Positions of Presbyterian Church in America Clergy

	% Agreeing
The federal government should do more to solve social problems such as unemployment, poverty, and poor housing.	12%
Education policy should focus on improving public schools rather than on encouraging alternatives such as private and religious schools.	7%
Sex-education programs included in the curricula of public high schools should be abstinence based.	94%
We need government-sponsored national health insurance so that everyone can get adequate medical care.	7%
African Americans and other minorities may need special governmental help in order to achieve an equal place in America.	18%
We need a constitutional amendment prohibiting all abortions unless to save the mother's life, or in cases of rape or incest.	83%
Homosexuals should have all the same rights and privileges as other American citizens.	37%
A lasting peace in the Middle East will require Israel to make greater concessions to the Palestinians.	23%

PCA pastors were equally uniform in their rejection of liberal policy positions. Only one in ten respondents supported a greater government role in solving social problems, improving public education, or creating a national health-insurance system. Only two in ten agreed with statements about the need for affirmative action and greater Israeli concessions to achieve peace in the Middle East. Almost four in ten (37 percent) PCA pastors agreed that homosexuals should have the same rights and privileges as other American citizens—a fairly strong showing for what many would consider a liberal social position. A close reading of the marginal comments, however, reveals a basic ambiguity in the question in the eyes of the survey participants. Many pastors agreed with the statement, but qualified it by saying "this is the case already" or "yes, without special rights as a group" or "doesn't include marriage." Thus we suspect the vast majority of PCA ministers would not wish to grant homosexuals special rights, including the right to marry or adopt children.

Table 11.5

Political Activities of Presbyterian Church in America Clergy in the Election of 2000

	% Reporting
Urged their congregation to register and vote	58%
Contacted a public official about some issue	33%
Prayed publicly for political candidates	39%
Took a stand from the pulpit on some political issue	39%
Prayed publicly about an issue	56%
Party Identification	
Strong Democrat	*
Weak Democrat	*
Independent, lean Democrat	1%
Independent	7%
Independent, lean Republican	14%
Weak Republican	19%
Strong Republican	59%
Vote Choice in the 2000 Election	
Al Gore	*
George W. Bush	93%
Pat Buchanan	*
Ralph Nader	*
Other	4%
Did not vote	3%

* = less than 1 percent

When examining how these political norms and conservative policy positions affected clergy behavior in the 2000 election, we find nearly 60 percent of PCA pastors identify themselves as strong Republicans, with 92 percent at least leaning Republican (see Table 11.5). But it still comes as some surprise that only one out of the 464 respondents admitted to voting for Al Gore. Fully 93 percent voted for George W. Bush, with only a smattering of ballots going to other candidates or no candidate. Bush support, however, was not particularly deep, since in the primary race less than half the clergy (46 percent) supported Bush, while 38 percent selected the fiery conservative Alan Keyes. No other major Republican candidate, including John McCain and Gary Bauer, received support from more than 2 percent of the respondents.

As for clergy political activity in 2000, more than half of the ministers surveyed prayed publicly about an issue. About the same proportion urged their congregants to vote. Significantly less than half the pastors said they contacted a public official, prayed publicly for a candidate or prayed for a political issue during the campaign.

CONCLUSION

The Presbyterian Church in America represents new growth on an old Presbyterian tree. Its theological and ecclesiastical roots are in the old Southern Presbyterian Church, once known for its strict adherence to the Westminster Standards, Presbyterian governance, and the spirituality of the church. The PCA's rapid growth, however, has taken it beyond its base in the American rural south into the nation's urban and suburban centers. Growth has brought the denomination into contact with the mainstream evangelical movement where, on the whole, it fits comfortably (Guth et al. 2003). But expansion has not come without internal cost. A cultural rift has developed within the denomination between the evangelical, more cosmopolitan wing of the church and a small but vocal traditional faction. The denomination has so far survived the major clashes, but the two sides have, by no means, settled all their differences. Schism, whether in the form of a dramatic break or a series of smaller withdrawals, is not out of the question.

The culture clash within the PCA has theological overtones, as traditionalists tend to emphasize the judgment of God and the need to live according to God's righteous standards, while the evangelicals preach a God of sinners saved by grace. These differences in theological tone, however, do not show up in our survey. PCA pastors uniformly conform to the traditional doctrines of the faith; they are staunch theological conservatives regardless of whether their cultural position is traditional or cosmopolitan.

PCA uniformity continues in the area of politics. Ministers identify themselves as Republicans, take conservative political positions and vote

Republican. They also tend to be politically involved, although more as individuals than as church leaders. In sum, PCA pastors are politically engaged, conservative evangelicals. They form a solid block in the Republicans' evangelical base.

Chapter 12

Christian Reformed Church

James M. Penning

The controversial and closely contested 2000 presidential election in the United States has provided scholars and journalists alike with unique opportunities for analysis and explanation. Some observers, for example, have noted specific regional patterns in the 2000 presidential vote, making distinctions between "red states," primarily heartland areas, which tended to vote for George W. Bush, and "blue states," mostly coastal regions, which supported Al Gore (Brooks 2001). Others have focused on demographic configurations in the 2000 vote, writing about variations in voting patterns based on such variables as income, race, ethnicity, age, and sex (Pomper 2001).

One variable that seems to have played a particularly important role in the 2000 election is religion. To use the terms of James D. Hunter (1992), George W. Bush did particularly well among evangelicals and the religiously orthodox while Al Gore tended to receive support from modernists and religious progressives. Certainly one can make a case that conservative evangelicals currently provide one of the core constituencies of the Republican Party (Hofrenning 1997 and 1998; Wilcox 1999). And given the closely contested nature of the presidential race, one might argue that conservative evangelicals played a key role in producing a Bush victory (Center Conversations 2001, Kellstedt et al. 2001).

The relationship between religion and voting choice is complex, with theological belief, denominational membership, and social networks playing important roles in shaping congregants' political behavior (Guth et al. 1997). For the purpose of this chapter, the primary focus is on the political role of the clergy. American clergy tend to possess important resources that, at least potentially, can be used to affect the political thought and behavior of their congregants (Welch et al. 1993). Specifically, ministers typically enjoy considerable social prestige, verbal ability, and high levels of education. In addition, they have access to resources such as church facilities, communications networks, and funding sources (Olson and Crawford 2001; Djupe and Gilbert 2001a). Yet, not all pastors are equally involved in politics, and not all who participate do so in the same fashion (Jelen 2001b). The characteristics of individual ministers play some role in this variation, as does denominational affiliation. There is growing evidence that clergy from various denominations tend to exhibit distinct configurations of political behavior (Green and Poloma 1990, Guth 1990, Guth et al. 1997, Crawford and Olson 2001). Thus it is important that we examine such patterns across denominations, and to that end, this paper examines one small but politically interesting denomination, the Christian Reformed Church in North America (CRC), during the period of the 2000 election.

HISTORICAL BACKGROUND

Dutch Calvinism has deep roots in North America; indeed the Dutch Reformed Church (now the Reformed Church in America or RCA) constitutes the nation's oldest Protestant denomination, tracing its origins to the Dutch settlement of New Amsterdam. During the nineteenth century, the RCA struggled with issues of theology and acculturation to American society as the denomination sought to assimilate waves of immigrants from the "old country." Many of these new immigrants were "seceders": Calvinists who had left the Dutch Reformed Church (Hervormde Kerk) in the Netherlands in the 1830s. The seceders, drawn primarily from the lower classes of Dutch society, objected to perceived theological drift in the Dutch Reformed Church (for example, downplaying traditional confessions), liturgical innovation (such as singing hymns in worship services), and structural reorganization of the denomination (Bratt 1984). The newer immigrants to the United States tended to settle west of the Allegheny Mountains in states such as Michigan and Iowa, producing an East (more modernist) versus West (more orthodox) division in the RCA which persists to this day. Internal divisions within the RCA grew so intense that, in 1857, a group of RCA members withdrew from the church and formed a new denomination, calling themselves the Christian Reformed Church (CRC) (Schoolland 1958; Swierenga and Bruins 1999). In part, the differences between the two groups were cultural, with the CRC members tending to resist Americanization more stubbornly, including the use of the English language and hymns in services. However, CRC members also objected to what they perceived as theological liberalism in the RCA as evidenced, for example, by the older denomination's refusal to condemn lodge membership, its apparent neglect of catechetical teaching, and its lukewarm support for the secession movement in the Netherlands (Bratt 1984, 39). One consequence of the schism was that, after 1880, the CRC attracted a majority of secessionist immigrants, bolstering its membership both in the United States and (during the twentieth century) in Canada as well. Nevertheless, today's CRC remains a small denomination of approximately 300,000 members.

Early immigrant settlement patterns have largely determined the location of CRC congregations in the United States. While churches exist across the United States, the denomination finds its greatest concentration of members in Western Michigan, Northern Illinois, and Northwest Iowa, and CRC congretations can also be found in such diverse states as New York, New Jersey, Indiana, and California. Indeed, the mobility of today's American population, coupled with the CRC's emphasis on missions has produced a denomination that is not only geographically but also increasingly ethnically diverse. While a majority of members continue to be of Dutch descent, growing numbers of CRC members trace their heritage to such places as Korea, Nigeria, and the Philippines.

The CRC today cannot be readily classified as a mainline Protestant denomination. The church has clung tenaciously to its orthodox theological roots and has tended to reject mainline conceptions of the social gospel and to refuse to join such mainline, ecumenical organizations as the National and World Councils of Churches. On the other hand, the CRC has also maintained an uneasy relationship with American evangelicalism, as indicated by its on-again, off-again membership in the National Association of Evangelicals (Penning and Smidt 2000 and

2001; Penning, Smidt and Brown 2001). While the CRC tends to share evangelicals' commitment to theological orthodoxy, the denomination has tended to place a greater emphasis on systematic theology, Christian education at all levels, and political and social engagement than have at least some of its evangelical counterparts.

The CRC has felt most comfortable with theologically conservative, sister Reformed denominations such as the Orthodox Presbyterian Church and the Presbyterian Church in America. Indeed, the CRC was among the founders and chief supporters of the National Association of Presbyterian and Reformed Churches (NAPARC). Ironically, the recent decision of the CRC to permit the ordination of women ministers and elders has created a rift between the CRC and NAPARC, resulting in the denomination's ouster from that organization.

Issues such as the ordination of women and the teaching of evolution have divided the CRC in recent years, resulting in the loss of some members to more conservative denominations such as the PCA and the newly formed United Reformed Church. However, a deeper and more longstanding division in the denomination exists between "pietists" and "transformationalists." Most of the early (nineteenth century) members of the denomination tended to share the secessionists' emphasis on personal piety and confessional orthodoxy. To these CRC members, secular society (and, in particular, American society) was antithetical to religious orthodoxy. Hence, they made every effort to separate themselves from American culture and to avoid political and social engagement.

However, around the turn of the twentieth century, such theological, social, and cultural isolation became increasingly difficult to maintain, as the denomination grew in size and as advances in transportation and communication challenged the isolation of CRC settlements in the New World. Equally important, many CRC members were influenced by the transformational theology and social ethics of the eminent Dutch minister, scholar, and politician, Abraham Kuyper. While Kuyper recognized the dangers of secularization, he also emphasized the sovereignty of God over virtually all aspects of life, and urged Reformed Christians to attempt to bring all of culture into harmony with God's will. So powerful and appealing was Kuyper's vision of this cultural mandate that it has inspired many CRC members to seek to transform society by participating in political and social affairs and by establishing distinctively Christian institutions such as schools, labor unions, hospitals, social welfare agencies, and political parties. As a result of this Kuyperian emphasis, the CRC, despite its small size, has tended to assume a leadership role not only intellectually but also in terms of social and political praxis among evangelicals, a factor contributing to the importance of examining the political role of CRC clergy.

NATURE OF THE STUDY

The data used in this chapter were collected in connection with the Cooperative Clergy Study Project, a massive examination of clergy from approximately twenty American religious denominations conducted during the spring of 2001. Using nearly identical written questionnaires, scholars from across the United States surveyed ministers from various denominations in an effort to produce a common dataset that could be used for the comparative study of the political roles of American clergy. Although most of the questions asked of the respondents were identical, regardless of denomination, scholars conducting the various surveys were also permitted to add a limited number of denomination-specific questions where appropriate or necessary.

The Christian Reformed data were collected by mailing questionnaires in the early spring of 2001 to virtually the entire roster of CRC parish ministers in the United States. One month later, a second wave of surveys was sent to non-respondents. From the 681 questionnaires mailed to CRC clergy, 399 usable responses were obtained, for an overall response rate of 59 percent. This high response rate may, in part, reflect the fact that the Cooperative Clergy Study Project was initiated at Calvin College, a CRC institution of higher education. Or it may stem from some Kuyperian-related interest in politics among the clergy, as noted before. In any case, the high response rate is most welcome, as it facilitates data analysis and may enhance confidence in the conclusions drawn below.

SOCIAL CHARACTERISTICS
OF CHRISTIAN REFORMED CLERGY

In terms of social characteristics, Christian Reformed clergy are, as seen in Table 12.1, a remarkably homogenous group. For example, despite the fact that, in 1995, the CRC sanctioned the ordination of female clergy and elders (Christian Reformed Church 1995, 733), the vast majority (99 percent) of its clergy today are males. While the percentage of female clergy will no doubt increase as opportunities for females in the ministry expand, this change is likely to be gradual since there is still considerable controversy in the CRC over the issue of female ordination.

The racial composition of CRC clergy is similarly homogenous, with 93 percent of the respondents classifying themselves as whites. Other groups represented among respondents include Asians (4 percent), African Americans (1 percent), Hispanics (1 percent), and Native Americans (less than 1 percent). Although the CRC has worked diligently in recent years to broaden the ethnic and racial composition of both its membership and clergy, change has come slowly. One notable exception, however, has been the rapid growth in Korean CRC members, many of whom emigrated from Korea and settled in California. The relatively large number of Asian CRC clergy reflects this growth. Not only are Christian Reformed ministers largely white and male, they are also homogenous in terms of marital status. Fully 95 percent of CRC clergy fall into the "married/never divorced or widowed" category. In contrast, only 2 percent of the responding pastors were "single, never married" and another 2 percent reported being "divorced and remarried."

Table 12.1

Social Characteristics of Christian Reformed Clergy

	% of Clergy
Gender: Male	99%
Race: White	93%
Marital Status: Married, never divorced	95%
Education	
College Graduate	99%
Seminary Graduate	99%
Age	
Under 35 years of age	7%
Over 55 years of age	29%
Community Size	
Farm or small town	32%
Small or medium-sized cities	23%
Large cities	45%

In view of the fact that ordination to the CRC ministry normally requires seminary training, it is no surprise that the clergy also tend to be very well educated. Indeed, fully 99 percent of the responding ministers reported that they are seminary graduates.

On the whole, CRC ministers are not particularly youthful, with a mean age of 49.8 years. As one would expect, given this age distribution, most of the pastors are relatively senior, with a mean of 19.2 years in the ministry and 6.4 years at their current congregation. While the CRC no doubt benefits from its relatively experienced ministers, there are long-term concerns within the denomination about the apparent graying of the clergy and the difficulty of attracting new seminarians.

THEOLOGICAL POSITIONS HELD BY CHRISTIAN REFORMED CLERGY

Past research on Christian Reformed clergy (e.g. Guth et al. 1997) has suggested that they tend to fall closer to the orthodox than to the modernist end of the theological spectrum. Table 12.2 confirms this perspective. Indeed, with respect to the first six questions included in the table —items which are often included in indices of theological orthodoxy (Guth et al. 1997, 44–45)—CRC clergy demonstrate considerable support for more orthodox positions. For example, the pastors responding to the survey were nearly unanimous in their agreement with both the statement that "Jesus will return to earth one day" and that "Jesus was born of a virgin" (each with 99 percent response rates). Further, the survey participants were nearly as supportive of the orthodox positions that "the devil actually exists" (98 percent) and that "there is no other way to salvation but through belief in Jesus Christ" (96 percent).

Table 12.2

Theological Views Held by Christian Reformed Clergy

	% Agreeing
Jesus will return to earth one day.	99%
Jesus was born of a virgin.	99%
The devil actually exists.	98%
There is no other way to salvation but through belief in Jesus Christ.	96%
Adam and Eve were real people.	90%
The Bible is the inerrant Word of God, both in matters of faith and in historical, geographical, and other secular matters.	58%
The church should put less emphasis on individual sanctification and more on transforming the social order.	10%

Yet, CRC ministers were somewhat less supportive of other positions that have traditionally been associated with theological orthodoxy. As Table 12.2 demonstrates, while 90 percent of the responding clergy affirmed the orthodox position that "Adam and Eve were real people," fully 10 percent did not agree with the statement. Moreover, agreement levels proved even lower (58 percent) concerning the statement that "the Bible is the inerrant Word of God, both in matters of faith and in historic, geographical, and other secular matters."

These findings demonstrate that while they do indeed tend to be theologically orthodox, CRC ministers also feel free to deviate in certain respects from traditional perspectives. In particular, they tend to separate, at least to some degree, from orthodox positions concerning the reality of Adam and Eve and biblical inerrancy. In this respect, the Christian Reformed clergy may differ somewhat from ministers in more fundamentalist denominations.

The final response in Table 12.2, concerning the view that "the church should put less emphasis on individual sanctification and more on transforming the social order," differs from the previous six statements in that it primarily concerns social ethics rather than theological orthodoxy. It is a particularly interesting and important question to ask CRC ministers. As noted before, there is a longstanding division in the CRC between pietists, who prefer to emphasize personal salvation and sanctification, and Kuyperians, who tend to place a greater emphasis on communal responsibility and societal transformation. Table 12.2 reveals that the pietistic emphasis seems to find greater support among CRC clergy than does the Kuyperian position. Indeed, only 10 percent of the responding pastors asserted that the church should shift its emphasis from individual sanctification and place a greater burden on transforming the social order. It is, of course, possible that these responses simply reflect the belief of some ministers that the CRC is already making a maximum effort to transform the social order. Yet, the overwhelmingly pietistic responses would seem to suggest that Kuyperianism is not the dominant approach accepted by CRC clergy.

POLITICAL ENGAGEMENT
OF CHRISTIAN REFORMED CLERGY

This section of the chapter focuses on three important questions, including the political norms held by Christian Reformed clergy today, the specific policy positions they tend to advocate, and finally, the political activities they engaged in during the 2000 election.

A number of the political norms held by the CRC ministers responding to the survey are included in Table 12.3. The data reveal that they are sensitive about the particular appropriateness of actions taken from the pulpit. On one hand, nearly all the respondents (96 percent) approved of ministers taking a stand from the pulpit on some moral issue. And yet, the clergy tend to be leery of supporting, from the pulpit, specific political issue positions. Indeed, only a minority (44 percent) of the respondents approved of such actions. The survey responses do not tell us why CRC pastors are hesitant to take political positions from the pulpit, but one might assume that both legal prohibitions against such activity and practical concerns over church unity may be involved.

Table 12.3

Political Norms of Christian Reformed Clergy

	% Approving
Take a stand while preaching on some moral issue	96%
While preaching, take a stand on some political issue	44%
Publicly (not preaching) support a political candidate	53%
Contribute money to a candidate, party, or political-action committee	78%
Form an action group in one's church to accomplish a social or political goal	59%
Participate in a protest march	70%
Commit civil disobedience to protest some evil	41%

Considerable variation exists among CRC clergy regarding their support for various types of nonpulpit political activities. As one might expect, only a minority (41 percent) expressed approval of committing "civil disobedience to protest some evil"; such action is, after all, both illegal and relatively extreme in the American context. Slight majorities of pastors expressed approval for publicly (not preaching) supporting a political candidate (53 percent) or for forming an "action group in one's church to accomplish a social or political goal" (59 percent). Again, it is possible that concerns about church unity may have suppressed pastoral support for these activities. Still, certain political activities did receive widespread support among the ministers. Large majorities approved of participation in a protest march (70 percent) and contributing money "to a candidate, party, or political-action committee" (78 percent).

While it is unclear why support for participating in a protest march received such high levels of affirmation, one might speculate that it may, in part, reflect the experiences of the baby-boomer generation of clergy with the antiwar marches of the 1960s.

When one examines the specific policy positions of CRC ministers (reported in Table 12.4), two important trends manifest themselves. First, the responses suggest that there is a high degree of consensus among them with respect to most issues of personal morality and that this collective opinion tends toward traditional, conservative values. For example, a substantial majority (92 percent) of the ministers surveyed agreed that "sex-education programs included in the curricula of public high schools should be abstinence based." In addition, approximately four out of five respondents (78 percent) agreed that "we need a constitutional amendment prohibiting all abortions unless to save the mother's life, or in cases of rape or incest." The exception to this pattern of consensus on issues of personal morality concerned the controversial issue of gay rights; CRC ministers proved divided on this issue, with only a slight majority (54 percent) agreeing with the position that "homosexuals should have all the same rights and privileges as other American citizens."

Table 12.4

Policy Positions of Christian Reformed Clergy

	% Agreeing
The federal government should do more to solve social problems such as unemployment, poverty, and poor housing.	46%
Education policy should focus on improving public schools rather than on encouraging alternatives such as private and religious schools.	18%
Sex-education programs included in the curricula of public high schools should be abstinence based.	92%
We need government-sponsored national health insurance so that everyone can get adequate medical care.	41%
African Americans and other minorities may need special governmental help in order to achieve an equal place in America.	50%
We need a constitutional amendment prohibiting all abortions unless to save the mother's life, or in cases of rape or incest.	78%
Homosexuals should have all the same rights and privileges as other American citizens.	54%
A lasting peace in the Middle East will require Israel to make greater concessions to the Palestinians.	54%

A second pattern apparent from Table 12.4 is that Christian Reformed ministers tend to have doubts about governmental efforts to reform society or deal with structural injustice, or at least they do not support specific policies aimed to further such goals. Thus, for example, only half of the respondents agreed that "African Americans and other minorities may need special governmental help in order to achieve an equal place in America." Moreover, less than half of the ministers agreed that "the federal government should do more to solve social problems such as unemployment, poverty, and poor housing" (46 percent) or affirmed that "we need government-sponsored national health insurance so that everyone can get adequate medical care" (41 percent). Even fewer clergy (18 percent) asserted that "education policy should focus on improving public schools rather than encouraging alternatives such as private and religious schools." While this last finding may, in part, reflect the same distrust of government solutions noted above, it no doubt also stems from the CRC's strong tradition of support for distinctively Christian education at all levels.

Table 12.4 reports ministers' positions on only one foreign-policy question, namely, whether "a lasting peace in the Middle East will require Israel to make greater concessions to the Palestinians." A slight majority (54 percent) of the responding clergy expressed agreement with this statement, suggesting the possibility that Christian Reformed pastors may not be as supportive of Israel as are some of their counterparts in other conservative, evangelical denominations.

The political activities of CRC clergy in the election of 2000 are addressed in Table 12.5, which reveals that, at least in comparison with the general public, these ministers were highly active politically in the election. Indeed, while only a slight majority of the total general electorate voted, fully 92 percent of the ministers reported doing so. Moreover, the pastors also engaged in a wide variety of other activities. Among the most common were "praying publicly about an issue" (67 percent), "urging their congregation to register and vote" (55 percent), and "praying publicly for political candidates" (54 percent). Each of these actions can be performed in a civic-minded and relatively nonpartisan fashion. On the other hand, only minorities of ministers engaged in "contacting a public official about some issue" (33 percent) or taking "a stand from the pulpit on some political issue" (25 percent). Nonetheless, even these levels of political activity suggest considerable political interest and involvement on the part of the respondents.

Table 12.5

Political Activities of Christian Reformed Clergy in the Election of 2000

	% Reporting
Urged their congregation to register and vote	55%
Contacted a public official about some issue	33%
Prayed publicly for political candidates	54%
Took a stand from the pulpit on some political issue	25%
Prayed publicly about an issue	67%
Party Identification	
Strong Democrat	3%
Weak Democrat	4%
Independent, lean Democrat	9%
Independent	9%
Independent, lean Republican	22%
Weak Republican	26%
Strong Republican	28%
Vote Choice in the 2000 Election	
Al Gore	11%
George W. Bush	79%
Pat Buchanan	*
Ralph Nader	2%
Other	*
Did not vote	8%

* = less than 1 percent

As one might expect, given the theological conservatism of CRC ministers, most of the pastors identify themselves as Republicans rather than as Democrats. Indeed, while a majority of the respondents (54 percent) identify with the GOP, only 7 percent align themselves with the Democratic Party. And while over one-quarter of the ministers (28 percent) stated they were strong Republicans, only 3 percent classified themselves as strong Democrats. While 40 percent of the CRC clergy indicated they are political independents, a majority of these independents lean toward the Republican rather than the Democratic Party. These patterns proved nearly identical to those reported in a 1996 survey of CRC clergy (Penning, Smidt, and Brown 2001), suggesting that their GOP identification has had considerable stability.

The Republican Party leanings of most Christian Reformed ministers are reflected in their presidential voting behavior in the 2000 election. Fully 79 percent of the ministers reported voting for the Republican,

George W. Bush, while only 11 percent said they selected Democrat Al Gore, and a mere 2 percent voted for the Green Party nominee, Ralph Nader. Overall, Bush did relatively better in 2000 than did his 1996 GOP counterpart, Robert Dole, who received only 69 percent of the ministers' votes. In contrast, the Democratic nominee in 1996, Bill Clinton, received 15 percent of the clergy's votes (Penning, Smidt, and Brown 2001).

CONCLUSION

Although the Christian Reformed Church is a relatively small denomination, its significance exceeds its size. It has deep roots in American culture, tracing its origins, through its theology and the Reformed Church in America, to America's earliest white settlers. Equally important, the CRC's Kuyperian tradition and its emphasis on education have enhanced its importance as a shaper of evangelical political and social thought.

The personal characteristics, theological views, political attitudes, and political activities of CRC clergy in the election of 2000, as examined in this study, suggest that they are a remarkably homogenous group. Demographically, CRC minisers are primarily married, well-educated, middle-aged, white males. Doctrinally, Christian Reformed pastors are highly orthodox, giving nearly unanimous assent to propositions concerning Jesus' return to earth, the virgin birth, the reality of the devil, and Jesus as the only way to salvation. However, somewhat less support was given to the reality of Adam and Eve, the inerrancy of Scripture, and (particularly) the desirability of shifting the church's emphasis from promoting sanctification to transforming the social order.

While the political norms of CRC ministers are firmly in the classical liberal, democratic tradition, pastors are not equally supportive of all forms of political activity on the part of clergy. In general, the surveyed individuals tended to be most reluctant to practice politics from the pulpit or to engage in activities prohibited by law. On the other hand, the ministers are highly supportive of such private activities as giving money to candidates and participating in a protest march.

An examination of the policy positions held by CRC ministers reveals high levels of agreement on issues of personal morality, as they tend to adopt conservative positions in those areas. On the other hand, the ministers demonstrated considerably less support for government efforts to transform society or address structural injustice, placing them closer to the pietest than to the Kuyperian tradition.

Finally, the Christian Reformed respondents proved to be highly active politically in the 2000 election, exhibiting, for example, a 92 percent voter turnout rate. Moreover, the ministers also reported engaging in a variety of other political activities, including contacting public officials and urging their congregations to register and vote. In overwhelming numbers, the pastors reported identifying with the Republican Party and voting for the Republican presidential candidate, George W. Bush. An examination of their political activities shortly after the 1996 presidential election revealed similar patterns, suggesting general stability in the political orientations and behavior of these pastors.

In recent years, the CRC has experienced some internal turmoil, particularly over the issue of the ordination of women. This conflict has resulted in an exodus of elements of the more conservative congregants and clergy from the denomination. This time period has also witnessed a concerted effort on the part of the CRC as a denomination to broaden its ethnic and racial composition. These shifts, along with more diffuse, secular changes in American society are altering the composition of both the CRC membership and its clergy. It remains to be seen whether this increased social diversity will translate into further political diversity, but that is indeed a possibility.

Chapter 13

Church of the Nazarene

Linda Beail and Greg Crow

The Church of the Nazarene is a denomination in the Wesleyan/ Holiness tradition, which has always held a strong commitment to social justice as well as to personal evangelism. One of the original founders, Phineas Bresee, wrote, "The evidence of the presence of Jesus in our midst is that we bear the gospel, primarily, to the poor. . . . Let the poor be fed and clothed; let us pour out our substances for this purpose; but let us keep heaven open, that they may receive the unspeakable gift of His love, in the transforming power of the Holy Ghost" (Smith 1983, 167–68). The tension between this emphasis on an individual's personal and salvific relationship with Christ, and the social-justice implications inherent in this faith, has always been felt by Nazarenes. "Heart holiness" is personal and internal but only truly evidenced by practicing a holy life, such as showing generosity and love for others. This heritage pushes Nazarenes to be conservative theologically, but opens the possibility for them to express more liberal views on social issues such as poverty, homelessness, and discrimination.

Today's Nazarene clergy reflect that history, while also reacting to the influence of more theologically fundamentalist and parachurch organizations, such as Focus on the Family (founded by the son of a Nazarene pastor, James Dobson), Promise Keepers, and the Bill Gothard seminars. As a result, "holiness" in contemporary American life may be increasingly understood in terms of condemning individualized choices and sins, to the exclusion of systemic and social ills. As a result, it is unclear whether Nazarene clergy, when taking their theological worldview into the political realm, will resemble the more fundamentalist clergy of the "Christian Right" or make some uniquely Wesleyan contribution to democratic polity.

HISTORICAL BACKGROUND

The Church of the Nazarene was established in 1908 in Pilot Point, Texas, when three independent Holiness groups from the Northeast, South, and California merged to form a single denomination. The denomination's theological roots lie in the doctrines of holiness and sanctification taught by John Wesley in the eighteenth-century English revival (Mead 1995). In fact, the church grew out of the Methodist and revivalist traditions: "four of the five [original] general superintendents of the Church of the Nazarene were former Methodist ministers, and the Nazarene Manual has been called a 'rewritten and modified Methodist Discipline'" (Mead 1995, 118).

Like other Wesleyan denominations, the Church of the Nazarene stresses the importance of a definite second work of grace, termed "entire sanctification," beyond the act of salvation (Mead 1995, 118). Entire sanctification is understood as "an act of God, cleansing the heart from original sin and filling the individual with love for God and humankind. This experience is marked by entire consecration of the believer to do God's will and is followed by a life of seeking to serve God through service to others" (Church of the Nazarene). Entire sanctification is also referred to as "heart holiness" or "being filled with the Spirit." Unlike Pentecostals, Nazarenes do not seek the gift of speaking in tongues; they do, however, emphasize the importance of the work of the Holy Spirit more than many other evangelical Protestants. Other doctrines of the Church of the Nazarene, typical of most evangelical denominations, include:

> belief in the plenary inspiration of the Scriptures as containing all truths necessary to Christian faith and living; the atonement of Christ for the whole human race; the justification, regeneration, and adoption of all penitent believers in Christ; the second coming of Christ; the resurrection of the dead; and the final judgment. (Mead 1995, 118)

Nazarenes are morally conservative, with guidelines that admonish members to abstain from activities such as dancing, using tobacco, drinking alcohol, and gambling. However, the denomination is distinguished from its fundamentalist counterparts by its Wesleyan theology. Instead of relying on a literal reading of the Bible as the sole revelation of God's truth, Wesleyans embrace reason, tradition, and experience as well as Scripture as means by which God can communicate His will to believers. Nazarenes have traditionally held to Wesley's maxim of "in essentials, unity; in all else, charity," thus avoiding theological dogmatism or schism.

The Church of the Nazarene is also characterized by a strong interest in evangelism and education. The church supports 590 missionaries in 109 world areas, and sends thousands of laypersons around the globe on short-term "Work and Witness" mission projects (Mead 1995; Church of the Nazarene). Although a relatively small denomination, the Church of the Nazarene supports eight liberal arts colleges and universities in the United States alone, as well as two graduate seminaries and forty-three Bible colleges worldwide (Church of the Nazarene). Church governance is relatively democratic and nonhierarchical, with local congregations maintaining autonomous control over choosing their own pastors and church boards. The denomination itself is governed by a board of six general superintendents, who are chosen by representative members at a general assembly of the church held every four years.

The Church of the Nazarene is the largest in the Wesleyan-Arminian tradition, with approximately 600,000 members in the United States and 1.3 million worldwide (Church of the Nazarene). Nazarenes are concentrated mainly in the middle section of the United States and are more likely to be found in rural than urban areas (Kosmin and Lachman 1993). Nazarenes have tended to be working class and lower middle class in social status; in the 1990 National Survey of Religious Identification, Nazarenes ranked twenty-fifth out of thirty denominations in socioeconomic status. Only 13 percent of Nazarenes in the survey were college graduates, with a median annual household income of $21,600 (Kosminand Lachman 1993). The researchers note that:

> Social studies of small California towns in the 1940s found that businessmen and the occupational elite tended to be Congregationalists and Methodists, while manual workers identified with the Church of the Nazarene or the Assemblies of God. This pattern is not just a historical vestige; it also operates in the modern business world. (Kosmin and Lachman 1993, 253)

With its combination of rural, blue-collar roots and Wesleyan doctrine, the Church of the Nazarene is "a major component of the conservative wing of the Holiness movement" (Kosmin and Lachman 1993, 69).

NATURE OF THE STUDY[30]

In October 2000, the General Secretary of the Church of the Nazarene agreed to provide us with a list of the names and addresses for all senior pastors found in its 5,103 churches located in the United States. A sample of 1,200 of these pastors was randomly selected to be surveyed. The first survey was mailed November 4, 2000 (November 6 for the West Coast recipients) to ensure that the pastors would receive the survey just after Election Day. Each hand-addressed envelope included only the survey instrument with its preprinted cover letter, signed by Ron Benefiel, the president of Nazarene Theological Seminary. The second wave of surveys was mailed on December 16, 2000.

The response rate for completed surveys was 51 percent (n=602), a reasonable rate for a mail survey. Of the 598 questionnaires mailed but not completed, three pastors returned them refusing to participate in the study, one was inadvertently sent to a United States address of a Canadian church, and twenty-one went to churches that were temporarily without a pastor.

SOCIAL CHARACTERISTICS OF NAZARENE CLERGY

The Church of the Nazarene pastors surveyed are overwhelmingly white (93 percent) and male (97 percent). They are primarily married (89 percent married, never divorced or widowed) and middle-aged (both the mean and median are fifty years of age). They tend to be fairly well educated: only 24 percent have less than a college degree, while 77 percent report holding a bachelor's degree. A little less than a majority (45 percent) has done some postgraduate work, with 36 percent reporting having a graduate degree from seminary. Of those who are seminary graduates, most pursued theological education at colleges and universities within their own tradition; nearly 82 percent were educated at the Nazarene Theological Seminary in Kansas City.

On average, the clergy have been in the ministry for twenty years (with a wide range of service among respondents, from less than one year to sixty years). Nazarene pastors tend to move between churches fairly frequently, given the high degree of local church autonomy; the ministers in our survey have served their present congregations for an average of six and a half years. Several of the respondents have served the same church for up to thirty-eight years, skewing the mean upward. The median length of service is a mere four years, and most pastors (80 percent) have been in their present church for ten years or less.

Table 13.1

Social Characteristics of Church of the Nazarene Clergy

	% of Clergy
Gender: Male	97%
Race: White	93%
Marital Status: Married, never divorced	89%
Education	
College Graduate	77%
Seminary Graduate	36%
Age	
Under 35 years of age	7%
Over 55 years of age	30%
Community Size	
Farm or small town	43%
Small or medium-sized cities	29%
Large cities	28%

Nazarene congregations are primarily located in rural areas or small towns (63 percent of ministers indicate they live in communities of 50,000 people or less), which is not surprising given the historical development of the denomination. Most congregations tend to be rather small; the average number of worshippers reported on Sunday mornings was 135 (again, this mean was skewed by the presence of a few very large churches, with five pastors reporting attendance of 1,000 or more). Large churches are atypical in the Church of the Nazarene; perhaps a better measure of church size is the median attendance of eighty persons on a normal Sunday. Finally, a sizable number of pastors characterize their congregations as primarily working class (40 percent) rather than middle class (32 percent), with the remainder denoting their churches as "mixed" in class status, which fits with previous survey findings about the blue-collar nature of the Nazarene denomination.

THEOLOGICAL POSITIONS HELD BY NAZARENE CLERGY

Pastors in the Church of the Nazarene hold highly orthodox views on theological questions, which would be expected from members of a conservative evangelical denomination. As is evident in Table 13.2, they are nearly unanimous in their belief in the virgin birth, the existence of the devil, and the second coming of Christ. Almost all ministers hold that salvation is possible only through belief in Jesus. This theological conservatism is further confirmed by responses to additional questions in the survey showing them united in their opposition to homosexual clergy, evolutionist theory, and both feminist and liberation theology.

The pastors' Wesleyan beliefs may be somewhat evident in the less emphatic agreement with the biblical literalism question. First, while a strong majority holds that the Bible is completely inerrant (86 percent), it is not universally affirmed. Second, an even larger percentage (90 percent) *rejects* a fundamentalist reading of Scripture that prohibits women from positions of church leadership and ordination, though a majority of Nazarene pastors agree with statements related to the Bible's historical veracity, such as "Adam and Eve were real people" rather than allegorical figures (96 percent), reflecting the degree to which fundamentalism may have begun to overshadow more traditional Wesleyan ideology of "plenary inspiration."

Table 13.2

Theological Views Held by Church of the Nazarene Clergy

	% Agreeing
Jesus will return to earth one day.	99%
Jesus was born of a virgin.	100%
The devil actually exists.	99%
There is no other way to salvation but through belief in Jesus Christ.	98%
Adam and Eve were real people.	96%
The Bible is the inerrant Word of God, both in matters of faith and in historical, geographical, and other secular matters.	86%
The church should put less emphasis on individual sanctification and more on transforming the social order.	3%

Nazarene pastors also overwhelmingly agree (97 percent) that the church should stress individual sanctification more than transforming the social order, a likely result of holding personal heart holiness as a mainstay of the tradition. However, further analysis of questions juxtaposing social and individual morality yields somewhat more complex responses, given Nazarenes' historical pattern of taking stands against certain social ills. While rooted in the idea of personal cleansing, the church has historically seen sanctification as the beginning of a process that transforms the individual and then leads to social change, as one rejects worldly evils and seeks to serve others. Nazarenes have taken strong positions in support of temperance and against gambling, in part due to the social consequences of these activities, such as poverty and familial breakdown. Thus, the emphasis on individual sanctification comes not at the expense of social transformation, but as a necessary precursor to it in the minds of the Nazarene clergy. Further analysis of the data reveals that nearly two-thirds of the pastors agree "if enough people were brought to Christ, social issues would take care of themselves." There is further evidence that they seek to balance personal salvation with social transformation as well: almost 61 percent agree that "social justice is at the heart of the gospel."

POLITICAL ENGAGEMENT OF NAZARENE CLERGY

Church of the Nazarene pastors hold a positive view of most types of political activism, and they are especially supportive of activities that involve their official capacity as clergy members. As seen in Table 13.3, a majority approve of publicly taking a stand on political and moral issues from the pulpit (almost all are comfortable with preaching on "moral" issues; far fewer support doing the same on overtly "political" issues). More than half the respondents also think it appropriate to support particular candidates publicly, a potentially important cue-giving role for their congregations.

A majority of Nazarene ministers (57 percent) approve of giving money to political candidates, parties, and political-action committees, but they are much more ambivalent about direct political organizing, such as forming an action group in their churches or participating in a public protest. By far, the pastors are most uncomfortable with engaging in civil disobedience, as only 19 percent approve of this. As a group, the ministers seem to have a great deal of trust in the current political system and feel little need to reject or undermine it.

Table 13.3

Political Norms of Church of the Nazarene Clergy

	% Approving
Take a stand while preaching on some moral issue	97%
While preaching, take a stand on some political issue	58%
Publicly (not preaching) support a political candidate	54%
Contribute money to a candidate, party, or political-action committee	57%
Form an action group in one's church to accomplish a social or political goal	40%
Participate in a protest march	45%
Commit civil disobedience to protest some evil	19%

When asked about their policy preferences on a wide range of social and political issues, Nazarene pastors display a consistently conservative worldview. As Table 13.4 shows, most of them are opposed to "big government," with two-thirds lacking any desire to see it more actively engaged in solving social problems. They advocate private and individualized solutions to social problems, rather than political or group-oriented approaches. The ministers prefer encouraging private and religious schools rather than improving public education and generally oppose national health insurance (24 percent in favor). They see little need for affirmative action (22 percent), and even less for women's rights legislation (15 percent). A majority of Nazarene clergy also support welfare reform (58 percent), capital punishment (72 percent), teaching creationism (83 percent), and are in opposition to gun control (71 percent). On foreign policy, they are suspicious of the rest of the world: most support increased defense spending (68 percent), urge care in United States dealings with Russia (77 percent), and oppose giving China most-favored-nation trading status (85 percent). Like many evangelicals, they are extremely supportive of Israel, with only 22 percent believing that the Jewish state should make greater concessions to the Palestinians. This may reflect not only the pastors' eschatological understanding of the role of Israel but also their belief that there are usually "right" and "wrong" answers to political questions, not complexities or gray areas that require compromise.

The issues of sexuality and abortion generate widely held consensus in the responses of the clergy. Ninety-five percent believe that sex education in public schools should be abstinence based, with an astounding 64 percent strongly supporting that statement. The ministers are also vehement about the need for a constitutional amendment banning abortion, with 89 percent agreeing and 57 percent taking the strongest possible stance to approve of this survey question. Only 35 percent support civil rights for gays. These commonly held views are not a surprise in light of the Holiness theology that stresses purity of heart, mind, and activity: these are issues that deal with individual choices and behavior, not reforming institutions, and they directly relate to the concept of purity and holy living. Thus, these are the policy issues that Nazarene clergy seem to be most concerned with and on which they have the greatest certainty about their positions.

Table 13.4

Policy Positions of Church of the Nazarene Clergy

	% Agreeing
The federal government should do more to solve social problems such as unemployment, poverty, and poor housing.	37%
Education policy should focus on improving public schools rather than on encouraging alternatives such as private and religious schools.	21%
Sex-education programs included in the curricula of public high schools should be abstinence based.	95%
We need government-sponsored national health insurance so that everyone can get adequate medical care.	24%
African Americans and other minorities may need special governmental help in order to achieve an equal place in America.	22%
We need a constitutional amendment prohibiting all abortions unless to save the mother's life, or in cases of rape or incest.	89%
Homosexuals should have all the same rights and privileges as other American citizens.	35%
A lasting peace in the Middle East will require Israel to make greater concessions to the Palestinians.	22%

Nazarene pastors are very interested in the political sphere. Nearly all of them (80 percent) report being more than "mildly interested" in politics and the 2000 election campaign, and over three-quarters (87 percent) said they paid a lot of attention to news reports about the 2000 election process. Not only do they eagerly follow what is happening on the political scene, a majority (53 percent) express a desire for even more personal involvement in politics and also support additional efforts by the Nazarene church to expand involvement in social and political issues. Accounts of the denomination in earlier times gave the impression that Nazarenes, like many evangelicals, were fairly disengaged from civic life, focusing more on individual soul-winning and the life hereafter than on the political process and earthly concerns. Without longitudinal data, it is difficult to specify when the shift to greater political engagement occurred; perhaps it is linked to the rise of the Christian Right in the 1980s, when evangelicals as a whole became more energized about social and political issues. Certainly today's Nazarene clergy seem very interested in political events and lend importance to continued and increased involvement in this realm. The pastors display a certain naiveté about politics, though. More than one-third (37 percent) believe there is a single "Christian" position on political issues, and almost none (only 12 percent) acknowledge the necessity of compromise in the political process, preferring to "stick to one's principles at the risk of achieving little" (65 percent).

In addition to asking pastors about the political activities they supported in theory, the survey also inquired about actual political action during the 2000 election process. Table 13.5 reports the levels of activity in certain select political categories.

Table 13.5

Political Activities of Church of the Nazarene Clergy in the Election of 2000

	% Reporting
Urged their congregation to register and vote	76%
Contacted a public official about some issue	37%
Prayed publicly for political candidates	52%
Took a stand from the pulpit on some political issue	39%
Prayed publicly about an issue	65%
Party Identification	
Strong Democrat	2%
Weak Democrat	3%
Independent, lean Democrat	1%
Independent	6%
Independent, lean Republican	17%
Weak Republican	19%
Strong Republican	52%
Vote Choice in the 2000 Election	
Al Gore	5%
George W. Bush	90%
Pat Buchanan	*
Ralph Nader	*
Other	*
Did not vote	3%

* = less than 1 percent

By far, the most frequent activity in 2000 was urging parishioners to register and vote (76 percent). This is perhaps not surprising, given that voting is the most common and least costly (in terms of time and effort) form of political participation in the United States. Pastors appear to be taking deliberate steps to encourage their congregations to view good citizenship as part of being a good Christian, rather than withdrawing from the world. A majority of ministers also reported praying publicly about issues and candidates, and many also made their views on a political issue known from the pulpit (39 percent). For Nazarene ministers, taking action within their public role as pastor is a preferred mode of political activism. The data show that few of the clergy participated in conventional citizen activities like contacting officials, contributing money, attending political rallies, campaigning, or joining political organizations. Only three pastors in the entire survey group reported participating in civil disobedience, the least popular activity of all.

The pastors' concern about politics is not distributed across the ideological spectrum; they are a monolithic group, leaning toward the far right in their self-identification of ideology and political partisanship. Nazarene ministers are overwhelmingly conservative (87 percent); only 10 percent call themselves moderate, and a mere 4 percent identify themselves as liberal. In fact, most respondents believe that "it is hard to be a true Christian and a liberal" (72 percent).

The Nazarene clergy are almost universally Republican in their partisanship (88 percent), and most locate themselves within the staunchest segment of party loyalists: an astonishing 52 percent of Nazarene pastors chose the furthest end of the seven-point party identification scale, (strong Republican) as the category best describing them. Only 6 percent of Nazarene pastors identified as Democrats, which is somewhat surprising given the blue-collar, lower socioeconomic status of the denomination. However, these evangelicals may be among the "Reagan Democrats" who have realigned over the past thirty years over moral, racial, and other issues. In the year 2000, they were solidly in the Republican camp.

Nazarene pastors have turned out strongly at the polls, and they did not defect from their partisan identification in the 2000 presidential election. Ninety-seven percent of the ministers reported voting, and they overwhelmingly supported George W. Bush (90 percent). Clearly, in the 2000 election, Republican candidates could rely on the solid support of Nazarene pastors in the national campaign.

CONCLUSION

Church of the Nazarene clergy possess a Holiness theology that is both inward- and outward-looking, calling them to link personal purity and orthodoxy with radical social transformation. They translate this perspective into twenty-first-century American politics, in part by staying true to their theologically conservative heritage as they hold to highly orthodox views on theological questions, such as the virgin birth, the devil, and the second coming of Christ, while they differ from fundamentalists on significant issues such as the role of women in church leadership, as the vast majority of Nazarene clergy assert that all clergy positions should be open to women. They also refuse to choose between individual and social transformation, insisting that both are necessary. While they agree that individual sanctification should never be downplayed at the expense of social change, they view social justice as an inherent part of the gospel: social holiness will be the fruit borne of personal holiness.

On the other hand, Nazarene ministers have adopted an individualistic, and somewhat absolutist, approach to political issues. They oppose more government intervention into poverty, education, and health care, instead preferring private or personal solutions. The issues that unite and energize them are issues of sexual morality and "family values." The clergy are strongly in favor of abstinence based sex education and a constitutional ban on abortion, but overwhelmingly oppose gay rights. Most believe there is a "Christian" position on such issues and view the political world in fairly stark terms, where evil is easy to identify and good can be advocated for without question.

While Nazarene clergy may have been disengaged from politics in earlier times, focusing more on soul-winning than on winning election campaigns, today's Nazarene ministers are quite interested in politics and have a great deal of trust in the American political process. In the 2000 election campaign, Nazarene pastors were politically active from the pulpit, socializing their congregations by praying about issues and candidates and urging the church members to vote.

Nazarene clergy are rather monolithic in their ideological and partisan preferences. Nearly all define themselves as conservative and Republican, with a majority choosing the strongest possible identification with the GOP. Any holiness distinctiveness and sociodemographic background that might push the Nazarene clergy toward more liberal or communitarian positions are, at this moment, largely overshadowed by individualistic and fundamentalist influences.

Chapter 14

Assemblies of God

John C. Green

The Assemblies of God is the largest Pentecostal denomination in the United States. It originated in the Pentecostal revivals of the early twentieth century, one of several religious movements that operated on the fringes of American Protestantism and the margins of mainstream society. This outsider status extended to politics, where Pentecostals were widely regarded as apolitical, a tendency that was especially pronounced in their religious institutions and among their clergy. As the century progressed, however, Pentecostals carved out a prominent niche in American religion and moved steadily into the social mainstream, buoyed by strong religious institutions and prodigious evangelism. This trend eventually produced a high level of political engagement. Some Pentecostals followed the path of working from within party politics, of which U.S. Attorney General John Ashcroft is a good example. Others entered the political fray more as outsiders to party politics, such as Pat Robertson's bid to capture the 1988 Republican presidential nomination and the activities of the Christian Coalition (Hertzke 1993; Guth et al. 1995). Assemblies of God clergy were central to this political transformation (Green 1996), and by the 2000 election these ministers had become a bulwark of the Right in American politics. This essay describes the distinctive characteristics of the Assemblies of God clergy and their political engagement at the beginning of the twenty-first century.

HISTORICAL BACKGROUND

The Assemblies of God denomination was founded in 1914 at a meeting in Hot Springs, Arkansas, of three hundred clergy, evangelists, and lay persons from twenty states and several countries (Assemblies of God 2002a). The attendees were veterans of more than a decade of Pentecostal revivals, the first of which took place in 1901 at Bethel Bible College in Topeka, Kansas. Perhaps the most famous of these revivals occurred at the Azusa Street Mission in Los Angeles, California, between 1903 and 1913. The distinguishing characteristics of these revivals included speaking in tongues (uttering unknown languages during prayer) and other gifts of the Spirit during spontaneous and ecstatic worship. The participants interpreted these phenomena as the baptism of the Holy Spirit mentioned in the New Testament book of the Acts of the Apostles, which occurred on Pentecost. Thus, these spirit-filled Christians were soon called "Pentecostals." Although such revivals were distinctive, they were deeply influenced by other nineteenth-century religious movements among pietist Protestants, including the restorationist, holiness, premillennial, healing, and fundamentalist movements (Blumhofer 1993). Similar to these trends, Pentecostalism was a reaction to the inroads of modernist theology in the major Protestant denominations and shared an affirmation of orthodox Protestant doctrine, a commitment to evangelicalism, and the assumption that God was directly active in the lives of believers.

The purpose of the initial meeting in 1914 was to develop a cooperative fellowship able to address some practical problems that emerged from the Pentecostal revivals. These issues included the need for doctrinal unity, gospel literature, accounting of funds, and the approval and training of clergy and missionaries. Having originated from many religious backgrounds and viewing themselves primarily as a spiritual movement, the Hot Springs participants had little interest in forming a centralized denomination. Accordingly, they adopted a loose organizational structure, the General Assembly of the Assemblies of God, which united local congregations for certain common purposes but left them autonomous in other regards. In 1916 the general council promulgated a "Statement of Fundamental Truth," and within two years, the

Assembly had articulated a distinct theological perspective and moved its headquarters to the present location in Springfield, Missouri in 1918 (Blumhofer 1993, 137).

At its founding, the Assemblies of God encapsulated a tension between the spontaneity of religious movements and the order of denominational institutions (Poloma 1989). This tension helps define the relatively brief history of the Assemblies of God (Blumhofer 1985). From 1918 to 1940, the denomination developed basic religious institutions largely in isolation from other evangelical Protestants, including the fundamentalists, who rejected the gifts of the Spirit as false or even satanic. A period of contact with other evangelicals began in the 1940s, when the Assemblies of God accepted the invitation to join the newly founded National Association of Evangelicals and the National Association of Religious Broadcasters. A few years later, it joined the Pentecostal World Congress and the Pentecostal Fellowship of North America. At the same time, the denomination faced disputes with the "Latter Rain" movement, which put special stress on faith healing. By 1960, the Assemblies of God was beginning to achieve acceptance outside of the evangelical subculture and faced the challenge of the charismatic movement, which operated across the religious landscape and held a broader definition of the gifts of the Spirit. However, by the end of the century, these tensions had largely abated, and the Assemblies of God had become a force in a growing worldwide Pentecostal movement (Blumhofer, Spitller, and Wacker 1999).

In 2000, Assemblies of God was the largest Pentecostal denomination and the twelfth largest overall denomination in the United States, with more than 2.5 million members and some 12,000 congregations (Assemblies of God 2002a). In addition, the Assemblies of God claimed some 35 million followers and more than 200,000 congregations in 186 countries. This dramatic expansion was not consistent over time, including instead periods of rapid and slow growth, necessitating continual adaptation to changing circumstances. The Assemblies of God's ability to adapt resulted from its identity, mission, structure, and beliefs.

The Assemblies of God's "Visions 2000 Proclamation" (Assemblies of God 2002b) describes the church and its mission as follows:

> We are a people of the Spirit. We are a people of vision. Birthed in the fire of renewal, still less than a hundred years ago, we have now become a worldwide influence for worship, discipleship, and evangelism in the 21st century. What God has done, and is doing, should fill us with gratitude and awe, and should move us to deep prayer and faith in understanding

God's vision for us in this new century. Who can predict what the Holy Spirit may yet do before the return of the Lord? His vision is that the glory of Christ be revealed among every people and culture. Our church must proclaim Christ to this world in the 21st century with first-century fervor. . . . We believe the past is prologue to an unparalleled, sweeping outpouring of the Holy Spirit, as we surrender ourselves afresh to be used as a vital agency for the fulfillment of the Great Commission, bringing all the gospel by all means to all people.

The structure of the Assemblies of God has been described as "an unusual mix of presbyterian and congregational systems" (Mead 1990b, 189). Local congregations ("assemblies") are founded, financed, and governed independently, providing parish clergy with a wide scope for entrepreneurship and great local autonomy. The congregations are organized into fifty-seven districts ("district presbyteries"), where district officials are charged with pastoral ministry, licensing and ordaining ministers, and promoting evangelism. All licensed and ordained ministers belong to district councils, and all ordained ministers belong to the general council; each congregation sends one lay delegate to the district and national councils. The general council meets biennially to elect general officers ("executive presbytery"), set doctrinal standards, promote church growth, and attend to matters of common concern.

The Assemblies of God supports a publishing house, a seminary, and twenty Bible colleges. In line with the denomination's organizational structure, it is committed to establishing self-supporting national church bodies in every country in the world. To that end, the denomination has helped found more than 1,800 Bible schools abroad and is part of the World Assemblies of God Fellowship (Assemblies of God 2002a).

One observer describes the theology of the Assemblies of God as "Arminian" and "ardently fundamentalist" (Mead 1990b, 189), and another calls it "fundamentalism with a difference" (Blumhofer 1993, 5–6). The Arminian reference applies to the denomination's emphasis on personal religious experience and individual agency in accepting salvation. And the Assemblies of God is fundamentalist in its strident insistence on the "fundamental truths" of orthodox Protestantism. However, the church differs from classic fundamentalism by including distinctive doctrines concerning the Holy Spirit among the fundamental truths.

The Assemblies of God lists sixteen nonnegotiable doctrines in its Statement of Fundamental Truths (Assemblies of God 2002c), several of which are regarded as "cardinal doctrines" essential to the "church's core mission to reach the world for Christ." It is one of these cardinal

doctrines, the baptism of the Holy Ghost, that makes Pentecostals distinctive, and here the Assemblies of God has its own unique understanding. It affirms "All believers are entitled to and should ardently expect
and earnestly seek the promise of the Father, the baptism of the Holy
Ghost and fire, according to the command of our Lord Jesus Christ."
This "second baptism" is "distinct from and subsequent to the experience of new birth," namely, the "born again" experience or conversion
to Christianity. This subsequent baptism experience carries with it
"enduement of power for life and service, the bestowment of gifts, and
their uses in the work of ministries," including "overflowing fullness of
the Sprit," a "deepened reverence for God," and "more active love of
Christ, for His Word, and for the lost." In addition, the Assemblies of
God holds that the "initial physical evidence" of the second baptism is
speaking in tongues ("speaking with other tongues as the Spirit of God
gives them utterance"), a point that separates them from some other
spirit-filled Christians. Another cardinal doctrine is divine healing,
which is also considered to be a gift of the Spirit.

This emphasis on the gifts of the Spirit leads the Assemblies of God
and other Pentecostals to argue that they preach the "full gospel," one
that adds the regular experience of the divine to the traditional promise
of salvation. According to one commentator, for the Assemblies of God
the "paranormal is normal," (Poloma 1989, 21) or as another notes
"The Assemblies of God believe that all the gifts of the Spirit should be
evident in the normal New Testament church" (Mead 1990b, 189).
These practices include speaking in tongues and interpreting tongues;
the giving of prophecy; singing, dancing and being slain in the Spirit;
altar calls for special needs; testimonials of miracles; divine healing; and
deliverance services (Poloma 1989). These activities occur in the context
of ecstatic public worship and intense private devotionalism.

The Assemblies of God also hold other orthodox Protestants beliefs,
including the cardinal doctrines of "salvation through belief in Jesus
Christ" and the "second coming of Christ," which are central to its focus
on evangelism. The remaining principles in the Assembly of God
Statement of Fundamental Truths closely resemble the assertions of
other evangelicals: "Scriptures are the inspired word of God;" "there is
one true God"; "the deity of Jesus Christ"; "the fall of man"; the "ordinances of the church"; "individual sanctification"; the "purpose of
church and its mission"; the "ministry of the church"; the "blessed hope
of salvation"; "the final judgment"; and the "creation of a new heavens
and a new earth." Indeed, the cardinal doctrines of the Assemblies of

God fit logically into this sequence of beliefs, with the need for salvation resulting from the fall of man; the baptism of the Holy Ghost following the ordinances of the church (one of which is the "first" baptism); divine healing following the ministry of the church; and the second coming of Christ preceding the final judgment (Assemblies of God 2002c).

In recent years, the Assemblies of God appear to be more accepting of political activity—almost certainly more so than in previous generations. Indeed, it is widely accepted that Pentecostals were apolitical prior to the 1980s (Guth et al. 1997). The movement's focus on otherworldly matters and its cardinal doctrines are commonly offered as explanations for this lack of political engagement. But additionally, Pentecostals have historically tended to be of lower-class status, thus lacking the resources to participate in politics. Finally, the salient issues of previous political eras, especially economic and foreign-policy matters, did not arouse the interest of Pentecostals. In recent years, however, there has been considerable change on all these matters (Smidt et al. 1996). The Assemblies of God's dramatic growth has brought its members into closer contact with the world, and at the same time, its adherents have experienced considerable upward mobility. Perhaps most importantly, the appearance of moral issues on the political agenda has aroused Pentecostals, reducing potential theological barriers to political engagement.

These trends should not be overstated, however. Pentecostals still lag behind members of other denominations in many of these areas (Smidt et al. 1999), and the Assembly of God's official position on political engagement is a study in ambivalence. On the one hand, the denomination declares, "The Assemblies of God *does not* endorse systems of government or political parties" (emphasis in the original) and "The Assemblies of God is apolitical; that is it takes a neutral stance on purely political issues" (Assemblies of God 2002d, 2002e). After warning about the potential danger that politics could divide the church, the denomination continues that its members have an obligation to obey the civil government, to which God has assigned important duties separate from the church. In this regard, the Assemblies of God asserts that the principal mission of the church is spiritual rather than political.

On the other hand, the denomination notes (Assemblies of God 2002e):

> In recent years in America, however, the relationship between church and state has become increasingly complex and estranged. The reason for this change is a growing trend in government to redefine and politicize moral issues. This wholesale sell-out of these once concrete and absolute moral

values comes in direct opposition to the message of the church found in Scripture. . . .

More and more, government is defying biblical principles and interpreting sinful behavior as civil rights, i.e. abortion and homosexuality. The church as the body of Christ cannot stand by. . . .

While the Assemblies of God as an organization recognizes its calling and will continue to refrain from over-involvement in political issues, it will not abdicate its responsibility to speak out forcefully against immoral laws and oppose legislation which clearly defies Scripture.

The Assemblies of God thus urges its members to:

...influence society and the political process by voting, maintaining strong moral convictions and holy lifestyles, praying for government officials, encouraging and promoting legislation that strengthens the nation morally, and speaking out both corporately and individually against any political issue that would have an adverse effect upon the kingdom of God or His moral absolutes. (Assemblies of God 2002e)

With this perspective in mind, the Assemblies of God has prepared numerous position papers on issues, with a special emphasis on moral questions. It has even addressed such controversial matters as civil disobedience, where, for instance, the denomination recognizes the moral imperatives that may require defiance of the civil authorities and goes on to warn against apathy in the face of evil. However, it also cautions believers against "selfish justification of illegal protest" (Assemblies of God 2002f). This conflict was evident among Assemblies of God members in the 1980s (Poloma 1989), right before Pat Robertson's presidential campaign in 1988. Such ambivalence fits well with the denomination's orthodox beliefs and individualist social theology.

NATURE OF THE STUDY

As part of a cooperative research effort to study the role of clergy in American politics, a mail survey of Assemblies of God pastors serving local churches was conducted at the University of Akron. A random sample of 1,000 ministers was drawn from the official lists of Assemblies of God congregations published by the denominational headquarters. The surveys were mailed in the spring of 2001, and the sample was contacted four times. These efforts produced 336 usable returns, with a response rate of 45 percent (excluding undelivered mail). This return rate is similar for surveys of clergy in other evangelical denominations, but lower than for a 1988 survey of Assemblies of God clergy (Guth et al. 1997). The length of the common questionnaire may have contributed to a lower response rate in this survey.

The returned surveys were carefully inspected for response bias. In comparison to the original mailing list, there was a modest discrepancy by region, with slightly fewer returns from pastors of congregations in the South. Accordingly, the sample was weighted to correct for this deficiency. A comparison of the demographic characteristics of this sample with the 1988 survey of Assemblies of God ministers revealed only a few differences, particularly a somewhat older and better-educated clergy. This may simply reflect changes in the denomination in the intervening years, or it may be that this survey sample overrepresents somewhat older and better-educated clergy. With these few exceptions, the 2001 results do not differ significantly from the 1988 findings (see Guth et al. 1997 for all references to the 1988 survey).

SOCIAL CHARACTERISTICS
OF ASSEMBLIES OF GOD CLERGY

In demographic terms, Assemblies of God clergy are very similar to other evangelical clergy: 94 percent of respondents are male, and 88 percent are white (see Table 14.1). Some 94 percent of the clergy are married and never divorced, and almost half reported that their spouses work outside the home. These patterns differ very little from the 1988 survey demographics. The clergy in the 2001 sample tend to be middle-aged, with a mean age of forty-eight years. Some 11 percent of the pastors are thirty-five years old or younger, and more than twice that many (26 percent) are over fifty-five. In this regard, the 1988 and 2000 samples varied somewhat: in 1988, 21 percent were younger than thirty-five.

The geographical base of the Assemblies of God is primarily in the Sunbelt, particularly in small towns or rural areas. Nearly a plurality of the pastors (44 percent) serve congregations located in the South, while another one-quarter live in the West (24 percent) and a fifth in the Midwest (21 percent), with the remainder scattered throughout the Northeast. Approximately half of Assemblies of God clergy serve congregations in rural areas or small towns (46 percent), and fewer live in small or medium-sized cities (28 percent) or major metropolitan areas (26 percent). A relatively large portion of responding clergy serve racially diverse congregations, with one-quarter (26 percent) mixed, in ethnic or racial terms, and one-tenth (10 percent) minority. Reflecting their heritage, Assemblies of God clergy tend to serve working-class and lower middle-class congregations. Some two-fifths (41 percent) of the clergy responded that their congregations are working class, and nearly as many (37 percent) reported the members of the church as having mixed-class backgrounds. A little less than one-quarter (23 percent) evaluated their congregation to be middle class in character. The pastors reported serving small churches, with 68 percent of the clergy noting that their congregations have 120 members or less, and just 10 percent claiming 400 members or more.

Table 14.1
Social Characteristics of Assemblies of God Clergy

	% of Clergy
Gender: Male	94%
Race: White	88%
Marital Status: Married, never divorced	94%
Education	
College Graduate	43%
Seminary Graduate	19%
Age	
Under 35 years of age	11%
Over 55 years of age	26%
Community Size	
Farm or small town	46%
Small or medium-sized cities	28%
Large cities	26%

Nearly nine of ten respondents (88 percent) are ordained, with the rest being licensed ministers. A little more than two-fifths (43 percent) have a four-year college degree, and a little less than one-fifth (19 percent) are seminary graduates (the largest number attended the Assemblies of God seminary). The educational response differs from the 1988 survey, when fewer clergy were college graduates (26 percent), but about the same number (18 percent) had completed seminary. If these comparisons are accurate, then Assemblies of God clergy have experienced a substantial increase in educational attainment over the last decade.

Overall, Assemblies of God pastors who were surveyed are midcareer, professional ministers with a mean number of years in the ministry of twenty-two. Some mobility was exhibited in terms of the congregations they serve: the mean number of years the clergy have been at their present churches is eight years.

THEOLOGICAL POSITIONS HELD
BY ASSEMBLIES OF GOD CLERGY

The extent to which Assemblies of God clergy assert the official doctrines of the denomination are included in Table 14.2, which reports the percentage agreeing with six tenets of Protestant orthodoxy. The uniformity of the results is breathtaking: nearly 100 percent of the sample agree with these positions. From one perspective, the pattern is hardly surprising given the denomination's Statement of Fundamental Truths. As noted previously, two of the positions, that "Jesus will return to earth one day" and "There is no other way to salvation but through belief in Jesus Christ" are cardinal doctrines of the Assemblies of God. An inerrant view of Scripture is very close to the first of the doctrines listed in the Statement of Fundamental Truths, while the acceptance of the virgin birth, existence of the devil, and historicity of Adam and Eve all flow from such a view of scriptural authority. There was some variation on a few of the theological questions. For instance, only 83 percent *strongly* agree with biblical inerrancy as compared to 97 percent who *strongly* assert the second coming of Christ. These figures differ very little from comparable items in the 1988 survey of Assemblies of God clergy; if anything, the denomination's clergy in this survey are even more orthodox in their theological stands than those in 1988.

From another perspective, however, these findings are indeed surprising: one might well expect more variation based solely on individual differences, particularly in a denomination where there is great local autonomy and a lack of uniform education of the clergy. Under these circumstances, the very high degree of orthodoxy bespeaks potent religious and social experiences, just as one might expect from a self-conscious spiritual movement that sees itself in tension with the modern world. Although such spiritual/worldly conflict may have lessened in recent times, it is still sufficient to generate nearly uniform beliefs on matters central to the Assemblies of God identity among the religious professionals who lead the church.

Table 14.2

Theological Views Held by Assemblies of God Clergy

	% Agreeing
Jesus will return to earth one day.	99%
Jesus was born of a virgin.	99%
The devil actually exists.	99%
There is no other way to salvation but through belief in Jesus Christ.	98%
Adam and Eve were real people.	97%
The Bible is the inerrant Word of God, both in matters of faith and in historical, geographical, and other secular matters.	96%
The church should put less emphasis on individual sanctification and more on transforming the social order.	2%

Data not included in Table 14.2 support this conclusion. For instance, more than 90 percent of the sample identify themselves as charismatic or Pentecostal, similar to 1988 responses. Of the remaining respondents, three-quarters claim to be evangelicals (as do three-quarters of the entire sample). Although this survey did not ask specific questions about the Assemblies of God views on baptism of the Holy Spirit, the 1988 survey found strong agreement on this cardinal tenet of faith (84 percent), and furthermore, such agreement was strongly linked to doctrinal orthodoxy.

The final item in Table 14.2 taps the social theology of the clergy (Guth et al. 1997, 8). Virtually no respondents agree with the statement "The church should put less emphasis on individual sanctification and more on transforming the social order." Indeed, three-fifths of those surveyed strongly disagree; as previously noted, individual sanctification is one of the doctrines in the Statement of Fundamental Truths. This position reveals strong support for the traditional "private gospel," which places strong emphasis on transforming individuals rather than reforming the structure of society. Assemblies of God clergy demonstrate themselves to be highly orthodox in doctrine and at the same time distinctively Pentecostal.

POLITICAL ENGAGEMENT OF ASSEMBLIES OF GOD CLERGY

In spite of the ambivalence of the Assemblies of God toward politics, Table 14.3 presents evidence that the clergy still view various political activities to be appropriate, both inside and outside of the church. First, nearly the entire sample (99 percent) approves of taking "a stand while preaching on some moral issue." As in many denominations, moral instruction and exhortation is part of the role of Assemblies of God clergy. Fewer respondents, but still a sizeable majority, approve of explicitly discussing political matters: more than two-thirds (71 percent) agree with "taking a stand on a political issue while preaching," and nearly as many (69 percent) feel it is appropriate to "publicly support a candidate outside of the pulpit." Considerable support for pastoral discourse on political matters is shown in the survey responses.

Table 14.3

Political Norms of Assemblies of God Clergy

	% Approving
Take a stand while preaching on some moral issue	99%
While preaching, take a stand on some political issue	71%
Publicly (not preaching) support a political candidate	69%
Contribute money to a candidate, party, or political-action committee	61%
Form an action group in one's church to accomplish a social or political goal	44%
Participate in a protest march	41%
Commit civil disobedience to protest some evil	23%

On the other hand, Assemblies of God clergy are less supportive of other types of political activity. Just three-fifths (61 percent) approve of a pastor making a financial contribution to a candidate, party, or political-action committee. And only about two-fifths (44 percent) believe it appropriate to organize "an action group in one's church to accomplish a social or political goal" or participate in a protest march. Even fewer, just under one-quarter (23 percent), approve of "commit(ing) civil disobedience to protest some evil."

Taken together, these patterns suggest that Assemblies of God clergy are quite accepting of political activity and have become more comfortable with action in the political arena since 1988, especially with regard to preaching on political issues and publicly supporting candidates. Other evidence from the survey supports these conclusions. When asked if religious people should "withdraw from politics" (Thomas and Dobson 1999), merely 8 percent of the respondents agree. Moreover, nearly three-quarters of the pastors feel that people of faith should stay politically engaged. Only about one-quarter of those surveyed agreed that "some clergy in my denomination have gone too far in mixing religion and politics," while more than half of the ministers want to become more involved in social and political issues, and nearly as many want the denomination to be more active as well. On these last two items, however, the modal category was "same as now," with about two-fifths of the respondents expressing such a stance.

The issue positions of Assemblies of God clergy are recorded in Table 14.4 on a number of moral, economic, and foreign-policy statements. The highest levels of consensus are on positions related to moral issues. Nearly all (97 percent) of the responding pastors agree that sex-education programs in public high schools should be abstinence based, and almost nine of ten (87 percent) support the much more controversial stand of a constitutional amendment banning abortions "except to save the mother's life, or in cases of rape or incest." Fewer than one-quarter (23 percent) feel that "homosexuals should have all the same rights and privileges as other American citizens." Given the strong moral traditionalism of the denomination, these patterns are hardly surprising.

Table 14.4

Policy Positions of Assemblies of God Clergy

	% Agreeing
The federal government should do more to solve social problems such as unemployment, poverty, and poor housing.	40%
Education policy should focus on improving public schools rather than on encouraging alternatives such as private and religious schools.	14%
Sex-education programs included in the curricula of public high schools should be abstinence based.	97%
We need government-sponsored national health insurance so that everyone can get adequate medical care.	32%
African Americans and other minorities may need special governmental help in order to achieve an equal place in America.	14%
We need a constitutional amendment prohibiting all abortions unless to save the mother's life, or in cases of rape or incest.	87%
Homosexuals should have all the same rights and privileges as other American citizens.	23%
A lasting peace in the Middle East will require Israel to make greater concessions to the Palestinians.	9%

The respondents are more divided on traditional social-welfare questions. For instance, two-fifths (40 percent) agree that the federal government should expand its role in resolving unemployment and poverty, while fewer than one-third (32 percent) support national health insurance. These ministers are also quite critical of public schools, with a small number, only 14 percent, agreeing that formal policy should focus on "improving the public schools rather than encouraging alternatives such as private and religious schools." Fewer than one-sixth of Assemblies of God clergy (14 percent) express support for affirmative action for African Americans and other minorities (with three-fifths disagreeing). Thus, one common theme in the survey is opposition to public social programs, especially those administered by the federal government.

The final item in Table 14.4 is a foreign-policy issue, namely whether "a lasting peace in the Middle East will require Israel to make greater concessions to the Palestinians." Fewer than one-tenth (9 percent) of the Assemblies of God ministers agree with this statement, while three-quarters disagree, reflecting the strong support Pentecostals and other evangelicals have historically given for the state of Israel (Guth et al. 1996). Indeed, some 90 percent of surveyed Assemblies of God clergy agree with the statement, "modern-day Israel is a nation blessed by God."

The actual reported political activity of Assemblies of God clergy is included in Table 14.5, along with their reported party identification and presidential vote choice in the 2000 presidential election. About two-thirds (68 percent) of the sample reported having urged their congregations to vote—a relatively noncontroversial act. But only about two-fifths (43 percent) took a stand on a political issue from the pulpit, and just over one-third (36 percent) reported contacting a public official about an issue. Assemblies of God pastors were more likely to participate in public prayer: more than half (55 percent) prayed for political candidates, and some three-fifths (62 percent) reported praying publicly about an issue. Overall, these ministers appear to have been modestly more active in 2000 than in 1988.

At the turn of the millennium, Assemblies of God ministers were solidly Republican in party affiliation. Just over half (51 percent) describe themselves as strong Republicans and a total of almost nine-tenths (88 percent) identify in some way with the GOP (including those Independents who lean Republican). This is a significant change from the patterns evident among Assemblies of God clergy in 1988 when less than two-fifths of the ministers reported that they were strong Republicans. The Assemblies of God clergy apparently significantly intensified their Republican partisanship in the 1990s. Those pastors identifying themselves as Independents and Democrats remained very consistent over the same period. The two categories together constituted a little more than one-tenth of Assemblies of God clergy in 2001; this was also true in 1988.

Table 14.5

Political Activities of Assemblies of God Clergy in the Election of 2000

	% Reporting
Urged their congregation to register and vote	68%
Contacted a public official about some issue	36%
Prayed publicly for political candidates	55%
Took a stand from the pulpit on some political issue	43%
Prayed publicly about an issue	62%
Party Identification	
Strong Democrat	2%
Weak Democrat	2%
Independent, lean Democrat	2%
Independent	6%
Independent, lean Republican	15%
Weak Republican	23%
Strong Republican	51%
Vote Choice in the 2000 Election	
Al Gore	3%
George W. Bush	91%
Pat Buchanan	*
Ralph Nader	0%
Other	*
Did not vote	6%

* = less than 1 percent

Given their issue positions and partisanship, it is hardly surprising that Assemblies of God clergy voted overwhelmingly for Bush in the 2000 presidential election: 91 percent reported casting a ballot for George W. Bush, about the same proportion that voted for former President Bush in 1988. In the GOP primary race, George W. Bush was by and large their first choice for the presidential nomination as well: almost two-thirds of the respondents named Bush, with "no preference" running ahead of Alan Keyes and Gary Bauer, the next most popular GOP candidates. This pattern differs from 1988 survey results, when one-quarter of the Assemblies of God clergy backed Pat Robertson. Still, even in 1988, 53 percent of the Assemblies of God clergy reported that they had initially supported George H. Bush.

CONCLUSION

Assemblies of God clergy have become a bulwark of the Right on the American political scene. In this regard, they may be ahead of their congregations and some of their colleagues in other evangelical denominations (Smidt et al. 1996; 1999). But by 2000, evangelical Protestants as a group were solidly in the Republican camp (Kellstedt et al. 1996). Assemblies of God ministers advocate most of the surveyed avenues for political activity and express a desire for greater personal and denominational engagement in the political process. To a large degree, the pastors acted on these norms, particularly with regard to public discourse on moral issues. The reported political activity demonstrates a commitment to educating their congregations on moral issues, where the ministers hold very conservative personal views. Conservative positions were also displayed on government social programs and foreign policy.

In the area of party identification, the ministers are strongly Republican and voted heavily for George W. Bush in the 2000 election. More interesting, they also overwhelmingly backed Bush over conservative Christian candidates for the GOP nomination. Like John Ashcroft, himself a one-time aspirant for the 2000 GOP nomination, Assemblies of God clergy appear to have found a place in American political alignment.

The basis for this high level of political engagement arises in large part from the theology of the Assemblies of God church, including its Protestant orthodoxy and Pentecostal distinctiveness, but also from a distinctive social theology. Although strongly committed to the traditional "private gospel" of individual transformation, the Assemblies of God denomination also strongly favors political engagement, with a focus on moral issues. This ambivalence has allowed the church to maintain tension with modern society while at the same time being an active participant in it. It may well be that a decline in the salience of moral issues would lead Assemblies of God clergy away from political engagement and back toward their apolitical past. But, it is also possible that the new status of Pentecostalism, at both the institutional and personal levels, will continue to encourage a substantial level of political engagement—regardless of the content of the issue agenda.

Chapter 15

Evangelical Free Church of America

Kedron Bardwell

The Evangelical Free Church of America (EFCA) is a small, but growing, evangelical Protestant denomination within American religious life. Historically, its roots are grounded in Scandinavia, particularly in terms of church-state relationships within countries of that region. From its birth in 1880s America through the mid-twentieth century, the loose association of churches that would later merge into the EFCA was known for its immigrant and rural character. While the church still bears some distinctive marks from its historical development (including decentralized governance and concentration in Midwestern states), the EFCA's rapid and recent growth has revitalized the denomination, expanding its reach into suburban and urban areas, as well as to other regions of the country.

Today's EFCA is defined by an emphasis on the essentials of the Christian faith, a focus on local church growth, and a heart for global missions. Theologically (and for the most part socially and politically) conservative, the denomination is within the mainstream of evangelical Protestant churches. This chapter will address the history of the EFCA, including its roots in the Swedish and Norwegian-Danish free-church movements. It will describe the theological beliefs of the EFCA and then

195

sketch the growth of the denomination in the last two decades. Finally, it will examine the social, theological, and political characteristics of EFCA clergy based on the first survey of its kind in the history of the denomination.

HISTORICAL BACKGROUND

The Evangelical Free Church of America took form in 1950 with the merger of 275 congregations of the Swedish Evangelical Free Church and the Norwegian-Danish Evangelical Free Church Association (Melton 1993). The two groups had discussed a merger since their founding near the turn of the twentieth century, but language differences created a key obstacle to any union. The Swedish and Norwegian-Danish free churches in America shared much in common: immigrant and rural frontier origins, a focus on foreign and domestic missions, and a strong antidenominational inclination (Hanson 1990). Both groups were rooted in, and maintained ties to, the free church movements of Europe, which began within, but later moved outside, state churches. These movements emphasized lay leadership, a personal faith, and evangelism—providing traditions that had a clear impact on the organizational structure of the two groups. Both were loose associations whose main purpose was to coordinate missionary activity. In fact, the Swedish group operated without a president until 1927, and the Norwegian-Danish Association had only part-time leadership until the 1950 merger.

The traditions of the early free churches remain visible today in the EFCA and underlie the distinctive features of the denomination. The term *free* originally marked churches as free from state control, but in today's EFCA the designation is one signaling congregational governance (Hanson 1990). While not purely congregational, local churches in large part govern their own affairs; twenty-one geographic districts also have representation. This decentralization is incorporated into the EFCA statement of faith and can be illustrated through the process of clergy ordination. Local EFCA churches have the right to ordain candidates who have been licensed by the denomination for three years. Licensees must have a master of divinity degree from an evangelical (but not necessarily EFCA) seminary, adhere to a twelve-point doctrinal statement, pass a course on church history and doctrine, and be recommended by a district superintendent. It is the local congregation that calls and interviews candidates and, upon selecting a candidate, asks EFCA officials to perform the ordination service (Hanson 1990).

Another distinctive feature of the EFCA is its self-described emphasis on the essentials of the Christian faith. Theologically conservative, the denomination is in the mainstream of the orthodox evangelical movements.[31] The EFCA statement of faith affirms the inerrancy of Scripture as "the inspired Word of God, without error in the original writings," not only as it pertains to faith and doctrine but also to history and science (Hanson 1992, 187). Aside from confession of faith in Jesus Christ and agreement with the basic tenets of evangelical Christianity, however, minor differences on nonessential doctrinal points (those without bearing on salvation) are respected. Under a section labeled "Distinctives," the EFCA Web site quotes early church philosopher John Chrysostom: "In essentials, unity. In nonessentials, charity. In all things, Jesus Christ." (Evangelical Free Church of America 2002). Along these lines, the denomination describes itself as "inclusive, not exclusive" and "evangelical, but not separatistic." The official EFCA statement of faith affirms the basic tenets of Reformed Christian doctrine but is silent on issues that divide other Protestant denominations, such as predestination and modes of baptism (Reid 1990).

Today, the EFCA is one of the fastest growing denominations in the country. Between 1980 and 2000, the denomination experienced a 110 percent increase (from 649 to 1,365) in the number of churches in the United States. Not unexpectedly, the rate of membership growth has also been swift. Over the same time period, the number of EFCA adherents increased 300 percent, from about 70,000 to more than 285,000 (Jones et al, 2001).[32] Growth has changed the EFCA; its congregations are less rural and much less Scandinavian than in the recent past. For example, in just one decade California (which had 158 churches in 1990) overtook Minnesota (100 churches in 1980) as the state with the most EFCA congregations. Overall, however, the denomination is still concentrated in the Midwest. The states with the highest adherent rates per 1,000 in population are Nebraska (5.3), Minnesota (4.7), North Dakota (4.6), and Iowa (2.9). In keeping with its past, missions work is still a major focus of the denomination. The EFCA has several hundred churches abroad, and about one-third of all its members live outside of the United States (Melton 1993).

NATURE OF THE STUDY

In November 2001, the Center for Social Research at Calvin College mailed surveys to 676 pastors of the Evangelical Free Church of America. Contact information for these clergy was obtained from the official church and pastoral directory of the denomination. Those clergy who failed to return the survey after the initial mailing did not receive any subsequent mailings of surveys. As a result, a total of 261 surveys were completed and returned by EFCA pastors for a response rate of 39 percent.

SOCIAL CHARACTERISTICS OF EFCA CLERGY

While both branches of the early free church sent women evangelists into the mission fields (Hanson 1990), the church's official position is that women are not eligible for ordination, though they may participate in a variety of ministries. As a result, 100 percent of surveyed Evangelical Free Church pastors are male. Perhaps reflecting the recent growth of the denomination, the clergy are a relatively young group, mostly comprised of Baby Boomers. Only 5 percent are younger than thirty-five years of age, while 17 percent are over fifty-five. The mean age of EFCA pastors is forty-nine, with a mean length of time in the ministry of twenty years.

Table 15.1

Social Characteristics of Evangelical Free Church Clergy

	% of Clergy
Gender: Male	100%
Race: White	95%
Marital Status: Married, never divorced	97%
Education	
College Graduate	98%
Seminary Graduate	85%
Age	
Under 35 years of age	5%
Over 55 years of age	17%
Community Size	
Farm or small town	40%
Small or medium-sized cities	30%
Large cities	30%

As can be seen from Table 15.1, Evangelical Free Church ministers are a well-educated group, as more than five out of six (85 percent) are seminary graduates, with one-third (34 percent) having completed more intensive postgraduate work beyond their seminary education (a Th.D., for example). The official seminary of the denomination, Trinity Evangelical Divinity School, produced the plurality (42 percent) of pastors, while several other evangelical seminaries are represented, with the next largest share (15 percent) coming from conservative Dallas Theological Seminary.

The most pronounced social characteristic of EFCA clergy is their strong family orientation. More than 97 percent of the EFCA pastors surveyed are married and have never been divorced; only one minister in the entire pool of 261 survey respondents is single. While this might seem to suggest that these respondents exhibit ultratraditional values, over half (55 percent) of the pastors' wives are employed outside of the home. EFCA ministers are overwhelmingly white (95 percent), with small segments reporting Asian (2 percent), Hispanic (2 percent), or mixed-race backgrounds (2 percent).

Despite a lack of racial diversity among EFCA pastors, the geographic mix (rural vs. urban vs. suburban) of the denomination is diverse and about evenly split among small, medium-sized, and large communities. While 40 percent of EFCA clergy minister to congregations in rural areas and small towns (under 15,000), nearly one-third (30 percent) work with congregations located in small to medium-sized cities (15,000 to 100,000), and an equivalent number (30 percent) have congregations located in larger cities (over 100,000). Among the respondents, the average tenure of service in their present congregations is nine years.

EFCA churches come in many different sizes. Thirty percent of the pastors lead churches with an average weekly attendance of 100 or less, and 56 percent report attendance of 100 to 500 people. Fourteen percent of the pastors have congregations with 500 or more individuals attending weekly services.

THEOLOGICAL POSITIONS HELD BY EFCA CLERGY

In light of the decentralized nature of the denomination, the uniformity of the Evangelical Free Church pastors' theological views is somewhat surprising. As can be seen in Table 15.2, 100 percent of survey respondents agreed with the four statements that speak to an orthodox

Christianity and a literal interpretation of the Scriptures. In fact, 95 percent of EFCA clergy *strongly* agreed that "Jesus will return to earth one day" and "was born of a virgin," "the devil actually exists," and "there is no other way to salvation but through belief in Jesus Christ."

EFCA ministers voice strong views on other statements related to inerrancy and a literal interpretation of the Bible. More than 99 percent agree that the Adam and Eve of the book of Genesis were actual people and that "the Bible is the inerrant Word of God, both in matters of faith and in historic, geographical, and other secular matters." On these two questions, more than 92 percent of all pastors agreed strongly.

Table 15.2

Theological Views Held by Evangelical Free Church Clergy

	% Agreeing
Jesus will return to earth one day.	100%
Jesus was born of a virgin.	100%
The devil actually exists.	100%
There is no other way to salvation but through belief in Jesus Christ.	100%
Adam and Eve were real people.	99%
The Bible is the inerrant Word of God, both in matters of faith and in historical, geographical, and other secular matters.	99%
The church should put less emphasis on individual sanctification and more on transforming the social order.	2%

It is plausible to expect that orthodoxy among EFCA pastors in matters of theology and biblical interpretation will coincide with traditional and conservative attitudes on morality and social-policy issues (for example, abortion). A number of survey questions addressed the matter of social justice. One query, framed as an "either/or," asked clergy to choose between a focus on personal holiness and a focus on social justice; only 2 percent of EFCA pastors agreed that "the church should put less emphasis on individual sanctification and more on transforming the social order." However, when this trade-off between either individual morality or social action was removed, the ministers' views on social justice become somewhat more favorable, as 31 percent of EFCA pastors surveyed agree that "social justice is at the heart of the gospel."

The survey asked EFCA clergy about other theological issues which, while not reported in Table 15.2, are interesting to note. Almost all EFCA respondents reject the idea that "all of the great religions of the world are equally good and true" as well as the notion that "human nature is better understood as being basically good than basically evil" (99 percent and 97 percent, respectively). All EFCA pastors oppose the theological view that the sacraments are necessary for salvation. Yet, EFCA ministers do see the institutional church as crucial to the Christian life, with 91 percent of EFCA clergy disagreeing that "one can be a good Christian without attending church." On some of the most controversial issues confronting evangelical Protestant churches today, EFCA pastors are unwaveringly conservative. Ninety percent of pastors disagree (54 percent strongly) that clergy positions should be open to women, and all those surveyed rejected the view that the church should ordain practicing homosexuals.

POLITICAL ENGAGEMENT OF EFCA CLERGY

Given church history, the social backgrounds, and the theological views of Evangelical Free Church clergy, it is interesting to view the relationship between these factors and the pastors' political attitudes and activities. To allow for the comparison, the survey questioned EFCA ministers about their political norms, policy positions, and political activities.

First, EFCA pastors were asked about their views on political engagement by clergy, regardless of their own participation (or lack thereof) in such activities. Table 15.3 reports the respondents' level of approval for several activities. The survey participants are basically unanimous in their support of clergy who preach on moral issues, with about 72 percent voicing strong approval. However, approval declines when the question changes to preaching about explicitly political issues. Fifty-six percent of EFCA pastors are supportive, but only 15 percent strongly approve, and 17 percent are not sure. Private involvement in politics by ministers receives strong approval, including contributing money to political parties, candidates, and groups (76 percent approve).

Support is slightly lower, however, for more public kinds of political action. A bare majority of EFCA pastors believe it appropriate for clergy to (but not while preaching) support a political candidate publicly or participate in a protest march. Other types of political action by clergy receive a less than enthusiastic reception. For example, only 39 percent of pastors approve of a minister forming an action group in the church to fight for a political or social goal. Many other respondents (32 percent) are not sure whether or not this activity is appropriate. Along similar lines, more of the respondents disapprove (42 percent) than approve (27 percent) of clergy committing civil disobedience as a form of public protest. A likely explanation for this lower level of support is that these specific kinds of political action historically are associated with mainline Protestant denominations, due to their emphasis on issues of social justice.

Table 15.3

Political Norms of Evangelical Free Church Clergy

	% Approving
Take a stand while preaching on some moral issue	99%
While preaching, take a stand on some political issue	56%
Publicly (not preaching) support a political candidate	52%
Contribute money to a candidate, party, or political-action committee	76%
Form an action group in one's church to accomplish a social or political goal	39%
Participate in a protest march	55%
Commit civil disobedience to protest some evil	27%

Respondents were also asked about their level of agreement with statements of policy positions, ranging from poverty to education reform to health care to abortion. Again, consistent with the theology of the denomination, EFCA pastors are predominantly conservative on issues of economic, social, and morality policy. As shown in Table 15.4, fewer than 20 percent of the ministers support more federal government involvement in solving social problems (unemployment, poverty, and poor housing). A similarly small number support government-sponsored health care (16 percent) or the idea that minorities need special government help to achieve equality (18 percent).[33]

EFCA pastors' attitudes on education reform are also conservative. They are proponents of religious schools and hold traditional views about sex education. Only 14 percent agree that the government should focus on improving public schools rather than encouraging private or religious alternatives. EFCA ministers are nearly unanimous in their view that high-school sex-education programs should be abstinence based. Sixty-three percent *strongly* agree that this is the right message. On moral issues, the pro-life position dominates, with 85 percent favoring a constitutional amendment to ban abortion except to save the mother's life, or in cases of rape or incest. EFCA pastors' views on homosexuality are more divided. Equal shares of pastors (44 percent) agree and disagree that homosexuals should have the same rights as other citizens. As for United States foreign policy in the Middle East, most pastors are pro-Israel; only 23 percent assert that peace in the region will require Israel to make more concessions to the Palestinians.

Table 15.4

Policy Positions of Evangelical Free Church Clergy

	% Agreeing
The federal government should do more to solve social problems such as unemployment, poverty, and poor housing.	19%
Education policy should focus on improving public schools rather than on encouraging alternatives such as private and religious schools.	14%
Sex-education programs included in the curricula of public high schools should be abstinence based.	97%
We need government-sponsored national health insurance so that everyone can get adequate medical care.	16%
African Americans and other minorities may need special governmental help in order to achieve an equal place in America.	18%
We need a constitutional amendment prohibiting all abortions unless to save the mother's life, or in cases of rape or incest.	85%
Homosexuals should have all the same rights and privileges as other American citizens.	44%
A lasting peace in the Middle East will require Israel to make greater concessions to the Palestinians.	23%

Clergy were asked whether they had engaged in specific political activities, both public and private.[34] Table 15.5 reports the total percentage of pastors who "often" or "sometimes" engaged in the activities; the survey results demonstrate extensive political action on the part of EFCA pastors. Most ministers urged their congregations to register and vote; a majority have contacted public officials (but only eight percent report doing so often) and prayed publicly for political candidates (28 percent do it often). EFCA clergy are more reluctant to take a specific stand from the pulpit on political issues, with only 7 percent reporting that they do it often, and 38 percent sometimes—but 21 percent have never taken a political stand from the pulpit. Many more pastors are comfortable praying publicly about the issues (49 percent have done it often and 39 percent sometimes).

Table 15.5

Political Activities of Evangelical Free Church Clergy in the Election of 2000

	% Reporting
Urged their congregation to register and vote	88%
Contacted a public official about some issue	52%
Prayed publicly for political candidates	53%
Took a stand from the pulpit on some political issue	45%
Prayed publicly about an issue	88%
Party Identification	
Strong Democrat	0%
Weak Democrat	0%
Independent, lean Democrat	*
Independent	3%
Independent, lean Republican	18%
Weak Republican	28%
Strong Republican	51%
Vote Choice in the 2000 Election	
Al Gore	0%
George W. Bush	98%
Pat Buchanan	0%
Ralph Nader	0%
Other	*
Did not vote	2%

* = less than 1 percent

Finally, the survey asked EFCA clergy about their party identification and vote choice for president in the 2000 election. The party identification figures presented in Table 15.5 are consistent with the conservative theological views and policy positions of EFCA pastors. Seventy-nine percent of pastors identified themselves as Republicans, with 51 percent stating they were strong Republicans. Only 3 percent classified themselves as Independents who did not lean toward either party. In fact, only one EFCA pastor in the entire sample identified with any Democratic label. Not surprisingly, their voting behavior was consistent with these party leanings. Of respondents who voted, all but one pastor reported casting their ballots for George W. Bush. None of the EFCA pastors voted for Al Gore, and less than two percent stayed home on Election Day.

CONCLUSION

The theological and political attitudes and activities of clergy in the Evangelical Free Church of America are examined for the first time in this study, and the results clearly show that the theology and politics of its pastors are consistent with the evangelical and conservative history of the denomination. In light of the decentralized nature of the EFCA and its ordination procedures, the most striking finding is the near unanimity of responses to many theological and political questions. EFCA ministers consistently subscribe to the basic tenets of orthodox Christianity. They are united in their belief in the inerrancy of Scripture, the existence of evil, and salvation through faith in Jesus Christ alone. EFCA clergy overwhelmingly reject the idea that world religions are morally equivalent and oppose a worldview that emphasizes social justice at the expense of individual sanctification. And these pastors strongly oppose the recent trend in other denominations toward the ordination of women.

EFCA clergy are conservative not only on theological issues but also in their public policy positions and voting behavior. The EFCA respondents in this survey have little confidence that federal government intervention will solve social and economic problems like poverty, poor housing, and inadequate health care. They support traditionally conservative positions on education reform and government aid to racial minority groups. On foreign policy in the Middle East, the EFCA pastors are strong supporters of Israel. They are conservative on moral issues as well, asserting that sex-education programs should focus on abstinence and overwhelmingly favoring a constitutional amendment to ban abortion except in cases of rape, incest, or to save the life of the mother.

In areas of clergy political activism, EFCA pastors are comfortable with clergy taking moral stands, but they are divided on the question of whether ministers should explicitly support political issues or candidates, especially from the pulpit. The nuance in this position on clergy political activism is consistent with EFCA pastors' personal political activism. Huge majorities of ministers have prayed publicly about an issue and have urged their congregants to register and vote. EFCA pastors are personally active in politics (98 percent cast a ballot in 2000) and are uniformly Republican in their party affiliation and in their 2000 presidential preference. Yet just over half pray publicly for politicians, and less than half take stands on political issues from the pulpit. Taken together, these findings provide new insight into these ministers' philosophies about civic engagement. Many EFCA pastors draw a line of propriety between taking moral stands and voicing political views, and between private and public political activity.

Chapter 16

Mennonite Church USA

Lyman A. Kellstedt and James L. Guth

For few religious groups have political questions been more central to their identity than to Mennonites. As descendents of the Anabaptist wing of the Reformation, the Mennonites have focused above all on pacifism or nonresistance to evil. Adhering to a "two kingdoms" doctrine, they have respected the authority of the state as an instrument of God against evildoers, but have refused to participate in the state's use of "the sword." As members of Christ's kingdom of regenerated believers, Mennonites assumed a radical separation between the religious community and the kingdoms of this world, although they sometimes disagreed over the degree of separation.

In recent decades, however, traditional Mennonite rejection of political entanglements has been challenged by the social, theological, and political forces reshaping their communities. Some Mennonites have retained a posture of strict noninvolvement, while others have undertaken more active roles in influencing government on "peace and justice" issues (Graber Miller 1996). This emerging conflict is most visible in the largest Mennonite denomination, the Mennonite Church USA (MCUSA), produced by a 2001 merger between the Mennonite Church and the General Conference Mennonite Church. This chapter focuses on the political orientations of MCUSA clergy, who serve as important interpreters of Mennonite heritage for their congregations. As we will show, there are vital political differences emerging among the clergy—and incipient divisions between a majority of MCUSA laity and their pastors.

HISTORICAL BACKGROUND

The 2001 merger united the major institutional representatives of two important streams in American Mennonite history (Graber Miller 1996). The "Old" Mennonite Church traced its origins to migrations of German and Swiss Mennonites to North America during the seventeenth and eighteenth centuries. Although most settled initially in Pennsylvania and Ohio, others eventually moved west, and some, to Canada. Because of past persecutions by European governments, this wing usually practiced strict separation from the world, especially from government concerns. In theological terms, however, the emerging Mennonite Church tried to maintain a moderate position, and thus was subject to schisms from both right and left during the eighteenth and nineteenth century.

The second Mennonite stream consisted of the Dutch-Russian immigration, which was eventually institutionalized in the General Conference Mennonite Church (GCMC). Although of varied ethnic origins, these immigrants' more positive experience with local government during their sojourns in the Netherlands and Russia led them to be more open to Christian political involvement (except, of course, in military roles). Concentrating in the American Midwest and West, some of these Mennonites even ran for public office and served in local government, in state office, and occasionally in Congress. The GCMC was more strongly congregational in polity than the Mennonite Church, allowing a variety of theological and political shadings to persist without major schisms.

The theological and political beliefs of Mennonites have never fit comfortably within the usual American ideological frameworks. With their emphasis on the authority of the Bible, the saving role of Jesus, believers' baptism, and other familiar tenets of Christian orthodoxy, as well as their concern with personal morality, the Mennonites at first glance look like American evangelicals. But Mennonites have always focused on applying the message of Scripture in simple living, seeking peace and justice, and fostering Christian community in ways that have recently moved them into alliances with theologically liberal, mainline Christians.

During the twentieth century, a constellation of forces opened both theological and political divisions within the Mennonite community, making it more difficult to maintain the balance between conservative theology and liberal social concerns. These divisions appeared both within the Mennonite leadership, and to an increasing extent, between leadership groups and laity (Graber Miller 1996). Tensions first emerged from the modernist-fundamentalist controversy that rocked other American churches and the Mennonites during the early 1900s. Conservative church members accused college and seminary faculty of adopting modern critical perspectives on the Bible, leading to several purges. At the same time, outside fundamentalist groups wooed traditionalist Mennonites, with limited success, leading some congregations to join schismatic conservative groups (Redekop 1989).

In the second half of the century, theological divisions among Mennonites widened as the social transformation of the community accelerated: rapid migration into urban areas, increasing educational attainments, and movement into professional occupations encouraged new liberal-conservative fissures. In recent years, Mennonites have battled over theology, social issues such as abortion and homosexuality, and involvement in liberal social movements, especially those related to war and international politics. These quarrels have not only contributed to an incipient culture war among ordinary Mennonites, but also to a gathering storm in relations between Mennonite leaders and laity, as denominational officials are often more theologically and politically liberal than the majority of members in the pews (Kauffmann 1989).

Thus, while church leaders focus on a peace-and-justice agenda, many grass-roots Mennonites remain quite conservative on most political issues, identify and vote Republican, and understand the traditional Mennonite commitment to nonresistance in distinct ways. As a result, the Mennonite leadership's alliance with liberal religious groups in politics often produces backlash from other members of the denomination. For example, the Mennonite Central Committee's (MCC) office in Washington, D.C., is not only located in the United Methodist Building ("the God Box"), which houses many liberal religious and secular groups (including the National Council of Churches' Washington office), but the MCC also works hand-in-hand with these groups on social-welfare and foreign-policy issues. As conservative Mennonites often complain, the committee seldom speaks out on social issues that bother the conservatives, such as abortion and homosexuality, and almost never cooperates with more conservative religious lobbies, such as the National Association of Evangelicals (which does include some small Mennonite groups) or the Christian Coalition (Graber Miller 1996). Obviously, local clergy are a critical intermediary when it comes to resolving any such conflicts, explaining national policies to grass-roots members, and conveying lay concerns to national leaders.

NATURE OF THE STUDY

The following pages provide a profile of Mennonite Church USA clergy based on a survey of pastors that was conducted as part of the Cooperative Clergy Study Project, locating them in social, theological, and political continuums.[35] The names of the pastors within the MCUSA were obtained from a complete list of denominational ministers from the two merged groups that formed the MCUSA. Two waves of questionnaires were sent to 1,006 pastors in early 2001, with twenty-eight returned as undeliverable or noting that the recipient was no longer in the ministry. MCUSA clergy returned 384 usable responses, a return rate of almost 40 percent of the original sample. As part of our evaluation, we will also at times compare these clergy to those in the evangelical and mainline Protestant denominations that were surveyed as part of the larger project.

SOCIAL CHARACTERISTICS OF MCUSA CLERGY

Although Mennonites have made some inroads into minority populations in the United States, the great majority of Mennonite Church USA clergy still descend from the historically dominant white European ethnicities. They are also predominantly male (83 percent), although the percentage of female pastors is significantly higher than exists in evangelical churches, but somewhat lower than that for mainline Protestant denominations. Widespread support among both clergy and laity for women's ordination suggests that the number of women clergy will increase in the future (Kauffmann and Driedger 1991).

Most MCUSA pastors are married and have never been divorced. Four of five are college graduates, and more than half are seminary graduates. Although this no doubt reflects some increase in clerical education in recent decades (younger pastors generally have more college and seminary experience), MCUSA pastors are still less well educated than the ministers in most evangelical and mainline churches. They also tend to be somewhat older than clergy in other denominations, although the differences are not dramatic. Despite the rapid urbanization occurring within the MCUSA community, about half the pastors still serve churches in farm communities or small towns, a larger percentage than found in other surveyed groups. Finally, their congregations are rather small (an average adult membership of 178 and weekly service attendance of 161), once again below the statistics for other Protestants.

Table 16.1

Social Characteristics of Mennonite Church USA Clergy

	% of Clergy
Gender: Male	83%
Race: White	95%
Marital Status: Married, never divorced	92%
Education	
College Graduate	80%
Seminary Graduate	56%
Age	
Under 35 years of age	9%
Over 55 years of age	34%
Community Size	
Farm or small town	53%
Small or medium-sized cities	26%
Large cities	22%

THEOLOGICAL POSITIONS HELD
BY MCUSA CLERGY

One suspects that the doctrinal views of Mennonite Church USA clergy would be influenced by their Anabaptist roots, placing them securely in the camp of Christian orthodoxy with a few special Mennonite distinctives on nonresistance. On the other hand, their uneasy transformation to modernity may have pushed some pastors in theologically liberal directions. As Table 16.2 shows, MCUSA pastors adhere quite strongly to many elements of Christian orthodoxy. Large majorities affirm the second coming of Jesus, the virgin birth, the existence of the devil, and salvation obtained only through belief in Jesus

Christ. However, the percentages fall off dramatically when questions tap biblical literalism: only two-thirds believe that Adam and Eve were real people and just over half think the Bible is inerrant in all matters. Still, on most doctrinal matters, MCUSA pastors fall between evangelical and mainline clergy, but are much closer to the evangelicals. On the final item in Table 16.2, however, the Mennonites resemble the mainline: almost one-quarter want more stress on social transformation than on individual sanctification as an objective of the church, a goal shared by very few evangelical clergy. Note, however, that individual sanctification is still preferred by most MCUSA pastors.

Table 16.2

Theological Views Held by Mennonite Church USA Clergy

	% Agreeing
Jesus will return to earth one day.	94%
Jesus was born of a virgin.	88%
The devil actually exists.	87%
There is no other way to salvation but through belief in Jesus Christ.	86%
Adam and Eve were real people.	66%
The Bible is the inerrant Word of God, both in matters of faith and in historical, geographical, and other secular matters.	56%
The church should put less emphasis on individual sanctification and more on transforming the social order.	23%

The data in Table 16.2 hide some important theological variations. To investigate internal theological differences, we produced a factor-based orthodoxy score from the items listed in the table and looked for social factors that influenced the pastors' scores. As might be expected, clergy from rural and small-town areas (the historic origin of most Mennonites) are much more orthodox than suburban and big-city pastors (the new location of many Mennonites). In a similar vein, pastors from smaller congregations, men, and those with the fewer years of secular and theological education are more orthodox than their opposites. Finally, the impact of age is complicated. As we might anticipate, the oldest of the clergy (born before 1931) is the most orthodox, but the youngest pastors (born since 1961) include both the largest liberal contingent and a large group of very orthodox pastors as well. Thus, the dominant trend among recent entrants to the clergy seems to be theological polarization, rather than a simple march toward modernism.

To sort out the impact of these factors, we ran a multiple regression, which demonstrated that length of seminary education was the best predictor of deviation from orthodox theology, followed by congregation size, female gender, community size, and higher levels of secular education. Age, however, had no independent impact. These few variables did a remarkable job of predicting orthodoxy scores, accounting for over two-fifths of the variation.

These findings have important implications. As college and seminary education becomes more and more the norm, as female clergy increase in number, and as the denomination expands in suburban and urban America, with the concomitant increase in membership and attendance, the MCUSA will begin to look more like mainline and less like evangelical Protestantism. Nevertheless, this tendency is likely to be resisted by a strong minority of young traditionalist pastors, in combination with many Mennonites from "traditional" settings, increasing the level of internal controversy.

Other doctrinal questions designed to measure contemporary expressions of theological liberalism directly were also included in the questionnaire. The results varied widely, with strong pastoral support for some liberal perspectives. For example, 63 percent said that social justice is at the heart of the gospel, 62 percent supported the ordination of women, 46 percent saw important insights in feminist theology, and 44 percent supported liberation theology. On the other hand, only 12 percent endorsed the ordination of gays, and only 4 percent embraced the pluralist idea that all the religions of the world are equally good and true. These items formed a strong scale which had a powerful *negative* correlation with the orthodoxy measure (r=-.87), suggesting that theological liberalism is the mirror image of orthodoxy. As expected, well-educated pastors from large churches in metropolitan areas—and women clergy—anchored the liberal end of this scale.

POLITICAL ENGAGEMENT OF MCUSA CLERGY

One scholar has argued that "Mennonite participation in the political process has been, and is, minimal and very cautious" (Redekop 1989, 228), although that assessment is qualified by others, who point to considerable variation within the tradition (Graber Miller 1996). Whatever the historical case, the uneasy transformation of a rural, small-town community to one more in touch with mainstream culture suggests that historic preferences for a nonpolitical stance might be changing. If so, any new engagement should be reflected in the clergy.

We asked pastors to rank their level of approval for selected political activities by clergy ranging from within-church acts to those engaged outside of the church context (see Table 16.3). Clearly, MCUSA pastors are not averse to taking a stand on issues from the pulpit, but they distinguish between moral and political issues, with 97 percent approving the former but only 47 percent the latter. About half agree with formation of action groups within their congregations to deal with social and political problems. Not surprising, given Anabaptist history, MCUSA clergy also approve of protest and civil disobedience. On the other hand, they are far less likely to endorse conventional participation such as supporting candidates and contributing money to political causes, no doubt reflecting their separatist history. In comparison with evangelical and mainline pastors, MCUSA clergy have a distinct profile: on moral issues they look like everyone else, on political issues and electoral activities they approve such actions less than either evangelicals or mainliners, and when asked about action groups and unconventional protest, they match or even exceed the mainliners' high support.

Table 16.3
Political Norms of Mennonite Church USA Clergy

	% Approving
Take a stand while preaching on some moral issue	97%
While preaching, take a stand on some political issue	47%
Publicly (not preaching) support a political candidate	33%
Contribute money to a candidate, party, or political-action committee	35%
Form an action group in one's church to accomplish a social or political goal	49%
Participate in a protest march	62%
Commit civil disobedience to protest some evil	50%

Some strong differences exist, however, *among* MCUSA pastors. To analyze these variations, we constructed an overall approval score from sixteen items including those in Table 16.3. A multiple regression analysis reveals that, overall, the doctrinally orthodox are much less likely to approve a wide range of political activities by clergy, and the doctrinally liberal are significantly more supportive. This relationship is quite strong; indeed, theological perspective is the single best predictor of favoring political activism. Younger clergy, regardless of theological orientation, are also more likely to approve activism, as are pastors from larger communities. Finally, the extent of secular education is a vital predictor as well: the higher the education, the stronger the support for activism. Although female clergy, seminary graduates, and those from larger churches also are more likely to favor activism, these factors drop out of the equation as independent predictors when all the variables are taken into account.

Given the Mennonites' peace-church tradition and their strong involvement in social-justice matters at home and around the world, we might expect MCUSA clergy to hold relatively liberal attitudes about contemporary political issues. But on a measure of ideological self-identification, the pastors divide almost equally with 40 percent claiming to be liberal and 43 percent classifying themselves as conservative. (This ratio contrasts with a 51 to 19 percent *conservative* advantage among MCUSA laity in Kauffmann and Driedger's 1991 survey.)

Table 16.4
Policy Positions of Mennonite Church USA Clergy

	% Agreeing
The federal government should do more to solve social problems such as unemployment, poverty, and poor housing.	68%
Education policy should focus on improving public schools rather than on encouraging alternatives such as private and religious schools.	48%
Sex-education programs included in the curricula of public high schools should be abstinence based.	86%
We need government-sponsored national health insurance so that everyone can get adequate medical care.	60%
African Americans and other minorities may need special governmental help in order to achieve an equal place in America.	56%
We need a constitutional amendment prohibiting all abortions unless to save the mother's life, or in cases of rape or incest.	51%
Homosexuals should have all the same rights and privileges as other American citizens.	55%
A lasting peace in the Middle East will require Israel to make greater concessions to the Palestinians.	62%

In fact, MCUSA ministers fall between the conservative positions often taken by evangelical pastors and the more liberal stances of mainline clergy (see Table 16.4). On some items, they are closer to the conservative evangelicals (abstinence based sex education, gay rights), while on others (government involvement in social problems, health insurance, government assistance to minorities, peace in the Middle East) they are closer to the mainline. On the remainder, they fall between the two. There is an apparent and considerable difference *among* MCUSA pastors, reinforcing our theme of increasing political polarization within the church.

We constructed an overall measure of policy liberalism from the items in Table 16.4, and once again, ministers with advanced secular and seminary education, urban locations, and large churches are more likely to be politically liberal, as are women clergy. But these factors pale in importance compared to doctrinal factors: the more orthodox the pastor, the more conservative politically. Indeed, the chasm between the most and least orthodox is very wide. A multiple regression analysis shows that our two measures of theological orientation (orthodoxy and liberalism) are by far the most powerful, although seminary education and size of community also have modest independent effects in producing more liberal policy stances. In sum, MCUSA clergy are divided in their policy preferences; the divisions are deep, and theological persuasions are central to understanding the divisions. The contrast with the high level of policy agreement among pastors in many other denominations (conservative in evangelical churches, liberal in mainline denominations) is striking.

Finally, we consider the actual political involvement of MCUSA clergy. We have seen the differences within the denomination on approval of pastoral involvement in politics. The data at the top of Table 16.5 provides some evidence about whether these differences are reflected in actual participation rates. First, we should note that the overall level of activity among MCUSA pastors is quite low: 40 percent engaged in none of the surveyed activities in 2000. In particular, they were much less likely to urge their congregation to register and vote than were either the evangelical (58 percent) or mainline pastors (51 percent), suggesting little effort at political mobilization. On the other acts in Table 16.5 the same trend exists, although the differences with evangelical and mainline clergy are not as pronounced. Still, it is a consistent pattern, one which no doubt reflects a strong residue of the Anabaptist tradition of noninvolvement.

These results may tell only part of the story, however, since perhaps MCUSA pastors focus their efforts on the social and political values central to the Anabaptist tradition. When exploring the frequency of preaching on issues of war and peace and the simple lifestyle, more than one-third reported expositing on these topics numerous times a year, while only about 10 percent claimed never to raise these topics. Clearly, Mennonite pastors use the bully pulpit to discuss topics of social and political significance, although their overall level of conventional political activity is quite low.

Table 16.5

Political Activities of Mennonite Church USA Clergy in the Election of 2000

	% Reporting
Urged their congregation to register and vote	18%
Contacted a public official about some issue	27%
Prayed publicly for political candidates	30%
Took a stand from the pulpit on some political issue	33%
Prayed publicly about an issue	49%
Party Identification	
Strong Democrat	9%
Weak Democrat	14%
Independent, lean Democrat	22%
Independent	14%
Independent, lean Republican	15%
Weak Republican	14%
Strong Republican	13%
Vote Choice in the 2000 Election	
Al Gore	30%
George W. Bush	37%
Pat Buchanan	*
Ralph Nader	12%
Other	*
Did not vote	21%

* = less than 1 percent

What factors produce either conventional or Mennonite kinds of participation? On the activities included in Table 16.5, ideological liberals and Democratic identifiers are more active than their conservative, Republican counterparts. But a multivariate analysis shows that this advantage is the result of the social and institutional factors influencing the former group: pastors who have advanced secular educations, live in larger communities, and are younger, are more involved. Similarly, liberal theology and Democratic partisanship are the best predictors of preaching about Mennonite themes, suggesting once again that liberals have something of an advantage in activism.

That advantage does not extend, however, to partisan identification. As Table 16.5 shows, there are similar percentages of Democrats and Republicans among pastors when strong, weak, and independent leaning partisans are combined. This contrasts with the overwhelming Republican orientation of evangelical pastors nationwide, and the strongly Democratic propensities of most mainline pastors. The distribution also contrasts with those among MCUSA laity, in which the recent partisan division has favored the Republicans by a large (48 to 22 percent) margin (Kauffmann and Driedger 1991). MCUSA clergy also tend to cluster near the middle of the scale: they are far more likely to be Independents or Independent leaners than pastors in other surveyed denominations.

MCUSA clergy choices in the presidential election of 2000 are consistent with the previously discussed findings. First, a considerable number did not vote, conforming to the past practice of some Anabaptists. Second, there was a significant third-party vote for Ralph Nader (15 percent of those who voted). Nader did best among younger pastors, political Independents, theological liberals, and those who preach regularly on simple lifestyle and peace and justice issues. Finally, among those choosing from the major party candidates, George W. Bush had a small edge, receiving 55 percent of the two-party vote. Once again, previous studies of MCUSA laity suggest a much larger advantage for Republican presidential candidates among those who do vote (Kauffmann and Driedger 1991).

Clearly, MCUSA clergy are still less involved politically than pastors from most other Protestant denominations, although those with higher levels of education and stronger partisanship were more likely to vote. Those who are involved are equally divided in their partisan identification and in their vote choices. Once again, theological orthodoxy and liberalism rear their heads as significant sources of division when analyzing the choices selected. The pattern is actually quite simple: theological liberals are Democratic, the orthodox are Republican. Indeed, the strength of the theological division is impressive: in the 2000 presidential race, *100 percent* of the most liberal quintile of clergy voted for Gore, while 98 percent of the most orthodox quintile voted for Bush. Such a powerful relationship leaves little variation to be explained, although frequent preaching about simple lifestyles and about peace and justice issues also helped predict a Gore vote by that minister, as did a seminary or graduate degree. In explaining partisan identification, these same factors operate, with the addition of residence in a large community and higher levels of secular education favoring the Democrats.

CONCLUSION

The results of our survey of Mennonite Church USA clergy highlight the political changes facing a denomination which is emerging from a rural and small town geographical location to a more urban and suburban environment, with seminary and postgraduate education increasingly the norm for clergy. These changes have resulted in movement from relative isolation to increasing confrontation with the culture, and some are more accepting of these modernizing trends than others.

The denomination's clergy fall between evangelical and mainline pastors on theology and politics. They continue to resemble evangelicals more in their adherence to orthodox theology, although some movement can be detected toward theological liberalism. Traditional Mennonite concerns for peace and justice issues and simple lifestyles push clergy in the direction of theological liberalism, as does the church's routine cooperation with mainline denominations in Washington activities. Only the traditional orthodoxy of some clergy and many laity counters this trend. A polarization can be noted among the youngest pastors, with some defending traditional orthodoxy while others embrace theological liberalism, suggesting a potential battleground in ensuing years.

MCUSA clergy are divided in their policy stances, their partisanship, and their voting behavior. The more orthodox ministers tend toward conservatism, are Republican in identification, and generally vote for GOP candidates—and are probably more in tune with most MCUSA laity. This suggests a gathering storm: a serious division between ongoing conservatism within the laity while numerous pastors move toward mainline Protestant theology and political liberalism.

Such divisions are unusual within smaller denominations, where clergy and laity generally tend to be more in agreement. Will the future bring intensified conflicts of the kind that have divided denominations in the past generation—over ordination of women, abortion, homosexuality, biblical interpretation, and the like? Or will the MCUSA find a way to minimize differences as it falls back on its strong sense of community? Only time will provide the answer.

Part 4

Beyond the Two-Party Protestant System

Chapter 17

American Rabbis

Anand E. Sokhey and Paul A. Djupe

The 2000 election was groundbreaking for the Jewish community. Senator Joseph Lieberman (D-CT), an observant Orthodox Jew, was nominated to be the Democratic vice-presidential candidate. In addition, the presidential election events, especially in Florida, highlighted the important and sometimes central role of the Jewish community in American politics. And further, current events in Israel ensured that a core issue of the American Jewish community remained high on the national agenda. All these factors made the 2000 election a perfect time to assess the Jewish religious community's connection to United States politics. While the central place of American Jews within the Democratic coalition has been long established, and indeed continued in the 2000 election process, the role of rabbis in maintaining that partisan connection has not been explored empirically until now.

This chapter, therefore, examines the role of rabbis in sustaining Jewish community alliances within national politics. Three areas of inquiry are analyzed in the study: the theological positions held by rabbis and how those views translate into the political realm; the attitudinal and behavioral connections between rabbis and politics; and how engagement in electoral politics differs for rabbis of the four primary Jewish movements.

HISTORICAL BACKGROUND

Jews have lived in America since before the nation's founding and have always participated in politics, making their experience in America different from the history of Jews in other countries. This distinction was noted in a letter from President George Washington to a Rhode Island synagogue in 1790:

> The government of the United States of America which gives to bigotry no sanction, to persecution no assistance, requires only that they who live under its protection should demean themselves as good citizens in giving it on all occasions their effectual support. (quoted in Goldberg 1996)

While anti-Semitism has run as rampant in America as in any other country, the tools of the state have not served to single out the Jewish community. Moore (1986) suggests that in America, Jews found commonalities with other immigrant populations among whom they lived; these populations also could not aspire to occupy positions of high social status. In the United States, Jews did not suffer a different legal status from other nationalities.

The consequence of this status has been twofold, resulting in the evolution of pluralism within the Jewish community but also an attendant fear of community disintegration (Goren 1999). Ginsberg poses the question, "How long can America's Jews simultaneously lead the United States and resist assimilation by it?" (2001, 27). Indeed, in the long run, political involvement threatens the Jewish ability to remain ethnically and religiously distinct (Moore 1986). And yet, that same desire for divergence ultimately threatens Jewish political power: "[W]hen Jews were the victims of discrimination, there was no problem" (Ginsberg 2001, 27) since anti-Semitism "is the time-honored prejudice imposed on the 'outsider,' the 'stranger group'; it provides some Jews with a tangible referent for their identity" (Blakeslee 2000, 219). Paradoxically, anti-Semitism has united the Jewish community to work hard to secure and promote a vision of racial, ethnic, and religious acceptance and rights within American society.

The political agenda of the Jewish community has consisted of three prongs; combating anti-Semitism is at the forefront, accompanied by a concern for the state of Israel, and social welfare (Lipset 1995). Though the motivations of this agenda have been contested, especially by conservatives, most agree that a mixture of concerns drive it (Greenberg and Wald 2001). Anti-Semitism is seen as a civil-rights issue, and Jewish organizations have been careful to frame it in that light. Their pursuit of general civil-rights principles (as they apply to most any group) has granted Jewish groups special authority. Thus, while battling anti-Semitism may foundationally result from anxiety about personal and national security, the moral force of the Jewish community results from expressing that concern in terms of theological dictates having universal application.

The order of importance of the three issues, along with the particular referent, has shifted considerably over time in response to changing national and international political events. Prior to the 1950s, "the primary agenda of the Jewish community was combating anti-Semitism at home and abroad and the corollary of anti-Semitism, discrimination . . ." (Chanes 2001, 100). In the 1960s, elimination of anti-Semitism maintained importance within the Jewish community, but the focus shifted to demonstrate solidarity with overall civil-rights activism. The Soviet Jewry movement in 1963, coupled with the Six-Day War in 1967, served again to alter the attention of some Jewish groups. Concerns for economic justice and domestic issues were nudged over to make room for Jewish interests abroad.

In the 1980s, the shift toward conservatism and the right on the United States political landscape caused the Jewish community to reevaluate its positions. With the Reagan administration's restrictive policies and the rise of the Christian conservative movement, the Jewish community perceived a threat to constitutional protections. On the current political scene, following the collapse of the Soviet Union and with anti-Semitism found in exceedingly low levels, the Jewish agenda is again in a state of flux (Chanes 2001). However, Jewish security issues, a salient one being anti-Semitism, remain important both abroad and in the United States.

While it is common practice to theorize about one Jewish community, this reference is inappropriate. The Jewish community is highly fragmented organizationally, including an array of social, civic, political, and religious groups. The most visible Jewish associations are the so-called protective organizations: the American Jewish Committee, the American Jewish Congress, and the Anti-Defamation League. All three serve to represent the Jewish community, though in slightly different ways. Each of the groups raises, and keeps prominent in the national view, the issues that are central to maintaining the Jewish community. In addition, a number of Jewish organizations maintain affiliations with the major political parties: the National Jewish Democratic Coalition and the Republican Jewish Coalition, among many others.

The other major organizational forum within the Jewish community encompasses various religious movements generated in the United States. The different groups have developed within the Jewish community in a parallel process to the rampant denominationalism of American Protestantism.

Orthodox Judaism, the denomination of Senator Joseph Lieberman, is the smallest group in the United States, but holds a stronger position worldwide (particularly in Israel). Adherents view the Torah as recorded law, interpreting "its divine revelations as literal events" (Vara 2000). Orthodox Jews also believe in a set of orally passed laws and traditions called the *halakha*, and both the written and oral laws are seen as universally present and applicable. They strictly keep the Sabbath (choosing not to work from sunset Friday to sunset Saturday), wear *yarmulkes*, and hold particular conservative views regarding gender: in the synagogue, men and women are segregated, and women cannot become ordained rabbis. The Orthodox group attempts to maintain tradition in the face of modern changes.

The Reform movement of Judaism follows much Jewish ritual, but is more liberal than Orthodox Jewry in dealing with the Torah and halakha. Several theories guide Reform Judaism: first, "Judaism is evolving and is not based on a once-and-forever divine revelation. . . . Revelation can continue through great teachers and scholars" (Vara 2000, 1); and secondly, modern understanding and personal evaluations can be applied to the Jewish faith. The Reform movement of Judaism allows men and women to sit together during services and consents to the ordination of women as rabbis. The survey results show essentially all Reform rabbis in our sample agreeing that "women should be able to become rabbis." In 1983, Reform rabbis in the United States greatly angered Orthodox Jewry by voting to accept the patrilineal passing of the religion, breaking the ancient maxim that Jewish identity was passed exclusively from mother to child (matrilineal descent).

Conservative Judaism formed in reaction to the changes introduced by Issac M. Wise and other Reform movement leaders of the nineteenth century. While recognizing the necessity to change with the times, Conservatism upholds the observance of traditional religious traditions and laws. It does "not take the Torah revelations as literal but as the product of human inspiration influenced by God" (Vara 2000, 1). Conservative Jewry accepts the ordination of women, but disagrees with the personal autonomy of the Reform movement, as well as patrilineal descent.

The most recent faction within American Judaism, the Reconstructionists, is "a growing arm of liberal thought that focuses on social and personal improvement" (Vara 2000, 1). An offspring of Conservatism, the movement is based on the work of Rabbi Mordechai Kaplan and "rejects a God-centered theology, instead emphasizing Judaism as a distinctive religious civilization, with a unique tradition, culture, and land" (Chanes 1999, 10). Therefore, the Reconstructionists and Orthodox Jews share a common bond in their commitment to maintaining a distinctly Jewish community, though predicated on significantly different justifications.

NATURE OF THE STUDY

In the fall and winter of 2000, a mail survey was conducted which including rabbis within the four major movements of American Judaism—Reconstructionist, Reform, Conservative, and Orthodox. After obtaining membership directories from the rabbinical associations of each movement, questionnaires were sent to roughly half the rabbis (about 1,600 of 3,200). From the initial mailing and two subsequent waves, 517 surveys were returned, though not all were usable. The overall response rate, therefore, was approximately one-third. Participation, not surprisingly, varied by movement, declining with the increasing orthodoxy of the group: the response rate for Orthodox rabbis was 22 percent, 29 percent for the Reconstructionists, 30 percent for the Conservatives, and 32 percent for the Reform. Rabbis from the Reform movement dominate the dataset, with a slim majority of the sample.

SOCIAL CHARACTERISTICS OF AMERICAN RABBIS

Demographic characteristics, including gender and education, have been shown in past research to play a role in citizen motivation to participate in politics (Verba and Nie 1972). Demographics hint at the resources and roles that shape peoples' responses to invitations for involvement in the political arena.

The current survey included questions about the demographic characteristics of the respondents. As shown in Table 17.1, the majority of participating rabbis are male. Although women are absent from the Orthodox sample (due to the movement's positions on gender and ordination), female rabbis make up approximately half of the Reconstructionist responses as well as a portion, although small, of both the Reform (15 percent) and Conservative (4 percent) samples. The respondents are highly educated, with almost all holding post-graduate degrees, though some exceptions exist, especially among the Orthodox. In this demographic field, rabbis resemble mainline Protestant and Catholic clergy, who hold similarly high levels of education.

Table 17.1

Social Characteristics of American Rabbis

% of Clergy

	Reconstructionist	Reform	Conservative	Orthodox	Total
Gender: Male	50%	85%	96%	100%	89%
Education					
College Graduate	100%	100%	98%	82%	95%
Seminary Graduate	100%	97%	97%	75%	92%
Age					
Under 35 years of age	0%	14%	7%	33%	15%
Over 55 years of age	40%	35%	26%	24%	32%
Community Size					
Farm or small town	8%	4%	2%	2%	3%
Small or medium-sized cities	39%	30%	28%	15%	27%
Large cities	53%	66%	70%	83%	70%

The rabbis in the 2000 study represent a variety of communities. While few live in rural or farm areas, they are evenly distributed between small and medium-sized cities. A plurality of Orthodox, Reconstructionist, and Reform rabbis report living in a large city (over 250,000), while a plurality of Conservative rabbis classify their community as in the suburb of a very large city. The data indicate that a Jewish religious presence is not a new phenomenon in many of these areas, since across all four movements the average age of a rabbi's synagogue/temple is more than thirty years.

Experience in the ministry is extensive among the rabbis, with a mean of twenty-three years (the Reconstructionist rabbis fell somewhat behind in this category, with thirteen years in the ministry, which would be anticipated given that this movement is the newest group within the

Jewish faith). The respondents appear to be fairly well grounded in their communities as well: Orthodox, Reform, and Conservative rabbis have served the same congregations an average of more than ten years. Reconstructionist rabbis trail slightly behind that figure, having been with their current temples or synagogues an average of about seven and a half years.

Traditionally the Jewish community has been geographically centered in Democratic strongholds—data confirmed in our study. Approximately 75 percent of sample rabbis live in counties where Al Gore received over half of the vote; similarly, 72 percent reside in states carried by candidate Gore. There are predictable differences between the four movements: 94 percent of Orthodox rabbis, 82 percent of Reconstructionists, and just under three-fourths of Reform and Conservative rabbis live in counties delivering a majority of votes to Gore. Certainly the immediate political environments of survey participants appear conducive to maintaining traditional Jewish political attachments.

THEOLOGICAL POSITIONS HELD BY AMERICAN RABBIS

Significant theological differences exist between the major movements of Judaism (see Table 17.2). As noted earlier, Orthodox Jews stress the importance of religious law and tradition—they refuse to "update the faith." These particular conventions create an adversarial scenario, erecting barriers between Orthodox Jewry and the non-Orthodox Jewish world, though at times Conservative rabbis join their Orthodox colleagues to form a conservative coalition.

While only 7 percent of Orthodox rabbis believe that halakha (oral and written Jewish law) "must sometimes be ignored for the sake of Jewish unity," support for the statement is strong among the sampled rabbis of two of the other movements. The approval rate is highest for Reform participants, with just under three-fourths in agreement.

The difference between the Orthodox theological orientation and that of other Jewish clergy again surfaces in questions on gender. Only 4 percent of Reform rabbis assert that women should be segregated at the Western Wall in Jerusalem. The number in agreement is also fairly low for Reconstructionist and Conservative rabbis at 11 and 12 percent respectively. However, nearly three-fourths of Orthodox rabbis believe that women should be separated from the men. Similarly, only 3 percent of Orthodox rabbis agreed that "[w]omen should be able to become rabbis." The next lowest group in agreement was Conservative rabbis, at 94 percent.

Table 17.2

Theological Views Held by American Rabbis

% Agreeing

	Reconstructionist	Reform	Conservative	Orthodox	Total
Orthodox rabbis who refuse to recognize officially Reform and Conservative rabbis are right to do so.	9%	7%	4%	59%	19%
Halakha must sometimes be ignored for the sake of Jewish unity.	61%	71%	31%	7%	38%
In my eyes, the child of a Jewish father and a non-Jewish mother is a Jew.	73%	68%	4%	3%	47%
Women should be able to become rabbis.	98%	99%	94%	3%	75%
Women should be confined to the women's section at the Western Wall in Jerusalem.	11%	4%	12%	75%	24%

POLITICAL ENGAGEMENT OF AMERICAN RABBIS

The theological differences between rabbis translate into differences in political attitude and engagement as well. In particular, the walls constructed by Orthodox Jews between themselves and the outside world, somewhat ironically, result in a more politically conservative agenda. That said, there is still heavy emphasis placed on Israel and Jewish security issues. Taking all into account, however, Orthodox rabbis predominately remain in the Democratic partisan camp.

The conservative tendencies of Orthodox rabbis manifest to an extent in their reported policy positions, leading to significant differences between Orthodoxy and the other three movements. However, among the Reform, Reconstructionist, and Conservative branches, the policy positions demonstrate variations but not deep chasms. As Table 17.3 indicates, no Reconstructionist, and very few Reform or Conservative rabbis, agreed on the need for a constitutional amendment banning abortion; approximately one-third of Orthodox rabbis responded in the affirmative. Views on priorities in education also distinguish Orthodox survey participants: only 30 percent see a necessity to improve public schools before supporting alternative and religious schools. In fact, this position yielded a special public school for a Hasidic community ultimately created by the Supreme Court in *Kiryas Joel v. Grument* (1994, 512 U.S. 687). Rabbis of the other movements give this issue considerably more weight. Over 70 percent of Conservatives, 87 percent of Reform, and 95 percent of Reconstructionist rabbis agree that the public education system should be improved.

Table 17.3

Policy Positions of American Rabbis

% Agreeing

	Reconstructionist	Reform	Conservative	Orthodox	Total
The federal government should do more to solve social problems such as unemployment, poverty, and poor housing.	100%	91%	90%	62%	84%
Education policy should focus on improving public schools rather than on encouraging alternative private and religious schools.	95%	87%	71%	30%	70%
We need government-sponsored national health insurance so that everyone can get adequate medical care.	100%	81%	80%	66%	78%
African Americans and other minorities may need special government help to achieve an equal place in America.	90%	81%	60%	39%	61%
We need a constitutional amendment prohibiting all abortions unless necessary to save the mother's life, or in cases of rape and incest.	0%	2%	4%	33%	10%
Homosexuals should have all the same rights and privileges as other American citizens.	100%	95%	93%	52%	84%
A lasting peace in the Middle East will require Israel to make greater concessions to the Palestinians.	50%	47%	36%	22%	38%
We need to devote more resources against growing anti-Semitism in the United States.	14%	27%	12%	51%	29%

The differences in opinion extend to civil-rights issues as well. While nearly 100 percent of Reconstructionist, Reform, and Conservative respondents agree upon the need for gay rights, only half of Orthodox rabbis do so. Likewise, only 39 percent of Orthodox participants support affirmative action or its equivalent, but over 60 percent of Conservative rabbis, and over four-fifths of both Reconstructionist and Reform do.

Multiple interests obviously exist within the Jewish community; however, two issues have served to unite rabbis across movements: anti-Semitism and the state of Israel. Keeping in mind the importance of Jewish security issues, it is not surprising that rabbis do not readily agree that peace in the Middle East will require additional concessions to the Palestinians. Approximately half of Reconstructionist and Reform rabbis, 36 percent of Conservative rabbis, and only 22 percent of Orthodox rabbis recognize the necessity of compromise to achieve peace in Israel. Considerably fewer respondents assert that more resources should be devoted to combating anti-Semitism in the United States: 27 percent of Reform rabbis, 14 percent of Reconstructionist rabbis, and 12 percent of Conservative rabbis. Again, the Orthodox stand out with 51 percent agreeing that more needs to be done.

The political engagement of rabbis in the election of 2000 fits expectations based on theological orientation and agenda. The total percent of respondents who report having voted for Al Gore in 2000 echoes the percent that reportedly identify with the Democratic Party (approximately 90 percent). Orthodox rabbis are the exception, with the possibility of somewhat weakened connections with the Democratic Party, and by extension, the rest of the Jewish community. Since political engagement depends at least in part on how an individual's views resonate with a partisan agenda, the lower level of political-issue activity reported by Orthodox rabbis is not a surprise. On the other hand, over three-fourths of Reconstructionist rabbis publicly took a stand on a political issue in 2000. Although Reconstructionists share the Orthodox desire to preserve the Jewish secular community, they do not construct the same walls against the outside world. Reconstructionist rabbis share the concerns of other marginal groups in society, and their attention to a broader range of issues translates into a higher level of political action, despite their desire to remain separate.

Across all four movements, rabbis are most likely to engage in indirect political activities (those aimed at the congregation or wider public), but are unlikely to endorse publicly (not in a sermon) a political candidate. Eighty percent of Reconstructionist rabbis reported publicly taking a stand on a political issue in 2000, followed by 61 percent of Reform, 45 percent of Conservative, and 38 percent of Orthodox rabbis. Fifty-two percent of Reconstructionist rabbis publicly supported a

Table 17.4

Political Activities of American Rabbis in the Election of 2000

% Reporting

	Reconstructionist	Reform	Conservative	Orthodox	Total
Political Activities					
Urged their congregation to register and vote	60%	45%	46%	27%	42%
Contacted a public official about some political or social issue	67%	46%	41%	26%	41%
Took a stand, from the pulpit, on some political issue	67%	54%	60%	26%	49%
Publicly (not in a sermon) took a stand on a political issue	80%	611%	45%	38%	53%
Publicly (not in a sermon) supported a political candidate	52%	33%	16%	21%	28%
Party Identification					
Strong Democrat	78%	69%	63%	24%	58%
Weak Democrat	17%	16%	22%	31%	21%
Independent, Lean Democrat	6%	10%	10%	16%	11%
Independent	0%	2%	4%	5%	3%
Independent, Lean Republican	0%	0%	1%	9%	2%
Weak Republican	0%	2%	0%	5%	2%
Strong Republican	0%	1%	0%	10%	3%
Vote Choice in the 2000 Election					
Al Gore	100%	94%	96%	72%	90%
George W. Bush	0%	3%	2%	28%	9%
Ralph Nader	0%	2%	0%	0%	1%

political candidate in 2000, while only 33 percent of Reform, 21 percent of Orthodox, and a low of 16 percent of Conservative rabbis did so. For the Orthodox and Reconstructionist movements, respondents took a stand on a political issue in a sermon as frequently as they took direct action on a political issue, though the latter is probably an enterprise undertaken more out of personal, rather than communal, concerns. Undoubtedly, issues of perceived propriety likely exert some constraining effects upon rabbis' political activity. Overall, rabbis apparently do not make a major distinction between social and political positions and issues, as is common practice among, for instance, Lutheran and Episcopal clergy (Djupe and Gilbert 2003). Significant differences exist on issues and opinions between movements within Judaism, however, with an orthodox-modernist gap reminiscent of those once found among Protestants (Quinley 1974; Guth et al. 1997).

CONCLUSION

Significant theological differences exist between American rabbis of the four movements of Judaism, and to a certain extent, differences are also apparent in political opinion. This pluralism stems largely from the barriers constructed by some groups between themselves and the rest of the Jewish community, but it also reflects the impact of Jewish protective organizations. Indeed, a certain amount of fragmentation seems inevitable as multiple organizations and factions put their own spin on Jewish issues.

Overall, however, these political differences are limited. A certain amount of unity exists throughout the Jewish community that is absent when evaluating the political positions of evangelical Protestant clergy. Ultimately, Jewish security issues prove sufficiently important to shepherd a flock that is dispersed across theological and, on some issues, political landscapes.

One would be inclined to think that Lieberman's nomination for the vice presidency in 2000 would have united the Jewish religious community, as Kennedy's nomination did for Catholics in 1960. Though many rabbis expressed pride over Lieberman's nomination, there was no "Kennedy effect" in 2000. The nomination of the first Jew to a major party presidential ticket had no ostensible impact upon an already united front. Clearly Jewish security issues—including civil rights and Israel—overshadowed the varied interests of the community, thereby for now preserving the traditional Democratic Jewish coalition.

Chapter 18

Roman Catholic Priests

Ted G. Jelen

In recent years, there has been increased interest in the politics of Roman Catholicism among academic observers and political activists alike. Such attention to the political behavior of Catholics is not surprising; by any measure, Catholics are an enormous constituency, representing the largest religious denomination in the United States.[36] Further, this huge component of the U.S. population is disproportionately concentrated in large, urban, "swing" states rich in electoral votes (Bendyna and Perl 2000). Thus, the size and geographical dispersion of the Catholic vote renders American Catholics of great interest to observers of United States politics.

Recent scholarship has also emphasized the role of churches and clergy as sources of political learning for the general public (Crawford and Olson 2001; Jelen 1993; Guth et. al. 1997; Verba et. al. 1995; Welch et. al. 1993). Both scholarly evidence and common sense suggest that the clergy can be highly influential community figures and may provide consequential political cues for members of their congregations and the broader community. Our purpose in this paper is to examine the political attitudes and activities of Roman Catholic priests in the context of the 2000 presidential election.

HISTORICAL BACKGROUND

Although Roman Catholics were among the earliest Europeans to settle in North America, the Catholic presence in the United States became most conspicuous during three waves of immigration during the nineteenth and twentieth centuries. The first influx of Catholic immigration occurred during the 1840s and 1850s and consisted primarily of individuals from Ireland and Germany. The second major group came during the years surrounding World War I, bringing numerous immigrants from Southern and Eastern Europe to the United States. Finally, during the last third of the twentieth century, a large number of Catholic immigrants from Latin America and Asian nations with large Catholic presences (such as South Korea, Vietnam, and the Philippines) comprised the third wave of Catholics moving to the United States (Jelen 2001).

For much of American history, the politics of Catholicism have been inextricably linked with questions of immigration and nativism. During the late nineteenth and early twentieth centuries, issues such as public education and temperance divided Catholic from Protestant in many parts of the country (Abramson 1973). To this day, numerous state constitutions contain provisions directed at limiting the role of Catholics in public life.

There has been a strong link between Catholics and the Democratic Party for much of American electoral history. Indeed, during the late nineteenth century, the Democrats were labeled the party of "Rum, Romanism, and Rebellion." The alliance between Catholic voters and the Democratic Party was renewed by the presidential candidacy of Al Smith in 1928 (Clubb and Allen 1971), and solidified by the New Deal (Andersen 1979). The election of John F. Kennedy was thought by many to indicate the end of anti-Catholic prejudice in the United States, although studies of that election indicate that pro- and anti-Catholic attitudes were important predictors of vote choice (Converse 1966).

Since the 1960 presidential election, the story of lay Catholics in the United States has largely been one of assimilation and acceptance. White Catholics now exhibit levels of income and education comparable to white Protestants, and Catholics constitute a formidable political force in the suburbs. Numerous observers have predicted that these demographic trends would occasion a shift in the partisan loyalties of Catholics to Republican partisanship (see especially Prendergast 1999), but the ties between Catholics and the Democratic Party have proven quite resilient (Bendyna 2000; Brewer 2001). While some Republican presidential candidates have achieved success with Catholic voters in particular elections, the cultural conservatism of numerous devout Catholics has not resulted in major shifts toward the GOP (Jelen 1997). Nevertheless, many observers have characterized Catholics as a crucial swing vote in recent American elections (Catholic News Service 2000; Kenski and Lockwood 1991).

Outside the area of electoral politics, Catholic elites made several attempts to provide prophetic leadership during the final quarter of the twentieth century. In addition to the Church's traditional opposition to abortion, the National Council of Catholic Bishops took highly visible, public positions on nuclear war, American policy in Central America, and the moral imperatives surrounding the practice of capitalism during the 1980s. Although it is difficult to assess the effectiveness of these efforts (see Wald 1992), it is clear that the leadership of the Church has taken a politically assertive role in the United States during the most recent quarter century (see especially Byrnes 1991).

Thus, ample reasons exist to study the political attitudes and activities of Catholic priests. Priests provide the most consistent contact between a Church hierarchy that is occasionally politically assertive and a laity that, by its very size, constitutes an important electoral force in American politics. The extent and nature of the cues provided by Catholic priests may, potentially, be quite consequential for politics in the United States.

NATURE OF THE STUDY[37]

Data for this study were taken from a national mail survey of Catholic pastors in the United States. The mailing list came from two random samples of 1,000 Catholic parishes, which were drawn from the National Parish Inventory. The NPI, a database of all Catholic parishes in the United States, is maintained by the Center for Applied Research in the Apostolate (CARA) located at Georgetown University. Two mailings of the survey were sent to the first sample in January and again in March of 2001; a second random sample of priests received one mailing in February of 2002. These efforts yielded 454 usable questionnaires, for a somewhat disappointing response rate of 22.7 percent. While this is not unusual for a mail survey, the relatively small number of respondents suggests that the results should be interpreted with caution.

The relatively low response rate is difficult to explain. The survey instrument was quite long (over twelve pages, with nearly two hundred items), and many respondents may have been deterred by the time and energy necessary to complete the questionnaire. Perhaps more importantly, this survey is part of a larger, multidenominational survey of clergy in the United States. In order to achieve comparability across denominations, a large number of common items were included in the questionnaire, and many of these queries may not have been meaningful to Catholic priests; several instruments were returned with marginal comments to that effect.

SOCIAL CHARACTERISTICS OF ROMAN CATHOLIC PRIESTS

The demographic characteristics of our sample of Catholic clergy are quite similar to other studies of Roman Catholic priests. Thus, despite our low response rate, we are reasonably confident that our sample is representative of the population of Catholic pastors in the United States.

First, and most obviously, the entire sample of Catholic priests is male and unmarried, as only unmarried males are ordained to the priesthood. Catholic priests within the American context are also relatively homogeneous racially: respondents to the survey are predominantly white (93 percent). And, clearly, Catholic priests are highly educated: not only have all the respondents graduated from college and virtually all from seminary (99.5 percent), but almost all (94 percent) report some type of postgraduate training as well.

Much has been said about the aging and depletion of the ranks of the American Catholic priesthood, and our sample tends to reflect these noted sociological patterns. Only 1 percent of the respondents is below the age of thirty-five, while 60 percent are over fifty-five years of age. Not only is the sample relatively old, comparatively speaking, when the age distribution of the respondents is compared to that of clergy in other denominations analyzed in the study, but these priests tend to be relatively old in absolute terms as well (mean age = 59 years). Given their age, it is not surprising that they tend to be relatively stable in terms of their current assignments (mean years in present position = 7.2 years) and quite experienced in terms of parish service as well (mean years in the priesthood = 30.3 years).

Table 18.1

Social Characteristics of Roman Catholic Priests

	% of Clergy
Gender: Male	100%
Race: White	93%
Marital Status: Single, unmarried	100%
Education	
College Graduate	100%
Seminary Graduate	99%
Age	
Under 35 years of age	1%
Over 55 years of age	60%
Community Size	
Farm or small town	41%
Small or medium-sized cities	26%
Large cities	33%

Despite the stereotype of the Catholic Church as primarily an urban institution, slightly more than two out of five priests (41 percent) serve parishes located in rural or small towns, while one-third (33 percent) work in large cities or their suburbs. If one divides community size at a population of 50,000 people, then approximately half of the respondents (52 percent) report that their parishes are located in communities with populations under that number, with the remaining priests serving churches located either in cities with populations greater than 50,000 people or in the suburbs adjacent to such cities. However, as expected, the geographical distribution of the priests in terms of region of the country does reflect the traditional strongholds of Catholicism within the American context. Slightly more than three-quarters (76 percent) of the survey participants reside in either the East or Midwest, with the remaining portion serving parishes in either the South or West.

The size of the parishes also varies enormously: reported weekly attendance at Mass ranges from 20 to over 20,000, and the reported number of adult church members ranges from 45 to over 25,000. Most parishes are relatively large: medians for attendance and membership are 800 and 1,100, respectively.

THEOLOGICAL POSITIONS HELD
BY ROMAN CATHOLIC PRIESTS

Theologically, the respondents exhibit a fascinating mix of general Christian orthodoxy and Roman Catholic distinctiveness. On certain doctrinal matters, Catholic priests adopt positions that resemble the patterns exhibited by clergy of conservative Protestant denominations. For example, almost all Catholic priests believe that Jesus will return to earth some day (87 percent), that Jesus was born of a virgin (96 percent) and that the devil actually exists (86 percent). However, on other doctrinal matters, the pastors assert positions that clergy of many conservative Protestant denominations are less prone to express. Less than one in five Catholic priests (17 percent) state their belief in the literal existence of Adam and Eve, and only one in ten regards the Bible to be the inerrant Word of God.

Table 18.2

Theological Views Held by Roman Catholic Priests

	% Agreeing
Jesus will return to earth one day.	87%
Jesus was born of a virgin.	96%
The devil actually exists.	86%
There is no other way to salvation but through belief in Jesus Christ.	40%
Adam and Eve were real people.	17%
The Bible is the inerrant Word of God, both in matters of faith and in historical, geographical, and other secular matters.	10%
The church should put less emphasis on individual sanctification and more on transforming the social order.	28%

Surprisingly, only two of five Catholic priests surveyed (40 percent) responded that they believe that salvation is attainable only through belief in Jesus Christ. It is unclear why this figure is so low; it is possible that many respondents perceive the statement to be more characteristic of evangelical Protestantism and therefore reject the position for that reason. But it may also be reflective of some other factors. In particular, the position of the Catholic Church on matters related to the atoning work of Jesus Christ has shifted subtly over the past several decades. The position of the Church today seems to reflect the sentiment that faithful followers of non-Christian faiths are saved through the atoning work of Jesus Christ: it is Christ's life, death, and resurrection that saves, but non-Christians can be saved through faithfulness to their religion. If this is the understanding, then perhaps there is some ambiguity as to how to answer the question: one could believe that salvation is obtained through Jesus Christ, yet disagree that "there is no other way to salvation but through belief in Jesus Christ."

On the other hand, there seem to be some limits to this theological ecumenism. A somewhat larger percentage of participants (57 percent) believe that the sacraments of the Church are necessary for salvation, and relatively few (17 percent) agree that "all great religions are equally good and true." Further, the relationship between the stance that salvation is attained only through belief in Jesus Christ and the position that the sacraments of the Church are necessary for salvation is quite strong.[38] Still, overall, there seems to remain a substantial minority of Catholic priests with an ecumenical approach to personal salvation.

Finally, more than one-quarter of the survey participants (28 percent) agree that transforming the social order is more important than individual sanctification. While this figure may seem somewhat low at first glance, it is rather remarkable that, in an individualistic political culture such as the United States, over a quarter of Catholic priests would endorse such an unequivocally communal response. This seems strong evidence of a communal ethic among U.S. Catholic clergy (see Tropman 1995; Bendyna 2000).

POLITICAL ENGAGEMENT
OF ROMAN CATHOLIC PRIESTS

The sample of Catholic pastors exhibits interesting patterns of political attitudes and involvement. Indeed, the election of 2000 provides an interesting opportunity to examine the general characteristics and dynamics of priestly political attitudes and behavior.

By and large, Catholic priests approve of several forms of political activity on the part of clergy, while opposing others.[39] As Table 18.3 shows, respondents are virtually unanimous (96 percent) in approving preaching about a particular moral position, and nearly three in four (73 percent) favor the formation of social-action groups and participation in protest marches (72 percent).

On the other hand, Catholic priests are nearly evenly divided on the appropriateness of taking positions on political issues while preaching

(58 percent approving), and fewer than half (48 percent) approve of making financial contributions for political purposes. Only two in five (40 percent) believe priests may engage in civil disobedience, and just over one-quarter (27 percent) of all respondents favor publicly supporting a political candidate even if done when not preaching.

Table 18.3

Political Norms of Roman Catholic Priests

	% Approving
Take a stand while preaching on some moral issue	96%
While preaching, take a stand on some political issue	58%
Publicly (not preaching) support a political candidate	27%
Contribute money to a candidate, party, or political-action committee	48%
Form an action group in one's church to accomplish a social or political goal	73%
Participate in a protest march	72%
Commit civil disobedience to protest some evil	40%

These findings would suggest that priests are not hesitant about approving participation in the public sphere, but draw a line at participation in "politics," when this term is construed to mean partisan or electoral activity. Not surprisingly, most priests exhibit hesitation about breaking the law when asked about civil disobedience.

When attention is turned to the policy positions advocated by Catholic priests on major political issues of the day, a moderately complex pattern of responses is again observed, as can be seen in Table 18.4. In general, Catholic clergy seem unusually liberal on economic issues such as federal involvement in solving social problems or in establishing national health insurance. The respondents are also generally supportive of gay rights and greater Israeli concessions in the Middle East conflict, and are divided on the question of affirmative action.

Not surprisingly, since the Catholic Church operates the largest system of private schools in the nation, most priests oppose government promotion of public education at the expense of encouraging private or religious alternatives. However, the lack of support for abstinence based sex education in public schools and the low level of agreement with a constitutional amendment limiting abortion are both surprising patterns.

The responses to the abortion question, in particular, are quite unanticipated, given that the Catholic Church has advocated what is known as a "seamless garment" position regarding the sanctity of life. From the Catholic perspective, human life is sacred, a gift from God, and the sanctity of life must be protected. Human life begins with conception and should be protected from that point onward; abortion is the taking of human life. However, this position shapes perspectives on other life-and-death matters as well. The Catholic Church stands in opposition to both capital punishment and euthanasia based on the same sanctity-of-life argument.

Table 18.4

Policy Positions of Roman Catholic Priests

	% Agreeing
The federal government should do more to solve social problems such as unemployment, poverty, and poor housing.	84%
Education policy should focus on improving public schools rather than on encouraging alternatives such as private and religious schools.	18%
Sex-education programs included in the curricula of public high schools should be abstinence based.	39%
We need government-sponsored national health insurance so that everyone can get adequate medical care.	73%
African Americans and other minorities may need special governmental help in order to achieve an equal place in America.	55%
We need a constitutional amendment prohibiting all abortions unless to save the mother's life, or in cases of rape or incest.	38%
Homosexuals should have all the same rights and privileges as other American citizens.	71%
A lasting peace in the Middle East will require Israel to make greater concessions to the Palestinians.	72%

Given the church's formal position, one possible conclusion is that the relatively low level of agreement with the abortion question may be a consequence of the particular wording of the statement. Some respondents may have disagreed because they do not approve of using the U.S. Constitution to mandate a particular policy outcome, while others may not approve of excluding rape or incest (or even saving the mother's life) from the general prohibition. In any event, the formulation of the abortion item appears to be problematic for these Catholic clergy.

The seemingly difficult nature of the abortion question became even more apparent in light of the virtually unanimous opposition expressed by the respondents to the death penalty. Not only did nine out of ten priests (90 percent) indicate agreement with the statement "I oppose capital punishment," but 65 percent of those surveyed expressed strong agreement with the statement, and only 5 percent of the respondents disagreed with the query. This strong opposition to capital punishment suggests not only that these priests embrace the sanctity-of-life position, but that the church and its clergy may well take an active, prophetic role in opposing capital punishment as that issue reemerges on the political agenda.

Table 18.5

Political Activities of Roman Catholic Priests in the Election of 2000

	% Reporting
Urged their congregation to register and vote	54%
Contacted a public official about some issue	38%
Prayed publicly for political candidates	23%
Took a stand from the pulpit on some political issue	33%
Prayed publicly about an issue	48%
Party Identification	
Strong Democrat	14%
Weak Democrat	14%
Independent, lean Democrat	20%
Independent	21%
Independent, lean Republican	12%
Weak Republican	8%
Strong Republican	11%
Vote Choice in the 2000 Election	
Al Gore	31%
George W. Bush	59%
Pat Buchanan	*
Ralph Nader	6%
Other	*
Did not vote	4%

* = less than 1 percent

Table 18.5 records the actual level of political engagement reported by Catholic priests in the election of 2000; such activity seems to have been somewhat limited in nature. Only a bare majority of respondents (54 percent) publicly took the unexceptionable position of urging the members of their congregations to register and vote, and just less than half of the priests in the sample (48 percent) prayed publicly about a political issue. A minority of these priests engaged in other political activities: less than two of five (38 percent) Catholic clergy had contacted a public official about some issue; only one-third (33 percent) took a stand on some political issue while preaching; and less than one-quarter (23 percent) prayed publicly for political candidates.

Despite the expectations of some analysts (see especially Prendergast 1999), Catholic priests remain largely Democratic in their personal political identifications. Just under half (48 percent) report identifying with the Democratic Party, while only 31 percent consider themselves Republicans.[40] However, the pattern of party preference is distinctive in another sense. Given that the distribution of partisan identification among clergy in many other denominations examined in this volume are skewed in the direction of one particular political party, the relatively equal distribution of Catholic priests within each category of partisan identification tends to be unique. In addition, given the older age of many of the priests surveyed, it is noteworthy that there is a higher proportion of Republican Party identifiers among younger, rather than older, priests. Thus, to the extent that Catholic priests provide partisan cues to their congregants (which, given our data, seems limited), the priesthood may serve as a source of partisan inertia among American Catholics.

The general tilt toward Democratic partisan identification by the surveyed priests did not prevent George W. Bush from winning a substantial majority of their vote in the 2000 presidential election. Al Gore, the Democratic Party candidate, garnered less than one-third (31 percent) of the votes cast by respondents, while George W. Bush captured nearly two-fifths (59 percent) of their ballots.

Further analysis of the survey results suggests some interesting dynamics. The study not only revealed that Bill Clinton won a narrow majority of the votes of Catholic priests in 1996, but that the election of 1996 seemed virtually devoid of short-term forces. When we attempt to account for priestly vote choice in 1996, the only variable whose effects attained statistical significance was party identification. By contrast, in 2000, priestly positions on abortion, assistance to private schools, and school prayer all caused significant Democratic defections to Republican candidate George W. Bush. Aside from his advantage in partisan identification among priests, the only issue which helped Al Gore among respondents was the death penalty (not surprising, given the strong opposition to capital punishment among Catholic priests and Bush's record on the death penalty while governor of Texas).

CONCLUSION

Roman Catholic clergy exhibit a combination of anticipated and unexpected patterns in their theology, political attitudes, and political behavior. Theologically, the priests express views that are both conservative and liberal in their theological interpretation. On some doctrinal matters, Catholics pastors are highly orthodox in their theological understandings and stand in agreement with many conservative Protestant clergy; on other theological matters, they adopt positions that stand in stark contrast to such conservative pastors and appear to be more liberal in their theological beliefs than many mainline Protestant ministers.

Politically, the results of this survey clearly justify the characterization of Catholics as a swing-group vote. While nearly a majority of priests identify with the Democratic Party, short-term forces specific to the 2000 presidential election (quite possibly the scandals associated with the Clinton administration) caused substantial defections. It seems possible that Catholic priests are a basis for both political inertia and political change for many members of the laity.

In an era of privatization and widespread skepticism about governmental social programs, priests (given their economic liberalism) seem a likely source of support for aggressive public measures to assist the disadvantaged. As the issue of capital punishment becomes more salient and more controversial,[41] the Church, through its priests, can provide impressive moral and rhetorical resources to those who wish to limit or abolish the death penalty. On such matters, Catholic priests are well positioned to provide a prophetic voice for American politics. However, given their apparent relative lack of political activity, it is less clear whether they may be willing to fill that role.

Chapter 19

African Methodist Episcopal Church

Eric McDaniel

Following the end of the Civil War, the black church emerged as the dominant institution within black communities. Not only was the church central in the lives of African Americans, but it became the "womb of black culture" and mothered other major social institutions as well. It is difficult to underestimate the historical importance of black churches within the communal life of black Americans. The church contributed to the survival and liberation of enslaved and segregated African Americans. It provided comfort to and aided in the transition of those blacks who, looking for work, moved to the North in the Great Migration. It was the base for much of the civil-rights movement, and it continues to play an important role in efforts related to electoral politics. Thus, historically speaking, the black church has served as the central institution that empowers black people in the United States.

This chapter examines the clergy of the African Methodist Episcopal Church (AME), the largest of the black Methodist denominations and the first denomination formed by African Americans. The group's history involves several firsts. The AME is unique in that it is the first major religious denomination whose origin can be traced to sociological, rather than theological, differences (African American). It elected the first black bishop, Richard Allen, in 1816, and in 2000 the AME General Conference elected the first black female bishop. Finally, it might be noted that the first AME congregation, Bethel AME of Philadelphia, Pennsylvania, is still located on the oldest piece of land that has been continually owned by blacks in the United States.

HISTORICAL BACKGROUND

Born out of protest, the roots of the African Methodist Episcopal Church can be traced to 1787 when numerous black members of the Methodist Episcopal Church (MEC; known today as the United Methodist Church) became dissatisfied with the treatment of blacks and the practice of segregation within church services (Childs 1980; Lincoln and Mamiya 1990; Mead 1995; Cone 1997). The precipitating catalyst was a conflict that transpired in Philadelphia's St. George's Methodist Episcopal Church: during a service in 1787, Absalom Jones, a black member, was pulled up from his knees because he was praying in the wrong part of the church. In response, several members of the congregation walked out, led by Absalom Jones, Richard Allen, and William White. These dissident members withdrew from the church in protest, built a chapel, and obtained their own black pastor.

These particular actions by the dissidents were not initially intended to create a separate denomination. Rather, those involved styled themselves, for the most part, as African Methodists—they were of African descent and Methodists. Their desire was simply to implement freedom of worship and rid themselves of the humiliation of segregation, especially in church.

Richard Allen established the first church within the "denomination," though almost three decades passed before the AME was eventually founded. It became clear that the AME was to be a distinct body, separate from the MEC, when, in 1816, Allen invited five other black Methodist churches that had formed under similar circumstances to join a General Convention in Philadelphia; the convention established the African Methodist Episcopal Church. Allen, in turn, became their first bishop.

Although Allen broke with the MEC, he did not want to leave Methodism, as he believed that Methodism was the only faith that would fit the needs of blacks (Lincoln and Mamiya 1990). As a result, the young denomination accepted Methodist doctrine and discipline almost in its entirety. Both the tenets espoused by the church and the polity established by the denomination were detailed in *The Book of Discipline*, modeled after the original MEC (Lincoln and Mamiya 1990), with the AME denomination's motto being "God Our Father, Christ Our Redeemer, Man Our Brother." Thus, the split was based more on racial, rather than theological, grounds.

The AME has a long history of focusing on education. Much of this emphasis on education was initiated through the work of Bishop Daniel Payne. Payne helped to create Wilberforce University, the first institution of higher education built by blacks in America. The AME supports other colleges as well as two seminaries: Payne Theological Seminary and Turner Theological Seminary (Lincoln and Mamiya 1990; Mead 1995). The denomination has also expanded its emphasis on education to the continent of Africa, where it has opened universities in western portions of Africa and South Africa. Based on its commitment to education, AME clergy have, on average, more years of schooling and theological training than clergy in many other black Protestant denominations.

Missions were also an early emphasis of the denomination, and the newly established church experienced rapid growth. However, membership in the AME was largely confined to states in the North prior to the Civil War. This regional basis of membership changed dramatically in the aftermath of the conflict, as the church sent hundreds of missionaries into the South, following the advances of the Union Army. Consequently, after the Civil War, the AME's membership witnessed a rapid increase in the southern United States. Today, the denomination has approximately 3.3 million members in 7,200 churches (Mead 1995).

The AME does not have a national headquarters or one chief administrative officer. The church is governed largely by its general conference, which is the supreme legislative body of the denomination, meeting once every four years. Between sessions of the general conference, the Council of Bishops serves as the executive branch of the church, providing supervision and oversight of the denomination's endeavors. A general secretary is elected to head the denomination, but the responsibilities of the office do not require its occupant to relocate (Lincoln and Mamiya 1990). Between meetings of the general conference, much of the "legislative" business of the AME is conducted through some thirty committees, which operate under the authority and provision of the general conference.

Throughout its history, the AME has encouraged activism among its members. The founder of the denomination, Richard Allen, established the Free African Society, a group that fought for abolition. The Denmark Vesey Slave Revolt in South Carolina was planned in an AME church in Charleston. The first black U.S. Senator, Hiram Revels, was an AME minister. Studies of the civil-rights movement have also documented this focus on political activism within the AME (Morris 1984; Payne 1995). And the denomination continues to be active in the National Congress of Black Churches as well as various international religious organizations.

Since the late 1930s, the AME has historically held close ties to the Democratic Party, with these links growing even stronger in recent years. During the 2000 election campaign, for example, Democratic presidential candidate Al Gore spoke at the denomination's general conference.

NATURE OF THE STUDY

The African Methodist Episcopal pastors surveyed in this study were selected randomly from a directory of AME clergy. A total of 740 questionnaires were mailed to the ministers of the denomination. Those who failed to return the survey were sent an initial reminder a month and a half later. Despite these efforts, the return rate was relatively low in comparison to the responses from other denominations analyzed in this volume—slightly over 11 percent. However, the level of participation does compare fairly well to another recent national survey of black clergy that employed a much shorter questionnaire (Smith and Smidt 2003). Certainly, the low number of returned surveys necessitates some caution in generalizing the results of this research as reflective of the population being examined. Nevertheless, while the results cannot be viewed as conclusive, they are certainly suggestive. And, since the resultant data provide some vital information, these data are analyzed and presented for the purposes of this comparative study.

SOCIAL CHARACTERISTICS
OF AFRICAN METHODIST EPISCOPAL CLERGY

We begin our analysis examining the social characteristics of AME clergy, as presented in Table 19.1. First, the pastors of the denomination are almost universally African Americans (95 percent); those who reported otherwise indicated that they were "mixed" in terms of their racial composition.

Still, AME pastors are far from being socially homogeneous, and diversity becomes apparent within the ranks of the clergy in several ways, first in terms of gender composition: nearly one-quarter (23 percent) of the clergy are females. Another source of diversity is in marital status; nearly half the clergy (45 percent) report being married and never divorced, but one-quarter of the respondents have been divorced and remarried, and another tenth of those surveyed report they are divorced and presently single.

Table 19.1

Social Characteristics of African Methodist Episcopal Clergy

	% of Clergy
Gender: Male	77%
Race: Black	95%
Marital Status: Married, never divorced	45%
Education	
College Graduate	72%
Seminary Graduate	48%
Age	
Under 35 years of age	4%
Over 55 years of age	35%
Community Size	
Farm or small town	33%
Small or medium-sized cities	29%
Large cities	38%

AME clergy tend to be somewhat older, exhibiting relatively lengthy service to their current congregations. Few of the respondents are under 35 years of age (4 percent), while more than one-third (35 percent) report they are over 55 years of age, with the mean age being 54 years. It is not surprising, therefore, that these respondents exhibit a relatively high level of clerical experience: the mean number of years in the ministry for the surveyed clergy is twenty. The mean number of years they have served their current congregation is fifteen, a startling figure given that the AME has a strong hierarchy, which not only appoints pastors to churches but regularly moves or rotates its clergy among the various congregations within the denomination.

Generally speaking, AME ministers are well educated. As noted earlier, the denomination has historically stressed learning, and this emphasis is evident among its pastors. All of the responding AME clergy have at least a high school education, and nearly three-quarters of them (72 percent) are college graduates. Nearly half (48 percent) hold a seminary degree as well.

Finally, AME clergy exhibit considerable diversity in terms of the size of the communities where their congregations are located. A full one-third (33 percent) serve congregations in rural and small-town settings. Nearly an equivalent number (29 percent) of pastors have churches in small or medium-sized cities, while the plurality (38 percent) of ministers is found in urban contexts.

THEOLOGICAL POSITIONS HELD
BY AFRICAN METHODIST EPISCOPAL CLERGY

When attention shifts to the theological perspectives of the African Methodist Episcopal clergy (as shown in Table 19.2), it is clear that those surveyed are relatively uniform in the positions they express and generally orthodox in terms of doctrinal stands. First of all, virtually all the AME pastors (95 percent or more) express agreement with statements that reflect historic doctrines or articles of the Christian faith: that Jesus will return to earth one day; that Jesus was born of a virgin; that the devil actually exists; and that there is no other way to salvation but through belief in Jesus Christ.

However, less agreement was voiced on issues of biblical inerrancy and whether Adam and Eve were real people. But even on these two matters, the overwhelming majority of AME clergy assert their agreement with the Bible as the inerrant Word of God (85 percent) and the literal existence of Adam and Eve (81 percent). Finally, even given the historic activism of the denomination, most AME pastors appear reluctant to argue that the church should put less emphasis on individual sanctification and more on transforming the social order, with only 10 percent of the surveyed clergy expressing such sentiments.

This general level of theological orthodoxy expressed by AME ministers is not too surprising. While the church has historically taken stances similar to the larger United Methodist Church, the denomination remains a black organization, and African Americans are generally more theologically conservative than whites (Leege and Kellstedt 1993).

Table 19.2

Theological Views Held by African Methodist Episcopal Clergy

	% Agreeing
Jesus will return to earth one day.	96%
Jesus was born of a virgin.	96%
The devil actually exists.	96%
There is no other way to salvation but through belief in Jesus Christ.	95%
Adam and Eve were real people.	81%
The Bible is the inerrant Word of God, both in matters of faith and in historical, geographical, and other secular matters.	85%
The church should put less emphasis on individual sanctification and more on transforming the social order.	10%

POLITICAL ENGAGEMENT
OF AFRICAN METHODIST EPISCOPAL CLERGY

Given the history of the denomination, one would anticipate that African Methodist Episcopal clergy would be highly supportive of clerical political activism. As can be seen from Table 19.3, AME pastors are strongly supportive of clergy activism, and that support is not confined to electoral politics.

Almost all AME ministers (91 percent) assert approval for clergy taking a stand on some moral issue while preaching from the pulpit, and nearly two-thirds (63 percent) express support for taking a stand on a political issue while preaching as well. Thus, while more than one-third of the respondents do not advocate ministers taking political stands from the pulpit, the overwhelming majority clearly hold that sending political messages from the pulpit is part of their role as pastors. Nor are AME clergy hesitant to take a public stand on behalf of a political candidate, with nearly three-quarters (73 percent) indicating approval for public support of a candidate when off the pulpit. While this level of agreement clearly represents a drop from ratings regarding speaking to moral issues from the pulpit, it reveals a significant level of willingness to endorse a candidate publicly when compared to the opinions expressed by clergy in other denominations. Fewer ministers, but still a large majority (61 percent) express approval for pastors making financial contributions to political candidates and causes.

Table 19.3

Political Norms of African Methodist Episcopal Clergy

	% Approving
Take a stand while preaching on some moral issue	91%
While preaching, take a stand on some political issue	63%
Publicly (not preaching) support a political candidate	73%
Contribute money to a candidate, party, or political-action committee	61%
Form an action group in one's church to accomplish a social or political goal	76%
Participate in a protest march	75%
Commit civil disobedience to protest some evil	47%

AME respondents also advocate other kinds of activism on the part of clergy who seek to mobilize congregations and other individuals to political action. Three-fourths of the AME ministers approve of clergy participation in protest marches and of pastors organizing congregants into action groups within the church to address some social or political end. And while far fewer respondents sanction civil disobedience on the part of ministers, nearly half (47 percent) voiced approval for this type of activity as well—again a fairly high level when compared to responses from clergy in other denominations.

Finally, given the role African American ministers have played in American politics, it is perhaps not surprising that AME clergy also express a high level of approval of clergy running for public office, with nearly three-quarters (70 percent) of the participants doing so. Thus, while AME clergy hold theologically conservative positions, this conservatism does not translate into withdrawal from the political arena. Instead, AME pastors clearly approve of political activism on the part of clergy, almost regardless of the particular form of action taken.

When one examines the policy preferences of AME clergy, one finds that they generally favor an activist federal government that provides services for the poor and protection for minorities. These policy preferences are shown in Table 19.4. Nearly all (91 percent) AME ministers agree that the federal government should do more to solve social problems, including addressing issues of unemployment, poverty, and housing. Almost the same portion of those surveyed (88 percent) voice support for government-sponsored national health-care insurance. Finally, the overwhelming majority of AME pastors (84 percent) express the need for continued governmental support to improve public schools rather than encouraging and developing alternatives to public education.

Table 19.4

Policy Positions of African Methodist Episcopal Clergy

	% Agreeing
The federal government should do more to solve social problems such as unemployment, poverty, and poor housing.	91%
Education policy should focus on improving public schools rather than on encouraging alternatives such as private and religious schools.	84%
Sex-education programs included in the curricula of public high schools should be abstinence based.	75%
We need government-sponsored national health insurance so that everyone can get adequate medical care.	88%
African Americans and other minorities may need special governmental help in order to achieve an equal place in America.	82%
We need a constitutional amendment prohibiting all abortions unless to save the mother's life, or in cases of rape or incest.	48%
Homosexuals should have all the same rights and privileges as other American citizens.	53%
A lasting peace in the Middle East will require Israel to make greater concessions to the Palestinians.	38%

In addition to support for national government involvement in addressing economic needs, AME clergy tend to favor governmental protection for minorities and the socially disadvantaged. More than four out of five AME pastors (82 percent) agree that blacks and other minorities may need special governmental help to achieve equality within American society. Similarly, three out of five AME clergy stated that there should be more legislation to protect the rights of women. And, finally, a majority (53 percent) indicate they believe that homosexuals should have the same rights and privileges as other American citizens.

When analyzing issues that are cast in more moral, rather than economic, terms, there tends to be somewhat more variation in the opinions of those surveyed. On the one hand, three-quarters of AME clergy (75 percent) agree that sex-education programs in public schools should be abstinence based, while three-fifths oppose capital punishment—both issues demonstrate some significant agreement among the respondents. On the other hand, the respondents were nearly evenly split on the issues of a constitutional amendment banning abortions except to save the life of the mother, or in cases of rape or incest, with 48 percent voicing approval for such governmental action. Clearly, while there is general agreement on many social policies, the level of cohesion on such moral issues does not reflect the extent of agreement evident for the more economic issues discussed initially.

Overall, AME clergy tend to be very supportive of the role played by religion in American civic and political life. Well over 90 percent of those surveyed indicate they believe that religion has a positive effect on American life generally, while two-thirds assert that religion has a positive effect on American political life. But, it is also clear that AME pastors do not believe that all religions are equally beneficial for the health of American democratic life; two out of five clergy (42 percent) agree that some religious groups threaten American civil liberties.

Table 19.5

Political Activities of African Methodist Episcopal Clergy in the Election of 2000

	% Reporting
Urged their congregation to register and vote	94%
Contacted a public official about some issue	77%
Prayed publicly for political candidates	56%
Took a stand from the pulpit on some political issue	57%
Prayed publicly about an issue	83%
Party Identification	
Strong Democrat	59%
Weak Democrat	10%
Independent, lean Democrat	15%
Independent	14%
Independent, lean Republican	0%
Weak Republican	1%
Strong Republican	1%
Vote Choice in the 2000 Election	
Al Gore	94%
George W. Bush	4%
Pat Buchanan	0%
Ralph Nader	0%
Other	0%
Did not vote	3%

Table 19.5 reveals that AME pastors not only favor an activist clergy, they actually embody an activist group. Responding ministers almost universally report that they have urged their congregations to register and vote as well as being personally active in the campaign of some political candidate (94 percent and 98 percent, respectively). More than three-quarters (77 percent) have contacted a public official about some issue.

Their efforts are not, however, limited to campaign activities. The vast majority of AME clergy (83 percent) have prayed publicly about an issue. A majority of those surveyed state they have taken a stand on a political issue from the pulpit as well as having prayed publicly for political candidates from the pulpit (57 percent and 56 percent, respectively). AME clergy are also strong supporters of collective action, with nearly seven in ten (69 percent) reporting participation in a protest march. It is readily apparent that, overall, the AME clergy are highly engaged politically, both transmitting moral and political cues to their congregations and taking steps to mobilize their members.

Given the ties between the African American community and the Democratic Party, it is not surprising to find AME clergy showing high levels of commitment to the Democratic Party and overwhelmingly supporting its candidate in the presidential election of 2000. Almost three in five AME pastors (59 percent) report that they are strong Democrats in terms of their partisan identifications, while another quarter identify themselves as either weak Democrats or Independents leaning toward the Democratic Party. Only one-seventh of the respondents report that they consider themselves to be political Independents (14 percent), and virtually none (2 percent) indicate any psychological ties to the Republican Party. This strong identification with the Democratic Party easily translated into overwhelming support for Al Gore in the 2000 presidential election, as almost all of those surveyed (94 percent) report casting their ballots for Gore and very few (4 percent) voted for Bush. Also noteworthy is the fact that almost all the pastors (97 percent) voted in the 2000 election, adding additional weight to the interpretation of high levels of political activism among clergy in the denomination.

CONCLUSION

The African Methodist Episcopal Church was the first American denomination formed by African Americans. The denomination was born not over theological differences, but as a political act. Over its years of history, the political involvement and activity of the denomination's clergy have continued to be evident.

AME ministers are generally well educated. They are located in diverse settings, both rural and highly urban. And they are comprised of a sizable segment of female clergy. Theologically, they tend to be generally orthodox in their assent to various Christian doctrines.

While the clergy in the AME are more theologically conservative than other Methodists, this disposition clearly does not transform itself into a lack of activism. Further, their theological conservatism does not appear to affect the ministers' attitudes on certain policy and partisan preferences. The extent to which this is connected to race issues cannot be clearly determined, but compared to other religiously conservative denominations, the AME pastors appear to be far more liberal in their stances. Finally, when the partisanship of the clergy of the denomination is examined, it is clear that there is overwhelming support for the Democratic Party. This is true not only in terms of their partisan identifications, but also in their almost unanimous support for Al Gore in the 2000 election.

Chapter 20

Church of God in Christ

Eric McDaniel

The Church of God in Christ (COGIC) is the youngest and most theologically orthodox of all the historically black Christian denominations, and it is quickly becoming the largest of the black Protestant church groups. The denomination differs from the black Baptists and AME blacks both historically and theologically; it was not created out of racial differences or conflicts, but was generated as a result of theological differences.

The COGIC stresses sanctification, with the gift of speaking in tongues as a symbol of sanctification. The denomination is a prime example of the growth of Pentecostalism in the United States. The Pentecostal movement originated in the United States in the early part of the twentieth century, and it has not only grown rapidly over the last century on American soil but has gained a large number of adherents in the Third World. The COGIC played an important role in this growth and in the establishment of Pentecostalism in the United States, and today it constitutes the largest Pentecostal denomination in the country (Lincoln and Mamiya 1990; Mead 1995).

HISTORICAL BACKGROUND

The Church of God in Christ is the youngest, but largest, of the seven major black denominations in the United States and is associated with the Pentecostal movement that emerged during the early twentieth century. The founder and organizer of the COGIC was Elder Charles H. Mason, a black man who received his early training in the Missionary Baptist Church. In 1898, Mason was called to the ministry; he received his license from a local Arkansas Missionary Baptist Church but soon thereafter found his own beliefs to be at variance with those of the church in which he was ordained. Mason sought to establish a church with stronger appeal and greater encouragement for all Christian believers, one that would emphasize the doctrine of entire sanctification through the outpourings of the Holy Spirit.

As a result, the COGIC was organized in 1895, with headquarters in Memphis, Tennessee. After twelve years, the denomination consisted of ten congregations. The turning point for the denomination came in 1907, when Mason journeyed to Los Angeles, California, to attend a great Pentecostal revival led by William Seymour. During his visit, Mason received the gift of tongues, and upon his return to Memphis, he began to proclaim speaking in tongues as a New Testament doctrine.

Between 1907 and 1914, the COGIC was the only denomination that ordained Pentecostal ministers. As a result, many white, independent Pentecostal churches became associated with the denomination through Mason's ordination of white Pentecostal pastors as COGIC ministers. Whether these black and white churches worshipped together has not been clearly established, but many of the churches that later formed the Assemblies of God denomination had, at one time, been churches within the COGIC (Lincoln and Mamiya 1990; Sanders 1996). By 1924, the noteworthy—though brief—period of interracial worship and mission among black and white Pentecostals had ended (Lincoln and Mamiya 1990).

Bishop Mason led the COGIC until his death in 1961; due to his longevity as the leader of the denomination, its history is closely tied to Mason's life and actions. Under his direction, the church grew from ten congregations in 1907 to become the second largest Pentecostal denomination in America by 1961. A portion of this expansion can be attributed to the appeal of Pentecostalism among many African Americans, but certainly much of this growth was related to Bishop Mason's ability to cultivate leadership and delegate responsibility. Mason charged the bishops of the church with supervision of the districts to which they were assigned, but also gave them the responsibility of establishing new jurisdictions. He sent ministers to accompany African Americans moving to the North during the Great Migration of the early twentieth century, which resulted in newly planted churches and expanded membership. As a result of these efforts, the COGIC was transformed from a primarily rural denomination to a mainly urban one.

Following Mason's death, the denomination became more institutionalized as it drafted a formal constitution specifying offices and the authority possessed by the individuals holding those positions (Lincoln and Mamiya 1990). The denomination is currently organized into various ecclesiastical jurisdictions, each presided over by a bishop (in 1984, there were 116 such jurisdictions). These ecclesiastical areas of administration, in turn, are subdivided into district units, with the number of districts in each jurisdiction varying between two and forty-five; each district is generally composed of ten to fifteen churches. Jurisdictional assemblies meet semiannually, or at the discretion of the bishop, with participants consisting of all pastors and elders within the jurisdiction, one lay delegate from each district in that jurisdiction, and various other representatives from different departments of the church's ministries.

The chief legislative and judicial body of the denomination is the general assembly, which meets annually. Delegates to the general assembly include all jurisdictional bishops, all pastors and elders, as well as two district missionaries and one lay delegate from each jurisdictional assembly. Between sessions of the general assembly, a general board composed of twelve bishops acts as the executive arm of the church, providing general oversight of denominational operations. The general assembly elects the twelve board members from the board of bishops (comprised of all the bishops of the church); members of the Board of Twelve (as the general board is also known) serve four-year terms. The general assembly chooses one of the twelve to be the presiding bishop, who is the chief executive officer of COGIC and administers the affairs of the church on a day-to-day basis. The presiding bishop also serves a four-year term, but there is no restraint on the number of successive terms the presiding bishop may hold.

While local congregations are obligated to pay assessments to the national office, there is considerable autonomy for COGIC churches. Unlike the Baptist tradition, the autonomy is not actually congregational. Instead, local pastors themselves are relatively independent and able to act with very little restraint from superiors (Lincoln and Mamiya

1990). Bishops do not appoint and move pastors from one congregation to another; rather, pastors are encouraged to start their own churches. As a result, COGIC pastors have traditionally served their congregations for life, and many of their churches tend to be family churches (that is, when the pastor chooses to retire, the pastorate is passed on to another family member).

Consistent with its Pentecostal heritage, the COGIC is Trinitarian in doctrine, "stressing repentance, regeneration, justification, sanctification, speaking in tongues, and the gift of healing as evidence of the baptism of the Spirit" (Mead 1995, 114). Yet, despite shared theological emphases, there has been a history of animus directed toward the COGIC from predominantly white Pentecostal denominations, even though Bishop Mason offered his blessing on those whites who left to form the Assemblies of God. Only recently have these rifts begun to disappear, and the major white Pentecostal denominations today fully embrace the COGIC. Still, some distinct differences remain between black and white Pentecostal denominations that are most likely associated with racial differences. In particular, the COGIC's strong alliance with the Democratic Party (Lincoln and Mamiya 1990; Mead 1995; Sanders 1996) stands in contrast to the powerful ties with the Republican Party frequently evident among many white Pentecostals.

Historically, the COGIC has held both liberal and conservative stances. It preaches pacifism, and at one time required its members to ask permission before joining the armed forces. During World War I, Bishop Mason was arrested multiple times for speaking out against the war. While the denomination has taken liberal stances toward civil rights and war, it has also taken a strong conservative stance against women as clergy and does not ordain females. Women can, however, become evangelists, and over half of the graduates from Charles H. Mason Theological Seminary in Atlanta (the official seminary of the denomination) are women, but only under unusual circumstances will a woman become the pastor of a COGIC church (Lincoln and Mamiya 1990).

Today, the COGIC claims 6.5 million members in 12,186 churches and is the largest Pentecostal denomination in the world (Mead 1995). Some analysts have contended that Pentecostalism focuses on otherworldliness, diminishing the proclivity of its adherents to be engaged politically. Others have found that Pentecostalism need not be detrimental to political activity (Calhoun-Brown 1998; Harris 1999; McRoberts 1999); not only were members of the denomination active in the civil-rights movement, but the church holds close ties to the

Democratic Party (Lincoln and Mamiya 1990; Mead and Hill 1995; Sanders 1996).

NATURE OF THE STUDY

Since there is no published denominational directory listing all Church of God in Christ congregations and pastors, a random sample of COGIC congregations and their addresses was obtained from the listing of churches on the its Web site. Over 750 questionnaires were sent to pastors in these congregations, and the surveys were followed up with subsequent reminders.

Despite these efforts, the response rate was relatively low in comparison to that of other denominations analyzed in this volume—slightly over 11 percent. In part, this is because many COGIC congregations do not have mailboxes or church offices located at the address of their house of worship, resulting in many returned questionnaires. Still, the level of participation does compare fairly well to another recent national survey of black clergy that employed a much shorter format (Smith and Smidt 2003). Certainly, the low number of completed surveys necessitates some caution in generalizing the outcome of this research to be reflective of the population being examined. Nevertheless, while the results cannot be viewed as conclusive, they are clearly suggestive. And, since the data provide some vital information, they are analyzed and presented for the purposes of this comparative study.

SOCIAL CHARACTERISTICS OF COGIC CLERGY

Table 20.1 presents the social characteristics of COGIC clergy. Since the denomination does not ordain women to serve as pastors and allows women to serve as ministers only in extreme cases, it is not surprising that virtually all (99 percent) of the respondents are male. Nearly all (95 percent) are African Americans, with the remaining clergy indicating "mixed" in terms of their racial composition. Most of the participants (73 percent) are married, having never been divorced. However, when one adds those who were married but are now widowed, the figure rises to 90 percent of the clergy.

Table 20.1

Social Characteristics of Church of God in Christ Clergy

	% of Clergy
Gender: Male	99%
Race: Black	95%
Marital Status: Married, never divorced	73%
Education	
College Graduate	52%
Seminary Graduate	23%
Age	
Under 35 years of age	5%
Over 55 years of age	43%
Community Size	
Farm or small town	19%
Small or medium-sized cities	33%
Large cities	48%

Overall, as suggested by the number who report that they are widowed, COGIC pastors tend to be relatively old. More than two out of five (43 percent) are over 55 years of age, while only 5 percent are younger than 35 years. The average age of all the respondents is nearly 55 years, and given this fact, it is hardly surprising that the mean number of years in the ministry is twenty-six for the survey respondents.

As noted earlier, COGIC pastors tend to have greater autonomy than ministers in the African Methodist Episcopal Church, where bishops have the power to move clergy from one congregation to another. Pastors in the COGIC frequently start their own church and remain as its minister until retirement or death. While this is clearly the historical pattern, the survey data suggest that the pattern may be changing: while twenty-six years is the average number of years in the ministry for the survey respondents, fifteen is the average number of years in their present congregations.

COGIC clergy are fairly well educated. Historically, Pentecostalism has emphasized gifts of the Holy Spirit, rather than education, as the basis of qualification for the ministry. Nevertheless, only about one-fifth (19 percent) of the pastors have a high school education or less, while another one-quarter (29 percent) have at least some college education. The majority (52 percent) of the respondents are college graduates, with nearly one-quarter (23 percent) of all survey participants holding a seminary degree.

Finally, as expected, COGIC pastors tend to serve congregations in fairly urban contexts. Less than one in five (19 percent) report serving in rural or small-town congregations, while one-third serve churches in small or medium-sized cities. Thus, nearly half (48 percent) are ministering to congregations in large cities.

THEOLOGICAL POSITIONS HELD BY COGIC CLERGY

Because the Church of God in Christ is a Pentecostal denomination, one might expect that its clergy would express theological positions similar to other Pentecostals, such as the Assemblies of God. On the other hand, racial differences could also be evident in the way theological positions are expressed within Pentecostalism, leading COGIC pastors to differ from Assemblies of God ministers in the stances they adopt theologically.

However, when one analyzes theological beliefs in terms of various conventional understandings of the Christian faith, relatively little difference appears between the positions of Pentecostal clergy across the two denominations; pastors in both groups are highly orthodox in their beliefs (for a comparison, see Chapter 14). As reported in Table 20.2, all survey respondents affirm their belief that Jesus was born of a virgin and is the only way to salvation, while virtually all assert that the Bible is the inerrant Word of God (99 percent), Jesus will return to earth one day (96 percent), and Adam and Eve were real people (94 percent).

On the other hand, these theological positions tend to differentiate COGIC clergy somewhat from their fellow pastors in the African Methodist Episcopal Church (AME). Not only do COGIC ministers tend to be more likely to express theologically conservative positions than AME clergy, but they also emphasize individual sanctification more (and transforming the social order less) than AME pastors. One might anticipate that, as Pentecostals, COGIC clergy would be prone to stress personal salvation, and this pattern is clearly evident—only 6 percent of the pastors surveyed indicate their belief that the church should place greater emphasis on transforming the social order and less on individual sanctification.

In some ways, this high level of theological agreement among COGIC clergy is particularly striking, given the high level of authority afforded to each pastor and congregation within the denomination.

While there is some hierarchical structure to the COGIC, its bishops do not exercise a great deal of supervision over clergy at the congregational level. Given this lack of centralized structure and direction, the relative homogeneity of theological positions among COGIC clergy is all the more impressive.

Table 20.2

Theological Views Held by Church of God in Christ Clergy

	% Agreeing
Jesus will return to earth one day.	96%
Jesus was born of a virgin.	100%
The devil actually exists.	98%
There is no other way to salvation but through belief in Jesus Christ.	100%
Adam and Eve were real people.	94%
The Bible is the inerrant Word of God, both in matters of faith and in historical, geographical, and other secular matters.	99%
The church should put less emphasis on individual sanctification and more on transforming the social order.	6%

Also noteworthy is the fact that COGIC pastors exhibited more variation in their reported ability to speak in tongues than they did in their theological positions. Only four of five COGIC clergy (82 percent) report possessing the gift of tongues. Historically, the emphasis on speaking in tongues served to differentiate between Pentecostal and Holiness churches, as Pentecostals held speaking in tongues to be a sign of sanctification while Holiness denominations did not (Lincoln and Mamiya 1990; Mead 1995; Sanders 1996). Therefore, it is somewhat surprising that not every COGIC pastor claims the gift of tongues, thus possessing this particular sign of sanctification. On the other hand, Pentecostalism itself may be changing. Weber (1963, 60–61) points out that as movements become established, charismatic authority is transformed into an everyday form of leadership based on tradition or official capacity; this transmutation of influence usually compromises the ideals of the original message but is a necessary process for translating the ideal into practice. Thus, Pentecostalism may be changing, exhibiting fewer qualities of a religious movement, while expanding its religious boundaries and fostering greater institutionalization and routinization of charisma.

POLITICAL ENGAGEMENT OF COGIC CLERGY

In general, COGIC clergy support pastors using the pulpit to provide their parishioners with moral and political cues. Virtually all (96 percent) of the respondents expressed approval for clergy taking a stand on a moral issue from the pulpit. Even when the focus of such preaching shifts from moral to political statements, high levels of support for clergy to provide their congregants with cues continues; an overwhelming majority (74 percent) indicate that they approve of ministers taking a stand, while preaching, on a political issue. Support is also evident for cue-giving when clergy are no longer in the pulpit, as a large majority (72 percent) approve of pastors publicly supporting a political candidate. Clearly the COGIC ministers hold no strong animus toward sending moral or political cues to their members.

Table 20.3

Political Norms of Church of God in Christ Clergy

	% Approving
Take a stand while preaching on some moral issue	96%
While preaching, take a stand on some political issue	74%
Publicly (not preaching) support a political candidate	72%
Contribute money to a candidate, party, or political-action committee	53%
Form an action group in one's church to accomplish a social or political goal	49%
Participate in a protest march	52%
Commit civil disobedience to protest some evil	31%

On the other hand, COGIC clergy are far less likely to express approval for certain conventional forms of political participation. Only about half of the pastors surveyed believe it is appropriate for clergy to contribute money to a candidate, party, or political organization (53 percent) or to form action groups within one's church to accomplish some social or political objective (49 percent). And only half (52 percent) believe clergy should participate in protest marches. These patterns suggest that when the emphasis shifts from providing cues to congregants to actual engagement in the political process, there is much greater hesitation on the part of COGIC clergy to express approval of such activism.

In this regard, one of the most striking results included in Table 20.3 is that less than one-third (31 percent) of COGIC pastors approve of a member of the clergy committing civil disobedience. This response is surprising as many of the clergy surveyed are from the civil-rights generation, where civil disobedience was seen to be the norm. Yet, this pattern is consistent with the findings of Harris (1999), who has shown that blacks who are religiously orthodox will be politically active but refrain from political activity when their actions conflict with broader civic norms.

Research related to the politics of racial groups reveals that, in general, race plays an important role in how issues and the political parties are viewed among African Americans (Walton 1985; Dawson 1994). An examination of the positions adopted by COGIC clergy on matters of public policy reveals that they generally favor an activist federal government that provides services for the poor. As shown in Table 20.4, the vast majority (87 percent) of COGIC pastors agrees that the federal government should do more to solve social problems, including addressing issues of unemployment, poverty, and housing. Nearly the same portion of those surveyed (83 percent) voice support for government-sponsored national health insurance.

Table 20.4

Policy Positions of Church of God in Christ Clergy

	% Agreeing
The federal government should do more to solve social problems such as unemployment, poverty, and poor housing.	87%
Education policy should focus on improving public schools rather than on encouraging alternatives such as private and religious schools.	56%
Sex-education programs included in the curricula of public high schools should be abstinence based.	81%
We need government-sponsored national health insurance so that everyone can get adequate medical care.	83%
African Americans and other minorities may need special governmental help in order to achieve an equal place in America.	73%
We need a constitutional amendment prohibiting all abortions unless to save the mother's life, or in cases of rape or incest.	70%
Homosexuals should have all the same rights and privileges as other American citizens.	17%
A lasting peace in the Middle East will require Israel to make greater concessions to the Palestinians.	20%

When analyzing issues that are cast in more moral rather than economic terms, COGIC pastors continue to exhibit a high level of agreement on most issues. More than four out of five pastors surveyed (81 percent) favor sex-education programs included in public high school curricula being abstinence based, and more than two-thirds (70 percent) assert a need for a constitutional amendment prohibiting most abortions. Finally, relatively few reporting ministers (17 percent) favor ensuring that homosexuals have the same rights and privileges as other American citizens. Overall, COGIC clergy exhibit a relatively high level of cohesion on questions related to social policy, though that level is somewhat lower than the responses on economic positions.

When examining issues that may be more directly related to the black community, COGIC ministers adopt positions that may be somewhat surprising. As might be expected, nearly three out of four respondents (73 percent) agree that African Americans and other minorities may need special governmental help to achieve equality within American society.[43] But, on some other issues, COGIC pastors do not necessarily adopt positions that are strongly reflective of "racial politics." Two issues were included in the survey that, while not racial issues per se, are frequently framed in such a manner—positions related to capital punishment and welfare laws (Gilens 1999). Given the high number of African Americans in prison and the level of poverty evident in many black communities, one might anticipate that COGIC clergy would stand in opposition to capital punishment and agreement that "current welfare reform laws are too harsh and hurt children." With regard to both policy positions, COGIC clergy are inclined in such a direction, as a plurality of the pastors are opposed to capital punishment and current welfare reform laws. However, the surveyed ministers are fairly divided in the positions that they adopted. While a plurality of COGIC clergy (45 percent) express opposition to capital punishment, nearly a third (31 percent) indicate approval. And while a plurality of the pastors (43 percent) agree that current welfare reform laws are too harsh, nearly one-third (32 percent) disagree.

Nor are COGIC ministers necessarily active proponents of directing federal education funding only toward improving public schools, rather than encouraging alternatives to them; only a bare majority (56 percent) indicate approval for limiting governmental funding of education to public schools. Finally, in relationship to Middle East policy, COGIC clergy are not strong supporters of the Palestinian cause, as only 20 percent of those surveyed agree that a lasting peace in the Middle East will require Israel to make greater concessions to the Palestinians.

When the analysis shifts from policy positions to actual levels of political participation, it is clear that COGIC pastors are not hesitant to express political cues to their congregations. As shown in Table 20.5, nearly all (93 percent) report having urged their congregants to register and vote. More than four of five ministers (82 percent) indicate having prayed publicly about an issue, and approximately two out of three report having prayed publicly for political candidates (68 percent) or having taken a stand on some political issue from the pulpit (63 percent). In fact, more than half (53 percent) of the clergy surveyed report endorsing a political candidate from the pulpit.

Table 20.5

Political Activities of Church of God in Christ Clergy in the Election of 2000

	% Reporting
Urged their congregation to register and vote	93%
Contacted a public official about some issue	60%
Prayed publicly for political candidates	68%
Took a stand from the pulpit on some political issue	63%
Prayed publicly about an issue	82%
Party Identification	
Strong Democrat	58%
Weak Democrat	9%
Independent, lean Democrat	13%
Independent	9%
Independent, lean Republican	5%
Weak Republican	5%
Strong Republican	1%
Vote Choice in the 2000 Election	
Al Gore	77%
George W. Bush	14%
Pat Buchanan	0%
Ralph Nader	0%
Other	0%
Did not vote	9%

Previously, it was shown that COGIC pastors tend to mirror other Pentecostals in terms of their theological positions, and they also tended to express high levels of approval for policy positions reflecting "morality politics." Are COGIC clergy then closer to other Pentecostals in their partisan orientations or do they more fully reflect other African Americans in their approach to partisan politics?

Overall, the results tend to place the pastors on the African American "side," with heavy Democratic leanings. Nearly three out of five respondents (58 percent) indicate they are strong Democrats, and another one-quarter classify themselves as weak Democrats or Independents, leaning toward the Democratic Party. Yet, a remnant of COGIC ministers does identify with the Republican Party, though generally in a relatively weak fashion: only six percent indicate they are Republicans (11 percent, when Independents, leaning Republican are added).

In the election of 2000, however, nearly one in seven of the survey participants (14 percent) report having voted for George W. Bush, nearly twice the level of support generally reported for Bush among African Americans as a whole. Thus, to the extent that there may be an opening to the Republican Party among African Americans, it is possibly most evident among Pentecostal segments of the black community.

CONCLUSION

The Church of God in Christ is one of the most theologically orthodox denominations included in this study. As the fastest growing black denomination, it is clear that churchgoing blacks, like other active believers in America, are moving toward a more conservative theological stance.

However, this shift toward religious conservatism does not appear to indicate a sharp decline in political activism within the COGIC. The study demonstrates the clear willingness and predilection on the part of COGIC clergy to send cues to their congregations on moral as well as political issues. In addition, there is no apparent lack of mobilization on the part of these ministers; while they do not appear to approve strongly of clergy activism, they do take part in considerable levels of political activity, as mobilization tends to be directed toward specific involvement within the political arena.

Finally, this shift on the part of African Americans toward theological conservatism does not appear to affect their partisan identifications strongly. On the national level, the denomination has maintained strong ties to the Democratic Party; at the individual level, COGIC clergy tend to mirror the stance adopted by the national organization.

Chapter 21

Unitarian-Universalist Association

John C. Green

The Unitarian-Universalist Association (UUA) is the quintessential liberal denomination in the United States. Dedicated to a "free and responsible search for truth and meaning" and the "inherent worth and dignity of every person," the UUA embodies the modernist element in Christian thought as well as a rich variety of beliefs and perspectives from other sources. The UUA is a community of freethinkers, filling an important niche in the American religious landscape.[45] While the UUA is a relatively small denomination, its leaders and members are deeply involved in politics and public affairs. Such activism should come as no surprise: the UUA holds a longstanding commitment to social justice and political reform, dating back to before the origins of the republic. Hence, UUA clergy serve as a good basis by which to assess the level and conditions of political activism among self-conscious proponents of a liberal faith.

An examination of the social, theological, and political characteristics of UUA clergy can be made based upon a special survey that focused, in part, on the 2000 election. An analysis of the theological beliefs and the level and types of political activity among the UUA pastors reveals these clergy to be dynamos of liberal politics in the United States, with their extensive and diverse engagement in public affairs being strongly rooted in their liberal faith and related perspectives on politics.

HISTORICAL BACKGROUND

The 1961 merger of the American Unitarian Association and the Universalist Church of America created the Unitarian-Universalist Association. This union brought together two denominational bodies with different histories, but a common experience of conscious opposition to the dominant orthodoxy of American Protestantism (Buehrens and Church 1998).

For Unitarians, this opposition was centered on the question of official creeds and individual conscience (Wright 1989). Although anti-Trinitarian ideas were part of Christian thought since before the Protestant Reformation, the American Unitarian movement developed out of disputes within the Congregational Church during the late eighteenth and early nineteenth centuries. The key issue centered on opposition to requiring believers to affirm an official creed that was Trinitarian in nature, with those who opposed such an affirmation of faith being branded as Unitarians. The term became accepted as the name for an evolving liberal church that officially formed the American Unitarian Association in 1825. True to their origins, Unitarians never adopted a creed. This heritage is still maintained in the UUA: the denomination stipulates that no minister, member, or congregation "shall be required to subscribe to any particular interpretation of religion, or to any particular religious belief or creed" (Mead 1990d, 235).

For Universalists, opposition to Protestant orthodoxy resulted from the belief that God's purpose is to save every member of the human race from sin (Howe 1993). While this idea and disputes surrounding it are as old as Christianity itself, American Universalism arose from original reflections on the concept within the crucible of late eighteenth- and early nineteenth-century Protestantism. Universalism first found organized expression in a series of conventions. The Philadelphia convention of 1790 published the first Universalist profession of faith and outlined a plan of church organization, including a congregational polity. A national denominational organization was eventually formalized in 1870, furthering the development of a separate identity as a "liberal" church. The Universalist's contribution to the UUA can be seen in the Association's embrace of diverse approaches to seeking truth and openness to religious innovation (Mead 1995).

In 2002, the UUA described its purpose as follows:

> The Unitarian-Universalist Association shall devote its resources to and exercise its corporate powers for religious, educational and humanitarian purposes. The primary purpose of the Association is to serve the needs of its member congregations, organize new congregations, extend and strengthen Unitarian-Universalist institutions and implement its principles. (Unitarian-Universalist Association 2002)

The principles that the UUA "covenants to affirm and promote" include:

- The inherent worth and dignity of every person;
- Justice, equity, and compassion in human relations;
- Acceptance of one another and encouragement to spiritual growth in our congregations;
- A free and responsible search for truth and meaning;
- The right of conscience and the use of the democratic process within our congregations and in society at large;
- The goal of world community with peace, liberty, and justice for all;
- Respect for the interdependent web of all existence of which we are a part.

Despite the absence of a formal creed, these principles arise from a set of core beliefs within a living tradition that is drawn from many sources:

- Direct experience of that transcending mystery and wonder, affirmed in all cultures which moves us to a renewal of the spirit and an openness to the forces which create and uphold life;
- Words and deeds of prophetic women and men which challenge us to confront powers and structures of evil with justice, compassion, and the transforming power of love;
- Wisdom from the world's religions which inspire us in our ethical and spiritual life;
- Jewish and Christian teachings which call us to respond to God's love by loving our neighbors as ourselves;
- Humanist teachings which counsel us to heed the guidance of reason and the results of science, and warn us against idolatries of the mind and spirit;
- Spiritual teachings of earth-centered traditions which celebrate the sacred circle of life and instruct us to live in harmony with the rhythms of nature.

Both Unitarians and Universalists were at the forefront of political reform in the nineteenth century. Both groups were among the earliest and most vocal opponents to slavery, they were deeply involved in efforts to reform prisons and improve working conditions for women, and they were among the strongest proponents of a strict separation of church and state. This activist heritage continues in the UUA today, where the denomination's Service Committee provides leadership and resources to foster social change. In recent times, Unitarian-Universalists were at the forefront of a variety of social struggles, including racial and cultural diversity; equality for women; the rights of gay, lesbian, and bisexual persons; and other progressive causes. Over the years, the denomination has taken stands on a wide variety of issues.

The UUA has been an especially vocal opponent of the Christian Right, and one of its documents, titled "Don't Agonize, Organize!" clearly illustrates the denomination's special commitment to political action.[46] The headings include:

- Subscribe! (to periodicals from the left and the right)
- Join! (a list of national progressive organizations)
- Read! (an extensive list of books on the religious right)
- Monitor! (local candidates, political organizations and the media, including "listen carefully to conversations in public places")
- Speak out! (express opinion through a variety of media and venues)
- Organize! (build local coalitions and "make sure everyone in your church or organization is registered to vote")
- Lobby! (all levels of government)
- Stay Strong! ("Spiritual discipline—prayer, meditation, holy house-cleaning—can give strength for the journey.")

The UUA is organized on a congregational model in which "free con-gregations" enter into a "covenant," promising one another "mutual trust and support." These congregations are organized into twenty geo-graphic districts and a national organization, which provides services to the congregations and helps foster denominationwide activities.

The UUA has historically been a relatively small denomination, a pattern that continues today. The 2000 Census of Religious Commun-ities reports some 147,000 members (182,000 adherents) in 999 con-gregations across the country (Jones et al. 2001). These figures represent less than one-tenth of one percent of religious adherents in the United States. However, the UUA represents a broader constituency in the pub-lic, including numerous individuals and organizations that are not formally part of organized religion. Surveys suggest that this extended group of religious liberals may account for a little less than one percent of the American adult population, nearly ten times larger than the UUA's official membership.

Like many religious minorities, Unitarian-Universalists tend to be dramatically overrepresented among liberal and progressive political activists (Green and Guth 1991b; Green, Guth, and Fraser 1991). For example, a 1998 survey of The Interfaith Alliance revealed that 8 percent of its members and 21 percent of its core activists were UUA members. In 2000, Unitarian-Universalists accounted for 2 percent of the delegates to the Democratic National Convention and 4 percent of major donors to Democratic presidential candidates.[47] This level of activism is much greater than one would anticipate based solely on the size of the UUA or its broader constituency in the public at large.

NATURE OF THE STUDY

In order to study the religious attitudes and political behavior of UUA clergy, a mail survey was conducted in the spring of 2001 at the University of Akron. The sample included all UUA pastors serving congregations (1,011 individuals), and was drawn from the *Unitarian-Universalist Association Directory 2000–2001* (2000). The clergy in the sample were contacted four times, producing 488 usable responses for a return rate of 65.9 percent (excluding undeliverable mail). The responses were carefully inspected for response bias, and none was detected.[48]

SOCIAL CHARACTERISTICS
OF UNITARIAN-UNIVERSALIST CLERGY

Given the distinctiveness of the denomination, Table 21.1 addresses whether the Unitarian-Universalist clergy are also distinctive in terms of their social characteristics. First, unlike clergy in many other denominations, the UUA pastors are nearly evenly divided between men and women. UUA ministers also differ in terms of marital status, with less than half of the clergy reporting that they are married and have never been divorced, while one-third indicate they have been previously divorced but are currently married. Like clergy in many other denominations, UUA pastors are generally well educated: virtually all (99 percent) report that they are college graduates and nearly all (92 percent) hold a seminary degree. Respondents are overwhelmingly white (94%), reflecting the history of the denomination.

Table 21.1

Social Characteristics of Uniterian-Universalist Clergy

	% of Clergy
Gender: Male	51%
Race: White	94%
Marital Status: Married, never divorced	38%
Education	
College Graduate	99%
Seminary Graduate	92%
Age	
Under 35 years of age	4%
Over 55 years of age	40%
Community Size	
Farm or small town	21%
Small or medium-sized cities	36%
Large cities	43%

UUA clergy tend to be somewhat older than other clergy. Two-fifths report being over fifty-five years of age, while less than one in twenty (4 percent) are under thirty-five. Despite this age profile, many UUA pastors appear to have entered the ministry later in life, as the mean number of reported years in the ministry is fifteen. And they tend to be fairly mobile, as the mean number of reported years in their current congregation is 6.5 years. Only about one in five UUA pastors (21 percent) live in a small town or rural environment, while the plurality (43 percent) reside in large, metropolitan areas. Most UUA clergy are located in the Northeast, especially New England, the historic geographic base of the denomination.

THEOLOGICAL POSITIONS HELD
BY UNITARIAN-UNIVERSALIST CLERGY

A small portion of the numerous questions relating to theological beliefs that were included in the survey is shown in Table 21.2, illustrating the religious views of the UUA clergy. True to their heritage, the UUA ministers largely disagree with the major tenets of Christian orthodoxy. Relatively few responding pastors (3 percent or less) assert that Jesus was born of a virgin, that the devil actually exists, or that belief in Jesus Christ is the only way to salvation. In fact, of all the statements related to Jesus of Nazareth included in Table 21.2, UUA clergy were most inclined to agree that Jesus will return to earth one day—but only 5 percent hold that view.

Table 21.2

Theological Views Held by Unitarian-Universalist Clergy

	% Agreeing
Jesus will return to earth one day.	5%
Jesus was born of a virgin.	3%
The devil actually exists.	3%
There is no other way to salvation but through belief in Jesus Christ.	2%
Adam and Eve were real people.	2%
The Bible is the inerrant Word of God, both in matters of faith and in historical, geographical, and other secular matters.	2%
The church should put less emphasis on individual sanctification and more on transforming the social order.	77%

UUA pastors do not subscribe to biblical inerrancy, and relatively few believe that Adam and Eve were real people; in both cases, only 2 percent reported agreement with either item. However, they are much more prone than pastors in other denominations to stress the importance of social justice over individual morality, a position common among modernist clergy (Guth et al. 1997). More than three-quarters of the entire sample (77 percent) agree that "transforming the social order" should be the goal of the church, as opposed to addressing individual shortcomings.

Not surprisingly, UUA clergy perceive themselves to be religious liberals. When asked about their religious identity, they overwhelmingly choose to label themselves as liberal, as opposed to progressive or a variety of other self-identification categories.[49] Thus, UUA ministers fit the common image of being self-conscious proponents of a liberal religious faith.

POLITICAL ENGAGEMENT
OF UNITARIAN-UNIVERSALIST CLERGY

Role definitions frequently influence the way in which the professional duties of the clergy may influence the political engagement of pastors. Previous research has demonstrated that some clergy view political engagement as part of their professional responsibilities and that the strength of this view can be assessed, in part, by evaluating a minister's level of approval for specific political activities by pastors (Guth et al. 1997).

The data examined in Table 21.3 assess the norms of Unitarian-Universalist clergy relating to a range of political activities. As can be seen from the first statement reported, there is almost universal approval (99 percent) among UUA ministers for making moral pronouncements while preaching from the pulpit. Fewer, but still an overwhelming majority (86 percent) express approval of pastors taking a stand on some political issue from the pulpit. Clearly, UUA clergy see preaching as an appropriate means to address moral and political issues of concern to them and members of their congregations, a perspective often associated with more conservative denominations.

Table 21.3
Political Norms of Unitarian-Universalist Clergy

	% Approving
Take a stand while preaching on some moral issue	99%
While preaching, take a stand on some political issue	86%
Publicly (not preaching) support a political candidate	50%
Contribute money to a candidate, party, or political-action committee	89%
Form an action group in one's church to accomplish a social or political goal	89%
Participate in a protest march	97%
Commit civil disobedience to protest some evil	86%

Despite these high approval levels for clergy stances on moral and political issues from the pulpit, many UUA ministers are reluctant to agree that pastors should express public support for particular candidates, even outside of the pulpit. Only half the respondents expressed approval for such activity, opting instead for less visible forms of political support. For example, when asked about contributing money to a candidate, party, or political organization, nearly all those surveyed

(89 percent) voice approval. Yet, "visibility" is not the sole factor behind these opinions, since working publicly to accomplish political goals within the church context also receives a high level of approval: nearly all UUA clergy (89 percent) report agreement with clergy formation and organization of action groups within one's church to address social or political goals. Other highly visible forms of political engagement also garner their extensive support. Nearly all (97 percent) the respondents approve of clergy engaging in protest activities, and an overwhelming majority (86 percent) even agrees that ministers may engage in civil disobedience as a means to protest some evil. More than likely, such action is perceived to be less candidate related than issue oriented.

Table 21.4

Policy Positions of Unitarian-Universalist Clergy

	% Agreeing
The federal government should do more to solve social problems such as unemployment, poverty, and poor housing.	96%
Education policy should focus on improving public schools rather than on encouraging alternatives such as private and religious schools.	92%
Sex-education programs included in the curricula of public high schools should be abstinence based.	10%
We need government-sponsored national health insurance so that everyone can get adequate medical care.	91%
African Americans and other minorities may need special governmental help in order to achieve an equal place in America.	87%
We need a constitutional amendment prohibiting all abortions unless to save the mother's life, or in cases of rape or incest.	2%
Homosexuals should have all the same rights and privileges as other American citizens.	99%
A lasting peace in the Middle East will require Israel to make greater concessions to the Palestinians.	75%

The UUA clergy stands on issues are analyzed in Table 21.4, which addresses the policy positions of responding clergy on various selected issues that are prominent in contemporary American politics. Generally speaking, the UUA clergy strongly favor action on the part of the federal government to address social problems. For example, there is almost unanimous agreement among UUA pastors (96 percent) that "the federal government should do more to address social problems such as unemployment, poverty, and poor housing." Similarly remarkable high levels of assent are evident regarding the need for the government to provide national health insurance (91 percent expressing approval of the policy proposal) and for special government help for minorities to ensure an equal standing in American society (87 percent voicing agreement). UUA clergy are clearly supporters of public education, as nearly all pastors surveyed (92 percent) agree that "education policy should focus on improving public schools" rather than seeking alternatives through private education.

Shifting from economic to social policy, UUA clergy also hold liberal positions. Hardly any of those surveyed (only 10 percent) express support for sex-education programs in public schools being abstinence based, and virtually none (only 2 percent) indicate that they favor a constitutional amendment to prohibit abortions (even when the stated policy would permit particular exceptions). Likewise, there is almost universal agreement (99 percent approving) that "homosexuals should have all the same rights and privileges as other American citizens." Finally, even on matters of policy with regard to the Middle East, UUA clergy tend to stand apart from ministers in other denominations in their support for the Palestinian cause: a full three-quarters of the clergy surveyed voice agreement that, for any lasting peace to come to the Middle East, Israel will need to make greater concessions to the Palestinians.

Given these issue positions, it is not surprising that UUA clergy identify themselves as political liberals. When asked to classify themselves ideologically on a seven-point scale (ranging from extremely liberal to extremely conservative), more than one-quarter (27 percent) of the UUA pastors chose the label "extremely liberal," while another half (55 percent) designated themselves "liberal." Some (13 percent) selected the phrase "somewhat liberal," but hardly any (5 percent) chose from the categories of "moderate" or some variation of "conservative."

The political orientations of the UUA clergy translate into political action, and Table 21.5 describes the activities reported by pastors during the 2000 election. The patterns reflect several factors, including the difficulty of the task and the degree of controversy it entails. For example, several of the activities are neither particularly onerous nor especially subject to conflict, such as urging congregants to vote and praying publicly about either an issue or for political candidates. However, other options require more effort or can be somewhat more controversial, such as contacting a public official or taking a stand from the pulpit on a political issue.

Table 21.5

Political Activities of Unitarian-Universalist Clergy in the Election of 2000

	% Reporting
Urged their congregation to register and vote	66%
Contacted a public official about some issue	62%
Prayed publicly for political candidates	5%
Took a stand from the pulpit on some political issue	34%
Prayed publicly about an issue	35%
Party Identification	
Strong Democrat	56%
Weak Democrat	11%
Independent, lean Democrat	22%
Independent	7%
Independent, lean Republican	2%
Weak Republican	*
Strong Republican	1%
Vote Choice in the 2000 Election	
Al Gore	81%
George W. Bush	2%
Pat Buchanan	0%
Ralph Nader	15%
Other	1%
Did not vote	1%

* = less than 1 percent

The most commonly reported activity in Table 21.5 is relatively easy and non-controversial: urging congregants to register and vote. Approximately two-thirds of all UUA clergy (66 percent) report that they advocated that their congregants register and vote in the 2000 elections. But nearly the same portion of these pastors (62 percent) indicate that over the course of the past year they contacted a public official about some political issue—a much more time-consuming activity. Further, in terms of several other "easy" activities, relatively few UUA pastors report having engaged in such practices. For example, only a little more than one-third of responding clergy (35 percent) report having prayed about some political issue during the past year, and even fewer (5 percent) state that they prayed publicly for political candidates. It is unclear why there are relatively low numbers of pastors reporting having prayed for candidates and about issues, but it may simply be that prayer is a less common component of UUA worship liturgy and thereby, there is less opportunity to use prayer for such purposes.

In terms of partisanship, Table 21.5 indicates that UUA clergy are clearly on the Democratic side of the partisan divide. A majority of the pastors (56 percent) claim to be strong Democrats, and another one-third (33 percent) label themselves as either weak Democrats or Independents leaning toward the Democratic Party. Relatively few UUA ministers choose to identify themselves as complete Independents (7 percent) and virtually none (3 percent) select the Republican label. This proclivity toward the Democratic Party is evident in their presidential vote in the 2000 election: more than four-fifths (81 percent) of the clergy report casting their ballots for Al Gore, the Democratic candidate, while a negligible number (2 percent) voted for the Republican candidate, George W. Bush. In fact, Ralph Nader, the Green Party candidate, garnered more than seven times the votes received by George W. Bush, with more than one-sixth of the clergy (15 percent) stating that they had voted for Nader. Not surprisingly, nearly all UUA clergy (99%) voted in the 2000 election.

CONCLUSION

In conclusion, Unitarian-Univeralist Association clergy are distinctive in nature. Socially, they exhibit a higher proportion of female clergy, report a higher rate of divorce and remarriage, and enter the ministry at a later stage in life. Theologically, they reject many traditional tenets of Christian orthodoxy, in line with the history of the denomination. Instead, the UUA clergy hold liberal beliefs drawn from many sources, and are focused on a "free and responsible search for truth and meaning" and the "inherent worth and dignity of every person."

Politically, the UUA clergy fully approve of pastors addressing major moral and political issues from the pulpit and organizing congregants into action groups that seek to achieve social and political ends. They also hold strongly liberal positions on economic and social controversies of the day, and have a distinctive preference for the Democratic party. Finally, UUA ministers are engaged in a wide variety of political activities and can be described as dynamos of liberal politics in the United States.

Chapter 22

Willow Creek Association

Lyman A. Kellstedt and John C. Green

The growth of nondenominational Protestantism is one of the most significant developments in American religion in the past fifty years. While the independent Bible church movement originated in the late nineteenth century, most of America's large nondenominational churches came into existence only in the past generation. This growth not only reflects the enduring power of religious movements, especially those centered within evangelical Protestantism, but it also demonstrates a successful adaptation to contemporary society. As one scholar has put it:

> The last thirty years have witnessed a dramatic increase in the number of churches that meet in converted warehouses [or movie theaters], are led by ministers who never attended seminary [or are not seminary graduates], sing to melodies one might hear in a bar or nightclub, and refuse in their worship to separate mind, body, and soul. . . . These "new paradigm churches" . . . are reinventing the way Christianity is experienced and attracting large numbers of people who have felt alienated from institutional religion (Miller 1997: dust jacket).

The membership in these new-paradigm churches is significant. The 2000 census of Religious Congregations and Membership found that they accounted for about 1.5 percent of religious adherents (Jones et al.

2001). Other survey data from 2000 revealed a larger number, some 6 percent of the adult population.[50]

Part of this development has been the appearance of new postmodern organizations (Clegg 1990) among nondenominational churches. Some of these organizations have taken on the doctrinal and organizational trappings of denominations. Two examples of this phenomenon are Calvary Chapel, founded by Chuck Smith in California in the late 1960s, now with more than 600 congregations worldwide, and the Vineyard Christian Fellowship, a 1980s offshoot of Calvary Chapel stressing charismatic gifts (Miller 1997). Other such associations are more task-oriented and looser in structure, resembling the cross-denominational parachurch organizations long common among evangelical Protestants, though adapted for the twenty-first century (Carpenter 1997). A contemporary example of this second phenomenon is the evangelical renewal movement that is evident within many Protestant denominations (McKinney and Finke 2002). A second such example is the Willow Creek Association (WCA), founded by one of the nation's prototypical new-paradigm congregations, the Willow Creek Community Church of South Barrington, Illinois.

This chapter analyzes clergy whose churches belong to the WCA. These data give us a look inside a prominent postmodern church association, and its various religious elements. But it also allows for a review of the impact of the new-paradigm nondenominational Protestant churches as well as the potential for cross-denominational cooperation among clergy with common religious interests.

HISTORICAL BACKGROUND

Willow Creek Community Church (WCCC) was founded in 1975 under the leadership of Bill Hybels, who remains the senior pastor in 2004. It is best known as the preeminent seeker-oriented congregation, which is one version of the new-paradigm, nondenominational churches (Sargeant 2000). Its core ministry is the seeker-directed weekend worship services (see the church Web site at http://www.willowcreek.org). Designed specifically to appeal to people turned off by organized religion, the WCCC services make use of contemporary Christian music, drama, and a colloquial style in presenting Scripture and preaching. Visitors are considered guests and are asked not to make a financial contribution during the service. An introduction to the Christian faith as understood by evangelical Protestantism is at the heart of the sermons or "messages" ("Jesus—Up Close and Personal," "The Grace of God"), which regularly include the application of biblical principles to matters of everyday concern (marriage, money management, forgiveness, practicing compassion). Highly orthodox Protestant beliefs about the need for salvation and the requirements of the gospel are placed in a contemporary context.

By any measure, WCCC has been an enormous success. In its initial years, services were held in a movie theater in the northwest Chicago suburb of Palatine. Due to rapid growth, the church moved to its current campus in South Barrington in 1981. At the present time, WCCC holds four seeker services each weekend with a typical attendance of around 18,000, and two midweek services directed at its approximately 7,500 members.[51] In addition, the church puts great stress on involvement in small groups and also staffs over one hundred ministries serving a wide range of needs, mostly with volunteers from the congregation. Not surprisingly, WCCC has attracted considerable attention by scholars as well as the broader religious community (e.g., Sargeant 2000).

Because of this interest, and in keeping with its mission, the Willow Creek Association was founded in 1992. As of January 2004, the WCA had a membership of over 9,500 churches in the United States and around the world. Its goal is "to build prevailing churches everywhere in the world . . . biblically functioning churches that reach increasing numbers of unchurched people," and it describes itself as a group of "like-minded, action-oriented churches [linked] with each other and with strategic vision, training, and resources" (Willow Creek Association). The association conducts conferences and provides materials for member churches on music, the structure and content of worship services, functions of small groups, and church leadership. In return for the membership fee (just $249 a year), churches receive priority access to conferences at discounted rates, a bimonthly newsletter, and access to discounted worship materials and other publications.

If WCCC is a good example of a new-paradigm church, then the WCA is a prime example of a postmodern religious association. Such organizations have been described as follows:

> Its base of support is dues-paying . . . churches that wish to support the specific goals of this organization. There is no thought of becoming a "full-service" denomination. Rather, it is a specialized organization with an identifiable niche, capable of forging alliances for the purpose of pursuing specific short-term goals (Ammerman 1993, 900).

These associations seek out and fill specialized niches across the religious landscape. WCA is a place where clergy from all kinds of backgrounds can find help in implementing a particular vision of the local church. In this regard, WCA offers the results of "practical wisdom experiences," information and resources, and a network of clergy with similar interests in evangelism, and especially the seeker-directed approach.

The WCA itself is characterized by a strong commitment to core evangelical Protestant beliefs. The association has a statement of faith that affirms the fundamentals of orthodox Christianity in contemporary language. It speaks of the Bible as "the inspired, infallible Word of God" and the "final authority on all matters upon which it teaches." A number of paragraphs are devoted to the Trinity and another to the finality of death apart from belief in Jesus Christ. The statement has a contemporary, and Willow Creek, ring to it: "All people . . . matter deeply to [God]"; the goal of the local church is described as "reaching lost people and growing them into fully devoted followers of Christ" (Willow Creek Association). Given these statements of the WCA, it is unlikely that clergy would be inclined to be involved in the association if they did not have a high level of agreement with many of these assertions, regardless of their denominational background.

Although the WCA has no stated political agenda, the vision of the local church it promotes can have political implications. Spreading this vision to diverse churches across the country can thus encourage a certain kind of politics. However, a more important indirect effect is the networking of like-minded clergy, linking together nondenominational churches, but also creating bonds across denominational lines. Thus, the new-paradigm nondenominational congregations and their postmodern associations may foster particular connections between religion and public affairs.

NATURE OF THE STUDY

As part of a cooperative research effort to study the role of clergy in American politics, ministers serving churches that belong to the WCA were surveyed at the University of Akron. A random sample of 1,000 churches was drawn from the more than 8,000 churches on the WCA Web site. A questionnaire with common items was mailed to the sample during the spring of 2001. Pastors in the sample were contacted four times, producing 303 usable responses for a return rate of 39.9 percent (excluding undeliverable mail). A careful comparison of the characteristics of the respondents to the original mailing list revealed no obvious response biases.

SOCIAL CHARACTERISTICS
OF WILLOW CREEK ASSOCIATION CLERGY

Although the tables do not show the breakdown of denominational affiliations within the Willow Creek Association, perhaps the place to begin the analysis is with some explanation of this remarkable diversity. Nondenominational churches, interestingly, make up almost one-quarter of the sample, most being plain vanilla evangelical churches, coupled with a sprinkling of charismatic and Pentecostal congregations. Churches in evangelical Protestant denominations accounted for half of the sample, more than twice as many as the nondenominational group. Prominent in this category were clergy from the Assemblies of God, the Christian Reformed Church, and the Southern Baptist Convention. Churches in mainline Protestant denominations were the second largest group. At more than one-quarter of the sample, they outnumbered the nondenominational congregations. Indeed, United Methodists were the single largest group in the total sample, at about 12 percent, and the Presbyterian Church (USA), the Disciples of Christ, and the Evangelical Lutheran Church in America were also well represented.

Despite this denominational diversity, WCA clergy are quite homogeneous in social-demographic terms. As can be seen from Table 22.1, almost all the clergy surveyed are males (97 percent) and white (96 percent). Most are married, never having been divorced (90 percent), middle-aged (79 percent falling between thirty-six and fifty-five years of age), and midcareer (mean time in the ministry was twenty years). Almost all (95 percent) are college graduates, but only four of five are seminary graduates.

While WCA churches are found in all regions, nearly half are located in the Midwest and just over one-quarter in the South. What tends to distinguish WCA churches is that most (53 percent) are located in large metropolitan areas and tend to have large (mean = 600) and active memberships. With regard to these characteristics, only modest differences exist according to the denominational affiliation of the clergy, though the WCA mainline churches tend to be larger, and the nondenominational congregations tend to be more active.

Table 22.1

Social Characteristics of Willow Creek Association Clergy

	% of Clergy
Gender: Male	97%
Race: White	96%
Marital Status: Married, never divorced	90%
Education	
College Graduate	95%
Seminary Graduate	80%
Age	
Under 35 years of age	4%
Over 55 years of age	17%
Community Size	
Farm or small town	20%
Small or medium-sized cities	27%
Large cities	53%

THEOLOGICAL POSITIONS HELD
BY WILLOW CREEK ASSOCIATION CLERGY

Given their denominational diversity, how theologically unified would one expect these pastors to be? Surprisingly, considerable theological cohesion is evident in Table 22.2. Willow Creek Association pastors, on the whole, tend to agree with traditional Christian orthodoxy. Among the respondents, more than 90 percent agree that: Jesus will return to earth one day, Jesus was born of a virgin, the devil actually exists, and the only way to salvation is by faith in Jesus Christ. Even seven of ten pastors agree that Adam and Eve were real, historical people and that the Bible is the inerrant Word of God. And, very few of these clergy (3 percent) indicate that "the church should put less emphasis on individual sanctification and more on transforming the social order."

On these various theological questions, the mainline WCA clergy tend to be the outliers, expressing fewer orthodox positions on all the items, especially on questions of scriptural authority. However, they appear to express more orthodox beliefs and be more likely to stress evangelism than other ministers within their denominations. Similarly, the WCA clergy from evangelical denominations appear to be slightly less orthodox in their theological expressions than other pastors from such evangelical denominations. The nondenominational ministers are, by far, the most orthodox. Thus, the WCA clergy fall between their counterparts in the evangelical and mainline denominations.

Table 22.2

Theological Views Held by Willow Creek Association Clergy

	% Agreeing
Jesus will return to earth one day	96%
Jesus was born of a virgin	94%
The devil actually exists	93%
There is no other way to salvation but through belief in Jesus Christ	92%
Adam and Eve were real people	76%
The Bible is the inerrant Word of God, both in matters of faith and in historical, geographical, and other secular matters	72%
The church should put less emphasis on individual sanctification and more on transforming the social order	3%

More than four-fifths of the entire sample reported that they self-identify as "evangelicals," a figure that varies only a little across the sub-groups within the WCA. About half regard themselves as "conservative," but "charismatic or Pentecostal" and "fundamentalist" accounted for only about one-eighth and one-twentieth of these WCA clergy, respectively. These last three identifications are least common among the mainline Protestant clergy within the WCA. Far fewer respondents identify with what may be called "churchlike" movements—but roughly one-quarter claim to be "progressive" and "mainline." The former was only slightly more common among mainline pastors than other ministers within the WCA, but the latter term was primarily adopted by clergy from mainline Protestant denominations and rarely by clergy from evangelical denominations and nondenominational clergy. "Ecumenical" and "liberal" identifications were less common but found much more often among mainline clergy.

POLITICAL ENGAGEMENT
OF WILLOW CREEK ASSOCIATION CLERGY

The Willow Creek Association clearly approves of clergy taking stands on moral issues from the pulpit. As can be seen from Table 22.3, virtually all the pastors surveyed (97 percent) express approval for clergy doing so. While many respondents (50 percent) also expressed approval for ministers taking stands on political issues from the pulpit, they are far more reticent to grant such approval than they are when moral issues are the focus of the remarks.

Table 22.3

Political Norms of Willow Creek Association Clergy

	% Approving
Take a stand while preaching on some moral issue	97%
While preaching, take a stand on some political issue	50%
Publicly (not preaching) support a political candidate	44%
Contribute money to a candidate, party, or political-action committee	70%
Form an action group in one's church to accomplish a social or political goal	51%
Participate in a protest march	62%
Commit civil disobedience to protest some evil	43%

When the queries shift to political endeavors conducted more in the role of a private citizen than as pastor of a church, WCA clergy appear to remain somewhat hesitant about expressing approval for activities of a public nature. Whereas 70 percent of the WCA pastors indicated that they approve of clergy contributing money for political purposes (a fairly "invisible" political action), less than half (44 percent) voice assent for ministers publicly supporting candidates—even when done off the pulpit. It would seem, therefore, that a majority of these clergy would hesitate to place a campaign sign in their yards or a candidate bumper sticker on their cars. While they certainly have the legal right to do so, most of these ministers are hesitant to support such public displays of political choice by clergy, presumably because they are perceived to interfere with their effectiveness as pastors.

However, there is less hesitation to express approval for clergy seeking to organize congregants for particular social and political ends. A majority (51 percent) of the respondents affirm clergy choosing to form an action group within one's church to accomplish a particular social or political goal. Even more express approval for participation in protest marches (62 percent), and a fairly sizable portion of the pastors indicate acceptance of clergy engaging in civil disobedience to protest some evil.

When moving into specific policy positions, the WCA clergy tend to express relatively conservative views in some areas of public policy. Only two out of five (43 percent) agree that the federal government should do more to solve social problems; less than one-third indicate support for government-sponsored national health insurance or agreement that minorities may need special governmental assistance in order to achieve equality within American society (29 and 32 percent, respectively).

WCA clergy do not appear to be strong supporters of public education, with less than one-third (29 percent) of responding ministers agreeing that "education policy should focus on improving public schools rather than encouraging alternatives." This rather low level of support for public education among WCA clergy may be partially a function of the fact that a majority of those surveyed reside in large metropolitan cities.

Table 22.4

Policy Positions of Willow Creek Association Clergy

	% Agreeing
The federal government should do more to solve social problems such as unemployment, poverty, and poor housing.	43%
Education policy should focus on improving public schools rather than on encouraging alternatives such as private and religious schools.	29%
Sex-education programs included in the curricula of public high schools should be abstinence based.	89%
We need government-sponsored national health insurance so that everyone can get adequate medical care.	29%
African Americans and other minorities may need special governmental help in order to achieve an equal place in America.	32%
We need a constitutional amendment prohibiting all abortions unless to save the mother's life, or in cases of rape or incest.	73%
Homosexuals should have all the same rights and privileges as other American citizens.	45%
A lasting peace in the Middle East will require Israel to make greater concessions to the Palestinians.	36%

However, WCA clergy have mixed views on other social issues. Nearly three-quarters (73 percent) of the pastors express approval for a constitutional amendment to restrict abortions and even more (89 percent) indicate their belief that sex-education programs in public high schools should be abstinence based. Still, nearly a majority (45 percent) of these clergy indicate agreement that homosexuals should have all the same rights and privileges as other Americans. Not shown, but notable, is that, overall, these ministers are not especially fond of the Christian Right. Only about one-fifth of the nondenominational and evangelical pastors report feeling "close" to this movement, with the mainliners especially distant.

Given these patterns, it is not surprising that about half the sample claims to be politically conservative. Here the nondenominational clergy are the most conservative, at better than three-fifths. The WCA evangelical pastors are less conservative, at 49 percent; and the WCA mainliners, much less so, at 28 percent.

One reason for this gradient is the ministers' views on social-welfare and foreign-policy issues. As noted earlier, some two-fifths of the total sample agree that the federal government should do more to solve social problems, a figure that is only a little lower among the WCA's nondenominational clergy and their evangelical denomination members. In contrast, a majority of the WCA mainline ministers agree with the statement. A similar pattern occurs on foreign-policy issues, illustrated here by views on Israel and the Palestinians. Two-fifths of the entire sample support Israel in this dispute (by disagreeing with the statement), but this figure rises to three-fifths for the WCA's nondenominational clergy and falls to less than one-fifth for their mainline pastors.

How active were the WCA pastors in politics during the 2000 campaign? Overall, they were most involved politically within the context of church activity and least involved in acts of protest. For example, more than half of the entire sample reported urging their congregations to register and vote (56 percent) or praying publicly about an issue (54 percent), the most common in-church activities. Other in-church activities were reported less often. For example, slightly fewer than two of five pastors (39 percent) reported that they prayed publicly for political candidates, and fewer than a third (29 percent) indicated that they took a stand on some political issues from the pulpit.

In terms of the most common activities, the subgroups hardly differ. All told, the WCA mainline ministers were the most active, followed by the nondenominational pastors and then the WCA clergy in evangelical denominations. Nevertheless, for an organization that is explicitly apolitical, its member pastors appear to be fairly politicized, and much of the political action in which they engage occurs within the confines of the church. One additional statistic bears this out: Some two-fifths of the WCA clergy reported that in the run-up to the 2000 election there were conservative voter guides (such as those made famous by the Christian Coalition) available in their congregations. About half the

WCA's nondenominational pastors and evangelical clergy reported having voter guides in their churches, as did more than one-quarter of their mainline ministers.

Table 22.5

Political Activities of Willow Creek Association Clergy in the Election of 2000

	% Reporting
Urged their congregation to register and vote	56%
Contacted a public official about some issue	42%
Prayed publicly for political candidates	39%
Took a stand from the pulpit on some political issue	29%
Prayed publicly about an issue	54%
Party Identification	
Strong Democrat	3%
Weak Democrat	3%
Independent, lean Democrat	4%
Independent	8%
Independent, lean Republican	20%
Weak Republican	25%
Strong Republican	37%
Vote Choice in the 2000 Election	
Al Gore	13%
George W. Bush	85%
Pat Buchanan	0%
Ralph Nader	1%
Other	0%
Did not vote	1%

Overall, WCA clergy are highly Republican in their partisan identifications. The plurality (37 percent) of those surveyed report that they are strong Republicans. An additional quarter of the clergy state they are weak Republicans; and another fifth are Independents leaning toward the Republican Party. Only one in ten note any inclination toward the Democratic Party. Not surprising, therefore, the overwhelming majority (85 percent) of WCA clergy reported that they had cast their ballots for George W. Bush in the 2000 presidential election, although Gore did receive 13 percent of the votes cast. Nearly all the WCA clergy reported voting in 2000.

CONCLUSION

We find the Willow Creek Association to be quite diverse in terms of denominational affiliation, but fairly homogeneous in demography and theology. Important differences appear between the nondenominational ministers and the clergy who belong to mainline Protestant churches within the WCA. Overall, the WCA offers an indirect mechanism for coalition building between various kinds of conservative Protestant clergy not otherwise in contact with one another.

This exploration of the WCA clergy suggests several tentative conclusions about the new-paradigm, nondenominational churches and the impact of the postmodern associations to which they belong on the connection between religion and public affairs. First, although nondenominational churches are at the center of these new associations such as the WCA, their postmodern character can foster a diverse membership, drawn largely from evangelical and mainline Protestant denominations. Pastors from these diverse affiliations are brought together by a common vision of the local church and a commitment to evangelism. These common purposes are furthered by the WCA's limited scope, but also by the demographic and theological homogeneity of its members. To be sure, there are differences among the WCA clergy—especially between the nondenominational and mainline churches. While these differences do not appear to be sufficient to interfere with the special work of the WCA, they are probably large enough to prevent it from evolving into a denomination, as some other nondenominational associations appear to be doing.

From this perspective, it is probably a good thing that the WCA has no political agenda, for if it did, it could face serious internal divisions. However, the WCA does appear to have a potentially large indirect impact on politics and public affairs. The WCA provides a focus for networks of like-minded pastors to make common cause on particular issues. All the elements of the WCA clergy are aligned with the Republican Party and hold conservative positions on social issues, albeit with different degrees of intensity. These commonalities can support cooperative efforts in presidential elections as well as when social issues are at the fore. The high level of political activity of WCA clergy means that once such coalitions are arranged, they can be quite potent in mobilizing congregations, collecting resources for political action, and putting pressure on government officials.

Finally, our findings provide some additional documentation for the leadership of the new-paradigm, nondenominational Protestant churches. These pastors are highly orthodox in belief, closely identified with sectarian religious movements, and given to conservative social theology. They are also politically conservative, especially on social issues, and strongly aligned with the Republican Party. The WCA ministers are active in politics, and their churches are deeply involved in social programs. In these regards, the entire WCA sample nearly matches or exceeds the clergy in the mainline Protestant tradition, who have historically specialized in such worldly activities (and they are surpassed by WCA mainline clergy, who appear to combine both emphases).

In short, the WCA nondenominational clergy tend to fit the common image of the politically conservative, suburban megachurch. But rather than being islands of traditionalist fervor, they are linked to potential allies through the postmodern associations they create and animate. Ironically, these churches are well adapted to carry a premodern message into the postmodern world.

Part 5

Conclusion

Chapter 23

This World Is Not My Home?
Patterns of Clerical Involvement in
Politics over Time

Corwin E. Smidt

Religion and political life are not static in nature. A multitude of factors can affect either religious or political life, modifying or erasing previous patterns that characterized either domain. The chapters of this volume have analyzed the social characteristics, theological stands, and the political norms, policy positions, and political behavior of clergy across different denominations and religious faiths following the 2000 presidential election. This analysis has clearly demonstrated that there are important differences, theologically and politically, across religious bodies. The general pattern is one of theological and political consistency within denominations. Yet clergy from some denominations exhibit a high level of cohesion in their theological positions, but greater diversity in terms of their political positions, while ministers from other denominations are relatively diverse in the stands that they adopt theologically, but more cohesive in the political positions they hold.

Although this analysis has been informative, one question naturally arises in light of these findings: To what extent do the current patterns either reflect, or diverge from, those evident in the past? Consequently, this chapter seeks to assess patterns of change in (1) the theological stands of clergy, (2) the norms and practices of political engagement

301

among clergy, and (3) the political partisanship among clergy. More specifically, it assesses the relative level of change evident since 1989, when the last major cross-denominational surveys of clergy were conducted.[52]

In order to make the analysis and presentation more manageable, patterns of change are examined by religious tradition—in terms of change and stability among evangelical and mainline Protestant clergy—rather than by denomination. Because comparable data are not available for black Protestant clergy and Roman Catholic priests in 1989, it is impossible to assess changes within their ranks over time. However, survey results from these pastors and priests are also presented in the tables for purposes of comparison. But because the focus of this chapter is on assessments of change over time, their patterns will rarely be discussed.

It is important to note at the outset that any utilization of different denominations over time within either the evangelical or mainline Protestant category could affect the resultant findings.[53] Therefore, to eliminate such potential sources of contamination and ensure that differences across time reflect true change and not some methodological artifact, the evangelical and mainline Protestant categories contain clergy responses only from those denominations in which ministers were polled in both 1989 and 2001. Seven of the eight denominations surveyed in *The Bully Pulpit* were also included in the Cooperative Clergy Study Project: the Assemblies of God, the Christian Reformed Church, and the Southern Baptist Convention from the evangelical Protestant tradition; and the Reformed Church in America, the United Methodist Church, the Presbyterian Church (USA), and the Disciples of Christ from mainline Protestantism. Clergy from these seven denominations, therefore, serve as bases for the analysis presented in this chapter, with pastors from each of the seven denominations being weighted equally (N = 1,000) in both 1989 and 2001 to ensure that any disparate number of questionnaires received from pastors of the seven denominations, whether within or across time, would not color the results.[54]

THEOLOGICAL CHANGES OVER TIME

Theological understandings are central to the life and ministry of clergy. Consequently, in order to assess the nature of theological changes among ministers over time, a measure of Christian orthodoxy was constructed identical to that used by Guth and his associates in *The Bully*

Pulpit (1997). The authors of *The Bully Pulpit* were fairly constrained in the measures they could use to construct their index. Only three doctrinal questions were identical across all eight denominations involved in the study: agreement that Jesus is the only way to salvation, the Bible is inerrant, and the devil actually exists. Given the lack of other component measures, these three doctrinal items were combined and utilized as the measure of orthodoxy.

There are certain limitations to this particular measure. At least one item (inerrancy of Scripture) has a conservative, evangelical Protestant cast to it. Had a wider variety of theological questions been available across all eight denominations (e.g., agreement as to whether Jesus will return to earth one day or whether Jesus was born of a virgin), the relative distribution of orthodoxy across each denomination would have been different.[55] Nevertheless, the three component measures used to tap orthodoxy were highly correlated with other theological measures not included in every denominational survey, and the constructed measure of orthodoxy exhibited high reliability (alpha = .84, Guth et al. 1997, 45). Therefore, the three-item measure was deemed to be both a valid and reliable measure of doctrinal orthodoxy. More importantly for the purposes of this chapter, these measures provide an important baseline from which to assess change—as any increase or decrease in orthodoxy using the same items can be viewed as true change in the theological orientations of clergy across time.

With these caveats in mind, we analyze levels of theological orthodoxy across time. As can be seen from the data in Table 23.1, evangelical Protestant clergy in 1989 were clearly more orthodox in their theological stands than their mainline counterparts. A majority (55 percent) of evangelical Protestant pastors could be classified as highly orthodox—as they strongly agreed with all three items used as the component doctrinal measures of orthodoxy—while only 10 percent of mainline clergy could be so classified.[56] Another one-quarter of evangelical (27 percent) and another one-fifth of mainline Protestant pastors (20 percent) could be classified as orthodox, expressing at least agreement, though not necessarily strong agreement, with the items employed in the measure. Overall, therefore, four out of five evangelical Protestant ministers (82 percent) in 1989 could be classified as being orthodox in their theological positions, while only about one in three mainline Protestant clergy in 1989 (30 percent) stood in agreement with all three measures employed to assess theological orthodoxy.

Table 23.1

Orthodoxy among Clergy by Religious Tradition over Time

		1989	2001
Evangelical Protestants			
Most Orthodox	1	55%	62%
	2	27%	28%
	3	13%	8%
	4	4%	2%
Most Modernist	5	1%	1%
Mainline Protestants			
Most Orthodox	1	10%	13%
	2	20%	20%
	3	20%	18%
	4	27%	22%
Most Modernist	5	24%	24%
Black Protestants			
Most Orthodox	1	x	73%
	2	x	22%
	3	x	3%
	4	x	1%
Most Modernist	5	x	2%
Roman Catholics			
Most Orthodox	1	x	2%
	2	x	11%
	3	x	29%
	4	x	45%
Most Modernist	5	x	12%

x Not surveyed

In 2001, data are available for clergy outside the evangelical and mainline Protestant traditions. Of the four religious traditions examined in 2001, black Protestant pastors are clearly the most orthodox of the clergy surveyed. Roman Catholic priests, given this measure of doctrinal orthodoxy, appear to be highly modernist in their theological perspectives, though this low orthodoxy is, to a certain extent, a function of the particular measures employed.[57]

Most relevant for this chapter is the pattern of change in theological orthodoxy across time. Table 23.1 reveals that there has been an increase in theological orthodoxy within the ranks of both evangelical and mainline Protestant pastors over the past twelve years, with the level of increased orthodoxy being about the same for both religious traditions.

What accounts for these changes? Although the data in Table 23.1 cannot address directly the reasons for these changes, one possible explanation might be maturation effects, in which individual clergy change their theological positions over time. However, because theological understandings are foundational orientations for pastors, it is unlikely that many clergy would, over the course of their ministry, change their basic theological perspectives. Another possible explanation relates to varying patterns of recruitment to the ministry. It may well be that those choosing to enter the ministry today are more conservative theologically than those who began their ministry twenty or thirty years ago, regardless of religious tradition. Any such fresh influx of more conservative pastors would then be coupled with the related process of the graying and ultimate retirement of those holding more liberal theological perspectives. Certainly, clergy holding more liberal theological orientations are hardly on the verge of extinction, and there are many who choose to enter the ministry today who are relatively liberal in their theological orientations. But, since 1989, the ranks of the theologically orthodox have expanded at the expense of those espousing less orthodox views theologically, likely because their numbers entering the ministry have swelled in comparison to their more liberal counterparts.

Various factors may serve to shape one's theological orientations, including life experiences and educational socialization. Other analysts have noted that female clergy tend to be more liberal theologically (Hunter and Sargeant 1993; Guth et al. 1997) and that those pastors who are seminary graduates tend to be more liberal theologically than those ordained to the ministry without such educational training (Guth et al. 1997). Consequently, Table 23.2 examines the mean score on the orthodoxy measure exhibited by evangelical and mainline Protestant clergy while controlling for gender and seminary education.

The pattern of increased orthodoxy revealed in Table 23.1 is reflected again in terms of the mean scores presented in Table 23.2. It may be recalled that the three-component measure of orthodoxy was constructed to range from a maximum score of +6, indicating high orthodoxy, to a minimum score of -6, indicating strong disagreement with each of the three component measures used. The resultant mean scores for both evangelical and mainline pastors exhibit a net positive increase in their values between 1989 and 2001. While the mean orthodoxy score for all evangelical clergy in 1989 was 4.5, it was 4.8 in 2001.

Likewise, the mean orthodoxy score for all mainline Protestant clergy increased from 0.3 to 0.7 over the same period of time.

Table 23.2

Mean Orthodoxy Scores by Religious Tradition over Time Controlling for Gender and Seminary Education

Religious Tradition	Orthodoxy Scores 1989	Percent 1989	Orthodoxy Scores 2001	Percent 2001
Evangelical Protestant	4.5*		4.8*	
Male	4.5	98.7%	4.8	97.2%
Female	5.6	1.3%	5.0	2.8%
Non-Sem grad	5.5	43.3%	5.5	38.6%
Seminary grad	3.8	56.7%	4.4	61.4%
Mainline Protestant	.3		.7	
Male	.5	93.6%	1.1	75.8%
Female	-1.6	6.4%	-.8	24.2%
Non-Sem grad	2.6	8.9%	2.7	8.2%
Seminary grad	.1	91.7%	.5	91.8%

* Scores range from a -6 (reflecting strong disagreement with all three items used to measure orthodoxy) to +6 (indicating strong agreement with all three items).

However, several additional noteworthy patterns are evident in the table. First, it is clear from Table 23.2 that the proportion of female clergy is growing among both mainline and evangelical clergy, with the mainline percentage jumping markedly from 6.4 percent in 1989 up to 24.2 percent in 2001. Even among evangelical pastors, the proportion of women more than doubled over the same period of time, though the proportion of female clergy within the three evangelical Protestant denominations analyzed remains relatively small (about 3 percent).

Second, these changing gender patterns among clergy hold important implications for the level of orthodoxy expressed. Between 1989 and 2001, both male and female pastors within mainline Protestantism exhibited increased levels of orthodoxy. However, among mainliners, females tend to be less orthodox in their theological expressions than males. This was true in 1989 as well as in 2001. Thus, the lower level of orthodoxy evident among those women clergy, coupled with their growing proportions within the ranks of mainline clergy, tends to depress the overall level of orthodoxy exhibited by mainline Protestant clergy. Among evangelicals, female pastors are generally more orthodox than their male counterparts, largely because their numbers are found disproportionately within the ranks of Assemblies of God—a denomination whose clergy tend to be highly orthodox in their theological expressions (see Chapter 14). However, the orthodoxy scores among evangelical women pastors declined between 1989 and 2001, and, should this trend continue, female clergy within evangelical Protestantism will eventually be less orthodox in their theological stand than their male counterparts.

Third, the proportion of evangelical ministers who report graduating from seminary has also increased over time. The percentage of seminary graduates among mainline Protestant clergy remained high (92 percent) and unchanged over the twelve-year period. But seminary graduates are less common among evangelicals than mainliners, and, over time, there has been an increase in the percentage of seminary graduates among evangelical pastors—from 57 percent in 1989 to 61 percent in 2001—a trend that is likely to continue.

Fourth, it is clear from Table 23.2 that seminary graduates, as a whole, tend to be less orthodox than those pastors who did not graduate from seminary. This pattern holds across both evangelical and mainline Protestant denominations, and it was true in 1989 as well as in 2001. Thus, further expansion of the ranks of seminary graduates among evangelical Protestant ministers is likely to depress the level of orthodoxy expressed within the group.

In order to assess those factors that serve to shape the expressions of theological orthodoxy among the clergy surveyed in 2001, a Multiple Classification Analysis (MCA) was conducted, a procedure that enables one to use categorical variables in multivariate analysis. MCA first provides the mean score on the dependent variable for each category of the independent variable, which yields a bivariate measure of association (*eta*) between the independent and dependent variable. MCA then gives an adjusted mean score on the dependent variable for each category of the independent variables, reflecting the value of the mean score after controls have been entered for each of the other independent variables employed in the analysis. The resulting statistic *beta* represents the multivariate equivalent of *eta*.

Variables analyzed in the previous table (namely gender and seminary education) along with religious tradition, secular-education level, and years in the ministry were entered as independent variables predicting variation in orthodoxy. Table 23.3 presents the results.

As noted earlier, female clergy tend, as a whole, to be less theologically orthodox than male clergy. This can be seen in comparing the unadjusted mean orthodoxy score among women clergy (-0.3—a score slightly below zero, which serves as the midpoint of the measure) with that of male clergy (a mean score of 2.9). When the other independent variables presented in Table 23.3 are taken into account by means of MCA, the effects of gender on expressions of orthodoxy are clearly diminished. The adjusted mean orthodoxy scores are 0.8 for female clergy and 2.7 for male clergy. This reduction in the effects of gender on orthodoxy is revealed also in the decline between the magnitude of the *eta* (.317) and *beta* values (.194). Still, even after the effects of other independent variables have been entered into the analysis, gender continues to have an important effect on the expression of orthodoxy among evangelical and mainline clergy in 2001.

On the other hand, once the effects of the other independent variables are taken into account, the variable that measures the respondent's general level of education washes out as an explanatory factor, as its *beta* score is nearly reduced to zero (.032). Seminary education, however, continues to remain relatively important in explaining variation in theological orthodoxy (*beta* = .140) even controlling for the effects of the other variables, though it still trails gender in its effects.

Initially, there appears to be no particular pattern to the relationship between orthodoxy and the number of years in the ministry. But, once the effects of other variables have been taken into account, it is clear that those clergy who more recently entered the ministry are more orthodox than those who have served as pastors for a longer number of years. This is evident not only in the progressive diminishing of the adjusted mean score of orthodoxy as one moves from those with fewer years to more years in the ministry, but from the jump between the *eta* score of .010 to the *beta* score of .088 as well.

Of the variables analyzed, however, religious tradition is by far the one that most fully accounts for differences in expression of orthodoxy. It has a *beta* score of .465, more than double that of gender. Overall, the five variables included in the MCA explain a substantial amount of variation in orthodoxy, as the value of R squared is .380, indicating that the model explains 38 percent of the variation observed in the dependent variable.

Table 23.3

Theological Orthodoxy in 2000: A Multiple Classification Analysis

Grand Mean = 2.43	N	Unadjusted Mean	Eta	Adjusted for Independent Variables	Beta
Gender					
Female	1029	-.3*		.8	
Male	5971	2.9	.317	2.7	.194
Education					
Less than BA	840	4.3		2.5	
College degree	1433	3.7		2.6	
Postgrad	4727	1.7	.292	2.4	.032
Seminary Education					
Non-Sem grad	1616	4.6		3.4	
Seminary grad	4384	1.8	.322	2.2	.140
Years in Ministry					
Less than 13	1963	2.4		2.8	
13–24	2666	2.5		2.5	
More than 24	2371	2.4	.010	2.0	.088
Religious Tradition					
Evangelical Prot	3000	4.8		4.4	
Mainline Prot	4000	.7	.570	1.0	.465

Multiple R   = .617
Multiple R squared = .380

* Scores range from a -6 (reflecting strong disagreement with all three items used to measure orthodoxy) to +6 (indicating strong agreement with all three items).

CHANGES IN POLITICAL NORMS AND ACTIVITY OVER TIME

Are the changes in theological orthodoxy evident among evangelical and mainline Protestant clergy associated with political changes as well? Table 23.4 addresses this question, in part, by analyzing the level of approval expressed for different forms of clerical political activity by religious tradition over time. These data are not arbitrarily chosen to support some particular contention, as the table examines almost all such questions for which there is comparable data for clergy over time.[58] Fortunately, eight such questions are available—evenly divided between four questions that relate directly to within-church activities and four questions assessing activities that are generally, though not necessarily always, done as activities outside the church.

Table 23.4

Norms by Religious Tradition over Time

Approve	Evan Prot	Main Prot	Black Prot	Rom Cath
Church-based Activities				
Give sermon on a social/political topic				
1989	74%	83%	x	x
2001	75%	73%	69%	79%
Take stand from pulpit on a political issue				
1989	53%	58%	x	x
2001	60%	48%	68%	59%
Organize study group within church				
1989	65%	91%	x	x
2001	64%	81%	71%	78%
Organize action group within church				
1989	52%	75%	x	x
2001	46%	61%	63%	74%
Public (but not from pulpit) Activities				
Take a stand on a political issue				
1989	91%	92%	x	x
2001	83%	81%	85%	79%
Support a political candidate				
1989	73%	67%	x	x
2001	59%	46%	72%	26%
Contribute money to candidate or party				
1989	68%	80%	x	x
2001	64%	73%	57%	45%
Join a national political organization				
1989	52%	64%	x	x
2001	47%	54%	51%	35%

x   Not surveyed

In 1989, mainline Protestant clergy were more likely than evangelical Protestant clergy to approve of the various forms of clerical political engagement analyzed—though such differences tended to be greater in terms of church-based activities, where mainline Protestant clergy generally exhibited a higher approval rating by a margin of 10 percent or more (the exception being taking a pulpit stand on some political issue). Differences were also evident in relationship to more individually based activities, but neither as consistently so nor by such wide margins. For example, with regard to taking a stand on some political issue when off the pulpit, both evangelical and mainline Protestant clergy were equally strong in voicing their approval (with a little more than 90 percent of clergy expressing support within both religious traditions). And evangelical clergy were more likely than mainline clergy to approve publicly supporting a political candidate when off the pulpit (73 percent versus 67 percent, respectively). On the other hand, when asked about either joining a national political organization or contributing money to a candidate or party, a majority of clergy in both traditions voiced their approval in 1989, but mainliners were more likely than evangelicals to do so (by a margin of 12 percent).

Only a little more than a decade later, some important changes had occurred. First, the gaps in approval ratings for the various political activities between mainline and evangelical Protestant clergy were neither as consistent nor as large as those evident in 1989. Mainline Protestant clergy no longer consistently exceeded evangelical Protestant clergy in terms of their levels of approval expressed for church-based activities. While the mainline respondents continue to exceed evangelical Protestant clergy in their approval for organizing both study and action groups (by a margin of 15 percent or more), evangelical clergy now express greater approval than mainline pastors for taking a pulpit stand on some political issue (60 percent versus 48 percent, respectively). And, evangelical clergy are equally as prone as mainline counterparts to express approval for giving a sermon on some social or political topic (75 percent versus 73 percent, respectively). Thus, the gaps in approval ratings for the various political activities between mainline and evangelical clergy have become less consistent and generally more diminished in scope than was true roughly a decade and a half ago.

Second, in terms of differences over time, there has been a decline of 10 percent or more in the approval for almost all forms of clerical political activity among mainliners (the exception being contributing money to a candidate or party, which declined by only 7 percentage points). Among evangelical Protestant clergy, there are similar declines in expressed levels of approval for clergy political action—but neither as consistently nor by such wide margins.

Thus, overall, mainline ministers in 2001 were still more likely than evangelical pastors to express approval for various forms of clerical political activity—but not as consistently nor by as large a margin as was evident in 1989. More importantly, both evangelical and mainline clergy were far less likely in 2001 than in 1989 to express support for various forms of clerical political activity. This pattern was true for all forms of political activity among mainline clergy, while among evangelicals there was a consistent decline in approval for individually based political activities, though a more mixed pattern of change related to church-based activities.

Table 23.5

Behavior by Religious Tradition over Time

Behavior	Evan Prot	Main Prot	Black Prot	Rom Cath
Church-based Activities				
Touched on issue in sermon				
1989	74%	81%	x	x
2001	50%	49%	*	45%
Organized study group within church				
1989	6%	25%	x	x
2001	4%	10%	*	14%
Organized action group within church				
1989	8%	18%	x	x
2001	6%	9%	*	15%
Endorsed candidate from pulpit				
1989	5%	2%	x	x
2001	6%	2%	*	1%
Public (but not from pulpit) Activities				
Publicly took a stand on political issue				
1989	63%	66%	x	x
2001	52%	61%	*	38%
Publicly supported a political candidate				
1989	42%	40%	x	x
2001	36%	26%	*	13%
Contribute money to candidate or party				
1989	18%	34%	x	x
2001	18%	21%	*	17%
Joined a national political organization				
1989	13%	20%	x	x
2001	8%	13%	*	14%

x Not surveyed
* Question not asked in identical form

However, such changes over time are not confined only to a decline in the level of expressed approval for various political activities, but are also evident in the reported levels of such political action. Table 23.5 assesses the extent to which evangelical and mainline clergy report having engaged in certain specified forms of political behavior in both 1989 and 2001. Once again, the data are not arbitrarily chosen to support some particular contention, as the table examines almost all such questions for which comparable data for clergy exists over time.[59] The eight variables analyzed are evenly divided between four items concerning church-based activities and four measures tapping activities more public in nature.[60]

Several patterns are clearly evident from Table 23.5. First, in 1989, mainline Protestant clergy were clearly much more likely than evangelical Protestant clergy to engage in political activities.[61] In five of the activities examined, mainliners exceeded the rate of activity of evangelical clergy by a difference of 7 percentage points or more, with the largest difference found in terms of organizing a study group within the church. There were two exceptions to this pattern of higher political activity among mainline clergy: (1) the relatively rare behavior of endorsing a candidate from the pulpit, where evangelical clergy exceeded mainliners, 5 percent versus 2 percent, respectively; and, (2) supporting a candidate publicly when off the pulpit, where evangelicals were slightly more likely than mainline pastors to do so, 42 percent versus 40 percent, respectively.

Second, the magnitude of such differences between evangelical and mainline Protestant ministers, while still discernable, had diminished by 2001. The mainline Protestant respondents continued to be slightly more active politically than evangelical Protestants were, but only barely so. In 1989, mainline Protestant clergy exhibited a 7 percentage point lead or greater over evangelicals in five of the eight forms of political behavior examined. But, by 2001, there was only one type of political behavior in which mainline Protestant clergy demonstrated such a margin over evangelical Protestant pastors.

Third, and more significantly, there has been a consistent drop in reported activity for all forms of political behavior between 1989 and 2001 among both groups of pastors (the exception being a slight increase from 5 to 6 percent of evangelical Protestant clergy reporting having endorsed a candidate from the pulpit). These declines tend to be greater among mainline than evangelical Protestant respondents. But the overall pattern is clear: there was a decline in political activity among both evangelical and mainline Protestant clergy over the twelve-year period.

This decline in political participation becomes more evident when one examines the mean political participation score evident among evangelical and mainline Protestant clergy in 1989 and 2001, as displayed in Table 23.6. The mean participation score is based on activities for which comparable data are available across time. Ten such items are available across five denominations.[62] Clergy were asked whether they had participated in each of the ten acts during the past year,[63] so scores vary potentially from zero (no acts) to ten (all ten acts).

Table 23.6

Mean Political Participation Score by Religious Traditions over Time Controlling for Gender and Seminary Education

Religious Tradition	Pol. Participation Mean Score 1989	Pol. Participation Mean Score 2001
Evangelical Protestant	2.37	2.16
Male	2.36	2.29
Female	2.75	1.85
Non-Sem grad	2.34	2.19
Seminary grad	2.41	2.11
Mainline Protestant	2.92	2.15
Male	2.91	2.10
Female	3.10	2.26
Non-Sem grad	2.35	1.56
Seminary grad	2.99	2.25

The data presented in Table 23.6 reveal several important patterns. First, the decline in the overall rate of political participation among both evangelical and mainline Protestant clergy is again evident, with the mean score of political participation dropping for clergy within both religious traditions. Clearly, then, clergy in 2001 report being less active politically than in 1989—and this decline was evident regardless of the religious tradition within which the ministers were found.

Second, it is also clear that this decline is much more substantial among mainline than among evangelical Protestant clergy. The drop in the mean score of political participation is much less for evangelical Protestant pastors (from 2.37 to 2.16) than for mainline Protestant clergy (from 2.92 to 2.15). As a result, the mean level of political participation has become virtually identical for evangelical and mainline Protestant clergy in 2001.

Third, there is a different pattern of political engagement by gender among the evangelical and mainline groups. Among evangelicals, female pastors were more likely than males to engage in politics in 1989, but less likely to do so in 2001. This decline in participation among evangelical women is primarily a function of the drop in participation reported by female clergy in the Assemblies of God, as their numbers dominate the ranks of female evangelical ministers in both 1989 and 2001. Among mainliners, however, women were clearly more politically engaged than male clergy; this pattern was true in both 1989 and 2001. Thus, the decline in political participation among mainline Protestant clergy would have been even greater had the proportion of women clergy not swelled among mainliners between 1989 and 2001.

Are, then, religious tradition and doctrinal orthodoxy important predictors of levels of pastoral political participation? The answer is no when other variables are taken into account, as was made evident by a multivariate analysis in which the index of participation served as the dependent variable. As revealed by this multivariate analysis, the best predictors of political activity levels among clergy are: higher levels of educational attainment, greater interest in politics, older age, longer length of service in the congregation, strong ideological attachments, and strong moral- and social-welfare-issue positions. Religious tradition and orthodoxy, however, wash out in such a multivariate analysis.

CHANGES IN POLITICAL PARTISANSHIP OVER TIME

The period of the 1990s was a time of heightened partisanship and ideology in national politics. Do the patterns of change in partisanship and ideological orientation among clergy then reflect such increased partisanship and ideological polarization, or are their political stances largely divergent from this broader cultural pattern?

Evangelical Protestant clergy in 1989 were more conservative and more Republican than mainline Protestant clergy. But, over the course of the following decade, evangelical Protestant pastors became more homogenous in their ideological orientations and partisan identifications (becoming more conservative ideologically and more Republican in their partisanship), while mainline Protestant ministers became slightly more heterogeneous and polarized in their ideological orientations and partisan identifications.

The changing relationship between evangelical and mainline Protestant pastors and their political partisanship is much more fully evident in Table 23.7, which examines clergy positions on policy matters related to moral policy,[64] social-welfare policy,[65] partisan identification, and vote in the preceding presidential election. The scores presented in the table are converted to a metric in which scores range from 100 (fully Republican) to -100 (fully Democratic).

Table 23.7

Policy and Partisan Scores by Religious Tradition over Time Controlling for Gender and Seminary Education

	Moral Policy	Social-Welfare Policy	Party Identification	Pres. Vote
1989				
Evangelical Protestant	42	27	36	69
Male	42	27	36	69
Female	58	45	62	88
Non-Sem grad	61	52	46	85
Seminary grad	28	8	29	57
Mainline Protestant	-32	-19	-9	-11
Male	-29	-17	-7	-7
Female	-70	-47	-46	-72
Non-Sem grad	1	15	18	38
Seminary grad	-35	-22	-12	-16
2001				
Evangelical Protestant	43	30	53	76
Male	43	30	54	76
Female	43	22	21	66
Non-Sem grad	62	44	64	85
Seminary grad	31	22	46	70
Mainline Protestant	-32	-23	-9	-5
Male	-25	-19	1	8
Female	-60	-40	-39	-44
Non-Sem grad	+	4	16	32
Seminary grad	-36	-26	-12	-8

+ Less than 1, but greater than 0

Several important patterns emerge from the analysis presented in Table 23.7. First, evangelical Protestant clergy are consistently more

Republican than mainline Protestant pastors, regardless of whether one is examining issues related to moral policy, social-welfare policy, partisan identification, or votes cast in the most recent presidential election. The scores among evangelical respondents are always positive in nature (indicating a Republican stance), while the scores for mainline clergy are always negative in nature (indicating a Democratic stance). This was true in both 1989 and 2001.

Second, it is interesting that, in relationship to public policy, the magnitude of the scores is greater on moral rather than social-welfare issues for both evangelical and mainline clergy. While mainline Protestant clergy are frequently linked to expressions of concern related to social justice, it is the moral issues, and not the social welfare policies, that tend to divide the two groups more dramatically. The net difference in the scores on moral policy between evangelical and mainline clergy was 74 points in 1989 and 75 points in 2001, while the corresponding net difference on social-welfare policy was 46 points in 1989 and 53 points in 2001.

Third, the gaps between mainline and evangelical clergy are greater in 2001 than in 1989 on all four dimensions examined in Table 27.7. The gap is slightly larger on the moral-policy positions and the presidential vote, but much more substantially evident on social-welfare policy stances and partisan identifications. Apparently, then, the party polarization that characterized the Clinton-Gingrich years has become manifested more fully among Protestant clergy as well.

Fourth, it is clear that female clergy among mainline Protestants are much more Democratic in their inclinations than their male counterparts. Both male and female mainline pastors were clearly Democratic in their partisan inclinations in 1989 (since all four scores for both male and female mainline clergy were negative in nature). But, in every instance, the magnitude of those negative scores was far greater for female than male mainline pastors. In 2001, the scores for male mainline Protestant ministers moved in a net Republican direction in partisan identification and voting, but women clergy within their ranks remained Democratic in their partisan orientations. Clearly the consistent gap between the scores of male and female mainline pastors across all four columns indicates that the latter were still far more Democratic than the former in 2001.

Among evangelical Protestant clergy in 1989, both male and female pastors were clearly conservative and Republican in their policy stands and partisanship, although females were more so. By 2001, however, female evangelical clergy were less Republican than their male counter-parts. Still, female evangelical pastors continue to be rooted in the Republican camp, though the depth of that foundation is much shallower in 2001 than in 1989.

Finally, seminary education also has a clear impact on the policy perspectives and partisanship of clergy—one that is consistent in nature. Regardless of religious tradition and year examined, the scores of seminary-educated clergy are clearly less Republican and more Democratic than those exhibited by their counterparts who have not graduated from seminary.

In order to assess those factors that serve to shape the presidential voting decisions for respondents, a Multiple Classification Analysis (MCA) was conducted on the reported votes cast by evangelical and mainline Protestant clergy in the 2000 presidential election. This analysis is similar to the one conducted in Table 23.3, though the dependent variable has changed from orthodoxy to presidential vote, and the independent variables used to explain variation in the dependent are also different. The dependent variable is the same variable examined in the last column in Table 23.7 and uses the same metric of a -100 to a +100 employed there.[66]

The relative effects of five different independent variables on presidential voting decisions are examined: religious tradition, gender, level of theological orthodoxy, ideological orientation, and partisan identification. One would expect that the two political variables—namely, ideological orientation and partisan identification—would have the greatest effect on voting decisions. The question to be ascertained is whether, even after allowing ideological orientation and partisan identification to explain all they can explain in the variation of such voting decisions, can gender, theological orthodoxy, and religious tradition account for any of the remaining variance?

Overall, the five variables included in the analysis account for much of the difference in presidential voting of clergy in 2000, explaining about 68 percent of the variance (R squared = .679). Not surprisingly, the analysis reveals that ideology and party identification do, in fact, have a substantial influence in shaping voting decisions and that each rank fairly equally in terms of their capacity to explain such decisions. The *beta* coefficient for party identification is .396, with the corresponding beta for ideology being .375. However, even after the effects of party identification and ideology are taken into account in the analysis, it is clear that theological orthodoxy still has a relatively substantial effect in shaping such decisions, with the *beta* coefficient for orthodoxy being .116. Greater theological orthodoxy is still associated with an increased propensity to vote Republican, even after controlling for the effects of both ideology and party identification.

Table 23.8
Presidential Vote in 2000: A Multiple Classification Analysis

Grand Mean = 30	N	Unadjusted Mean	Eta	Adjusted for Independent Variables	Beta
Religious Tradition					
Evangelical Prot.	2774	77		36	
Mainline Prot.	3569	-3	.437	27	.050
Gender					
Female	921	-37		26	
Male	5508	43	.306	32	.023
Orthodoxy					
Very low	899	-73		16	
Low	1312	-30		17	
Medium	1039	47		40	
High	991	79		43	
Very high	2188	82	.658	36	.116
Ideology					
Very liberal	736	-82		-14	
Somewhat liberal	1048	-66		-23	
Moderate	1070	17		23	
Somewhat consv.	1608	81		58	
Very conservative	1968	92	.764	60	.375
Party Identification					
Strong Democrat	951	-91		-35	
Weak Democrat	491	-62		-19	
Independent	2121	27		33	
Weak Republican	1031	89		63	
Strong Republican	1701	97	.750	63	.396

Multiple R = .824
Multiple R squared = .679

Of course, had a multivariate analysis been employed, such as a path analysis in which orthodoxy is conceptualized as first shaping partisan preference and ideological orientation, then the effects of orthodoxy on vote choice would likely have been greater than either the direct effects of partisan preference or ideological orientation on the dependent variable. But, even without such a two-stage approach, the effects of orthodoxy on vote choice do not wash out even when partisan identification and ideological orientation have been allowed to explain everything possible about why clergy vote the way they do.

While gender appears initially to be fairly strongly related to presidential voting decision (*eta* = .306), its effects are largely washed out once the other four variables are taken into account, as its resulting *beta* coefficient is .023. Nevertheless, even after the effects of party identification, ideology, theological orthodoxy, and religious traditions have explained all they can, women remain more likely than men to cast their ballots in a Democratic direction (as the magnitude of their adjusted mean score is lower than that for men).

Finally, it is also clear that denominational location within a particular religious tradition has an effect on voting for presidential candidates, even after the other variables have been taken into account. Evangelical Protestant clergy were still more likely than mainline Protestant pastors to cast their ballots for Bush in the 2000 presidential election, even after one has controlled for their greater Republican partisan identifications, their greater political conservatism, their higher theological orthodoxy, and their relative uniformity in terms of gender.

CONCLUSION

This chapter has sought to assess change and stability evident among evangelical and mainline Protestant clergy over a twelve-year period that has witnessed significant changes in the United States and the world. Some things clearly have remained the same, while other things have changed—some fairly dramatically. Clearly, evangelical pastors continue to more likely than mainline Protestant ministers to exhibit theological orthodoxy. Likewise, those clergy who have obtained a seminary degree continue to be less orthodox than those who are not seminary graduates, as do female, in comparison to male, clergy. Evangelical pastors continue to be less active politically than their mainline counterparts, though such differences have narrowed, and evangelical clergy are more Republican in their orientations than mainline pastors.

Yet some important changes have occurred within the ranks of clergy over the past twelve years. Their social composition is changing, as the relative numbers of women continue to expand within the ranks of American clergy. Less dramatic, but also evident, is the growth in the proportion of ministers who are seminary graduates—particularly within evangelical Protestant denominations. Both changes move clergy in a more Democratic partisan direction.

At the same time, there has been an important decline in both approval for, and engagement in, political endeavors among clergy as a whole. This drop has been strongest among mainline Protestant clergy but is also evident within the ranks of evangelical pastors. And, ministers tend to be more polarized, though not dramatically so, in their partisanship at the advent of the new millennium than they were prior to 1990.

How are these changes likely to affect American religious and political life in the future? While gazing into the future is always somewhat hazardous, it is likely that there will continue to be a growing feminization and professionalization of American clergy. Associated with such changes will likely be a movement toward greater liberalism in moral- and social-welfare stands and an increased Democratic cast in terms of partisanship. This raises the specter of a division between clergy and laity within the ranks of the evangelical tradition similar to the one that has tended to characterize the mainline.

Less clear is whether there will continue to be a depoliticization of clergy engagement in American civic and political life. Perhaps the decline in political engagement since 1989 is largely linked to the continued numerical dwindling of mainline Protestant denominations. After all, the largest such drop in approval for political engagement as well as the reduction in political activity has occurred among mainline Protestant clergy. Various analysts warned several decades ago of a gathering storm in the churches and that conservative churches, because of the demands placed on their congregants, were the ones that were growing (e.g., Hadden 1969; Kelley 1977). Perhaps mainline pastors are less involved because of strategic decisions related to unifying, rather than dividing, one's congregations.

On the other hand, the depoliticization of American clergy over the past decade may simply reflect a growing exhaustion related to politics and the fact that, generally speaking, things change very slowly in political life. Clergy frequently confront the need to minister to relatively urgent, life-and-death matters among their congregants, and such calls can hardly be postponed to address that which, in the short term, is likely to be relatively inefficacious political action. Perhaps then the declining political engagement among American Protestant clergy is simply a reflection of the growing need to address the physical, spiritual, and emotional needs of a graying population within their congregations.

This depoliticization of American clergy does tend to counter, though certainly not eliminate, the effects of the increased partisan polarization evident among American pastors over the past twelve years. While evangelical and mainline Protestant clergy are far from standing on two totally different sides of some political and cultural divide in American social life, they had, by the turn of the millennium, moved farther apart politically than had been the case in 1989. Whether this political division will continue to hold true remains to be seen, but clearly such differences in partisanship are likely to continue to be a reflection of how clergy view political life through their different theological lenses.

Notes

Chapter 1

1.   For a further description of the Cooperative Clergy Study Project, see Smidt (2003).

2.   Of the different kinds of surveys available (e.g., face-to-face, telephone, and mail), mail surveys have the poorest response rates. The response rates for each denomination are discussed in each chapter, but of the approximately 22,750 surveys mailed, 8,805 usable surveys were returned—for an overall return rate of more than 38 percent. While higher response rates are always desirable, this response rate for mail surveys is typical, if not fairly good, given not only the size and scope of the study itself, the researcher's unknown quality to those to whom questionnaires were sent, and the length of the survey itself.

3.   The one exception relates to the chapter that examines the perspectives and behavior of American rabbis, as certain questions (e.g., certain theological questions) asked of Christian pastors would not be appropriate for inquiry among those outside the Christian faith.

4.   Different terminology has been used to denote the nature of the authority of Scripture within the Christian tradition: the infallibility versus the inerrancy of the biblical texts. Infallibility holds that the Bible is true and trustworthy, without falsehood, in all that it intends to teach—namely, the ways unto salvation. Inerrancy is a more stringent standard that the biblical texts, at least in terms of the original texts, are without error in all matters.

323

Chapter 2

5.   Jacques Ellul contends that confessionalism appropriates God's living word and remakes it into a dead human code. By so doing, even in the most sincere effort to defend God's word, we alienate ourselves from a living expression of God's love (1976, 145–46).

6.   Major splits in the history of the American Baptist Churches, USA, include: the formation of the Southern Baptist Convention in 1845, the formation of the National Baptist Convention in 1947, and the formation of the Conservative Baptist Association in 1895 (Ohlmann 2000). In 1992, the American Baptist Evangelicals organized within the denomination "to serve the renewal of American Baptist churches."

7.   A recent update of the list suggests that it was incomplete at the time the sample was taken.

8.   In order to summarize the theological orientations of American Baptist clergy and understand how theological education may play a role in developing these orientations, several theological types were first constructed. The consistently orthodox agreed with all of the first four statements in Table 2.2, while the heterodox disagreed with one or more of these statements. The consistently literal agreed with both the fifth and sixth items regarding biblical inerrancy and the primal pair. The relatively strong level of orthodoxy among American Baptist clergy is easily seen in that 81 percent are consistently orthodox and 57 percent are consistently literal, while only 13 percent are heterodox. Graduates of mainline seminaries are orthodox at about the same levels as clergy in the more liberal mainline denominations (e.g., United Methodist). Graduates of evangelical seminaries, who constitute 66 percent of all graduates in the sample, closely duplicate affirmation levels of clergy in moderate evangelical denominations. It would seem that the moderate theological orientation of American Baptist clergy is largely a result of what proportions have been exposed to various influences in their theological education.

9.   Theological orientation seems to have a significant impact on norms regarding political engagement. In particular, the more liberal heterodox respondents are considerably more approving than other clergy when it comes to creating alternative political structures and using unconventional means to achieve political goals.

10.   But this overall diversity of opinion masks much higher levels of consensus within opposing theological types. The relationship between theology and policy positions among American Baptist clergy is consistent with earlier findings for other Protestant denominations (Guth et al. 1997), where theological conservatives supported a moral-reform agenda while theological modernists advocated a social-justice agenda.

11.   Literalists are predominantly Republican (62 percent), while the majority of the heterodox are Democrats (54 percent), but the predominance of Bush supporters among the literalists (86 percent) and Gore supporters among the heterodox (81 percent) is striking. It would seem that the relationship between theological orientation and political orientation is exceptionally strong among American Baptist clergy.

12.   The relationship between theology and political participation in the election of 2000 for American Baptist clergy depends to some extent on the type of participation involved. There seems to be little difference in participation when it comes to nonpartisan politics, but the heterodox are significantly

more active in conventional politics. The greater political participation of the-ologically liberal clergy largely mirrors differences in norms regarding such participation.

Chapter 3

13.   http://www.disciples.org/discover/index.htm. Quote is from an earlier, no longer active site, http://www.disciples.org/general/dcmiss.htm.
14.   Background information on the Disciples of Christ is drawn in large part from the denomination's Web site http://www.disciples.org/history/htm.
15.   The 2000 Yearbook reports that there are 7,113 ordained Disciples clergy in the United States. Most, however, do not serve in a congregation, but hold other positions such as Christian educators, missionaries, administrators at the local, regional, and national level, counselors, ministers of music, and other positions. A large number are also retired. Only active ministers of rec-ognized congregations, a total of 2,575 pastors, were selected as the popula-tion from which the sample was drawn.
16.   http://www.disciples.org/discover/beliefs/htm

Chapter 4

17.   To a degree, this is not surprising. Lutherans amount to only 5 percent of the population while Catholics and conservative Protestants occupy approxi-mately 50 percent of the religious landscape. At best, Lutherans of the ELCA are subsumed in the larger category of mainline Protestantism.
18.   Notable exceptions include individual leaders, particularly in local and state government.

Chapter 7

19.   Unless otherwise noted, the material in this section relies heavily on Mead (1990c) and information from the United Methodist Web site at http://www. umc.org.

Chapter 8

20.   In data not reported, Southern Baptist clergy also strongly favor the death penalty, urge caution in dealing with Russia and China, support gun owners' rights, and back greater defense spending.
21.   Thus, in addition to the specific activities reported in the table, we found that a substantial number of clergy undertook other activities. Forty-eight percent reported taking a public stand on an issue (not from the pulpit), publicly sup-porting a candidate (35 percent), trying to persuade someone to vote for a particular candidate (26 percent), or preaching a whole sermon on a political issue (25 percent). In addition, 19 percent reported being at least somewhat active in supporting a presidential candidate during the primary season, and fully 59 percent claimed to be similarly engaged during the Bush-Gore fall presidential campaign.

Chapter 9

22.   In recent years, there has been a resurgence of interest in the historical foundation of the Churches of Christ. Some of the more interesting works include Hughes and Allen, *Illusions of Innocence*, 1988; Baker and Noll, eds., *Evangelicalism and the Stone-Campbell Movement*, 2002; Casey and Foster, eds., *The Stone-Campbell Movement*, 2002; Holloway and Foster, *Renewing God's People*, 2001; Allen, *Distant Voices*, 1993; Allen and Hughes, *Discovering our Roots: The Ancestry of Churches of Christ*, 1988.

23.   While there are a few congregations of the Churches of Christ that use instruments in worship, they are far and away the exception to accepted practice within the denomination.

24.   Not only do most ministers disagree with opening the clergy to women, 73.9 percent strongly disagree.

25.   In a survey completed in 1995 (Foster, Hailey, and Winter), 61 percent of the preachers had at least a bachelor's degree. One explanation of the "surprising" increase in the 2000 survey is a difference in sampling. Specifically, the 1995 survey found that smaller, less affluent congregations had less-educated ministers than larger, more affluent congregations. In the 2000 sample, Churches of Christ with fewer than fifty members were excluded from the survey since these congregations are not as likely to have full-time pulpit ministers.

26.   The following are from an incomplete list of common phrases used by the ministers: a moral compass, decline in morals, decline of morals, declining morals, hedonism, eroding moral foundation, immorality, moral breakdown, moral crisis, moral decay, moral decline, moral deficit, moral issues, moral laxness, moral perversion, moral relativism, moral values, moral relativity, and morality.

Chapter 10

27.   The LCMS model comports with H. Richard Niebuhr's "Christ and Culture in Paradox" as outlined in his 1951 seminal work, *Christ and Culture*.

28.   Generous financial assistance to complete the study was received from several institutional sources, including Concordia University Wisconsin's Office of the President, Office of the Vice President for Academics, and Cranach Institute, and the Ray C. Bliss Institute of Applied Politics.

Chapter 11

29.   Special appreciation goes to Laura McDaniel and Darcy Walker, whose help with the survey made this study possible. Thanks also to the 464 PCA pastors who filled out the survey and the Pew Charitable Trusts and Furman University for their generous financial support.

Chapter 13

30.   We would like to thank Patrick Allen, Provost of Point Loma Nazarene University for his encouragement and financial support of this project. We are also grateful to Kevin Archer and Holly Irwin-Chase, fellow members of the

Social Science Research Group at PLNU, for their help in collecting and entering data. Thanks to all of our students who volunteered their time and effort in helping us conduct the survey.

Chapter 15

31. The evangelical credentials of the Evangelical Free Church of America include affiliation with the more conservative National Association of Evangelicals rather than the more liberal National Council of Churches.

32. In Jones et al. (2001), the definition of "adherents" represents all attenders. People who attend may or may not be members, adults and children included.

33. It should be noted that unusually large numbers of EFCA pastors were unsure of their views on these two issues. Twenty-three percent were not sure about the need for government-sponsored health care, and 27 percent were not sure whether African Americans and other minorities need special government help to achieve equality.

34. Unlike most of the other surveys in this cooperative study, the EFCA survey questioned ministers about their general political activity rather than their specific activity in the 2000 elections. This choice was made because the EFCA survey was mailed in the winter of 2001–2002, when pastors' recall of activity during the 2000 campaign would have diminished. As a result, Table 15.5 reports how many respondents either "often" or "sometimes" engaged in these activities, rather than the share who did so during the 2000 elections.

Chapter 16

35. The authors wish to thank Rob Vickery for his assistance in collecting and preparing the data for this project.

Chapter 18

36. According to the Official Catholic Directory, there are nearly 64 million Catholics in the United States, constituting 23 percent of the population. Estimates based on religious self-identification tend to be slightly higher.

37. This research was supported by a UNLV SITE Grant, a Constant Jacquet Research Grant provided by the Religious Research Association, and research services generously provided by CARA and the Cannon Center for Survey Research at the University of Nevada, Las Vegas.

38. The magnitude of the correlation between belief in Jesus Christ as the only way to salvation and belief that the sacraments of the Church are necessary for salvation is a robust .455.

39. The question wording for these items refers to "ministers," rather than specifically to "priests." Thus, our results may be somewhat misleading if our respondents make a sharp distinction between Catholic priests and clergy from other denominations.

40. Because political scientists no longer consider party identification the "unmoved mover" in American electoral politics, we estimated several multivariate modes of party identification for our sample of priests. We found that partisanship is related more strongly to issues of economic justice than to

questions of personal morality or theological orthodoxy. This is not to say that many of our respondents did not take conservative positions on a variety of lifestyle issues. Rather, it is to suggest that attitudes toward abortion, vouchers, or creationism do not distinguish well between Republicans and Democrats.

41.   As this was being written, the U.S. Supreme Court issued two rulings relevant to the death penalty: the Court ruled that it is unconstitutional to execute people who are mentally deficient, and has required that death sentences be mandated by juries, not by judges.

Chapter 19

42.   Unlike most other surveys in the cooperative study, the African Methodist Episcopal Church (along with the Church of God in Christ and the Evangelical Free Church of America) surveyed pastors about their general political activities rather than specific activities during the 2000 elections. This distinction was made because the clergy surveys in these three denominations were mailed during the winter of 2001–2002, when pastors' recall of activity during the 2000 campaign would have diminished. As a result, Table 19.5 reports the percentage of pastors who report that they either "often" or "sometimes" engage in these activities (rather than "rarely" or "never"). Thus, these percentages do not reflect the actual percentages of those who engaged in the noted political action during the 2000 elections.

Chapter 20

43.   In contrast, only two of five COGIC clergy (43 percent) indicate a need for more legislation to protect the rights of women.

44.   Unlike the other surveys in the cooperative study, the African Methodist Episcopal Church, the Church of God in Christ, and the Evangelical Free Church of America surveyed pastors about their general political activity rather than specific actions in the 2000 elections. This choice was made because these three groups of surveys were mailed in the winter of 2001–2002, when pastors' recall of activity during the 2000 campaign would have diminished. As a result, Table 20.5 reports the percentage of pastors who report that they either "often" or "sometimes" engage in these activities (rather than "rarely" or "never"). Thus, these percentages do not reflect the actual percentage of clergy actions during the 2000 elections.

Chapter 21

45.   See the UUA Web site, http://www.uua.org for additional information.

46.   For example, see Don't Agonize, Organize at http://www.uua.org/uuawo/ new. The information provided comes from an earlier version of this site.

47.   The figures cited come from data collected by the authors in collaboration with other colleagues. The figures for the liberal faith in the mass public comes from the Third National Survey of Religion and Politics, conducted at the University of Akron in 2000. The data included all religious affiliations in the "liberal nontraditional" category. The figures of The Interfaith Alliances,

national convention delegates, and presidential campaign contributors come from mail surveys conducted leading up to or right after, the 2000 election. Further details on these data are available from the author.

48. A number of individuals chose not to participate in the survey because they were not ordained clergy. However, the sample does include 33 such individuals, who did not differ significantly from the ordained clergy making up the rest of the sample.

49. The respondents were allowed to check any combination of the following religious identities: fundamentalist, liberal, evangelical, ecumenical, progressive, charismatic/Pentecostal, mainline, conservative, or could write in a term of their own choosing.

Chapter 22

50. The survey estimate comes from the Third National Survey of Religion and Politics, conducted at the University of Akron in 2000. This survey made a special effort to measure nondenominational Protestants accurately.

51. Since 2002, WCCC has developed three "satellite churches in Chicago suburbs that are more than a thirty-minute drive from the main campus in South Barrington. The satellites serve over 2,000 people in both weekend and midweek services using videocasts from South Barrington for the preaching and other elements in the services.

Chapter 23

52. The data from 1989 are those used by Guth and his associates in *The Bully Pulpit* (1997).

53. As was evident earlier in this volume, patterns among clergy within the same religious tradition (e.g., Evangelical Lutheran Church in America [ELCA] and the United Methodist Church within the mainline Protestant category) are not identical. Thus, if one had data on United Methodist clergy time[1] but not at time[2], and conversely, had data on Evangelical Lutheran Church in American clergy at time[2] and not at time[1], and then employed United Methodist clergy to represent mainline Protestant clergy at time[1] and ELCA clergy to represent mainline Protestant clergy at time[2], one could not be sure whether any differences noted between time[1] and time[2] were reflections of true change among mainline Protestant clergy or simply functions of the employment of different denominational clergy at the two different points in time.

54. Despite the utilization of identical denominations across time, changes in the theological or political orientation of clergy within a particular religious tradition can still be affected by the presence of greater or smaller numbers of clergy from the included denominations existing within that category over time, as the theological positions of clergy, their expression of political norms, and the level of clerical engagement in politics varies from denomination to denomination. Therefore, in order to address this potential contamination factor, the numbers of clergy in the evangelical and mainline Protestant categories were weighted equally. In other words, each denomination was weighted to reflect that each denomination had 1,000 clergy both within and across time. Consequently, any noted theological or political changes across

time cannot be a function of different numbers of specific denominational clergy within the category either within or across time.

55. This is evident, for example, if one examines Table 18.2. Roman Catholic priests are much more orthodox theologically when one examines their responses at the top of the table (the two questions about whether Jesus was born of a virgin and whether he will return to earth one day), than when one examines items regarding the inerrancy of Scripture and the historicity of Adam and Eve.

56. Given that the three questions employed to tap orthodoxy were constructed in a Likert format, ranging across five categories from strongly disagree to strongly agree, the combined measure could range from a value of 3 to a value of 15. The net score was then recoded in such a fashion that the midpoint value on the scale was 0 with the highest score being +6 (strong agreement on all three measures) and lowest score being -6 (strong disagreement on all three measures). For purposes of this table, this measure of orthodoxy was collapsed in the following fashion: most orthodox (+6), orthodox (5,4,3) modernist (2,1,0), and most modernist (-1 thru a -6).

57. This is evident by the fact that had the measure of orthodoxy been composed of the three items tapping belief in the virgin birth, the existence of the devil, and that Jesus would return to earth one day, the percentage of Roman Catholic priests falling into the most orthodox category, given the same coding procedures, would be 37 percent, while another 46 percent would fall in the orthodox.

58. Those two variables for which there are comparable data over time but which are omitted from the table are: approval for participation in protest activities and approval for the practice of civil disobedience.

59. One question for which there is comparable data over time that is not reported in this table is whether or not the respondent had run for public office.

60. Black Protestant data are not included in Table 23.5 because the form of the question did not inquire about their activities over the past year but whether they had ever done so.

61. CRC and RCA clergy are not included in the evangelical and mainline Protestant categories in Table 23.5 because the form of the question used in 1989 for the two denominations was different from that asked of clergy in the other denominations. For CRC and RCA clergy, the question in 1989 asked them to indicate whether they had ever, over their careers, rather than in the particular election year under study, specifically done a particular action.

62. CRC and RCA clergy were dropped from the analysis because, as noted in the note above, the nature of the questions related to political participation was structured differently for CRC and RCA clergy in 1989, preventing comparability over time.

63. These ten items assessing political participation included whether during the past year the respondent had: contacted a public official, publicly (but not from the pulpit) supported a political candidate, endorsed a candidate from the pulpit, engaged in any protest activity, participated in civil disobedience, organized a study group in church, organized an action group in church, joined a national political organization, contributed money to a candidate or party, or voted in the election for president.

64. The moral-policy variable was composed of responses to the same three questions (abortion, the death penalty, and gay rights) in 1989 and 2001. The three queries loaded heavily on one factor at both points in time, with the fac-

tor explaining 70 percent of the variance in 1989 and 67 percent of the variance in 2001.

65.   The social-policy variable was composed of responses to the same three questions (the role of government in addressing social problems, free enterprise, and affirmative action) in 1989 and 2001. The three questions loaded heavily on one factor at both points in time, with the factor explaining 56 percent of variance in 1989 and 68 percent of the variance in 2001.

66.   In this case, a vote for Gore was scored as -100, while a vote for Bush was scored a +100. Those who did not vote or voted for a third-party candidate were assigned a score of 0.

Works Cited

Abramson, Harold J. 1973. *Ethnic diversity in Catholic America.* New York: Wiley.

African Methodist Episcopal Church. http://www.amecnet.org

Ahlstrom, Sydney E. 1972. *A religious history of the American people.* New Haven: Yale Univ. Press.

Alvis, Joel L. 1994. *Religion and race: Southern Presbyterians, 1946–1983.* Tuscaloosa: Univ. of Alabama Press.

Ammerman, Nancy T. 1990. *Baptist battles: Social change and religious conflict in the Southern Baptist Convention.* New Brunswick: Rutgers Univ. Press.

———. 1993. SBC moderates and the making of a postmodern denomination. *The Christian Century* 110:896–903.

Andersen, Kristi. 1979. *The creation of a democratic majority, 1928–1936.* Chicago: Univ. of Chicago Press.

Assemblies of God. 2002a. About the Assemblies of God: our history. http://www.ag.org/top/about/history.cfm (accessed August 17, 2002).

———. 2002b. About the Assemblies of God: our vision 2000 proclamation. http://www.ag.org/top/about/vision.cfm (accessed August 17, 2002).

———. 2002c. Assemblies of God beliefs. http://www.ag.org/top/beliefs/truths.cfm (accessed August 17, 2002).

———. 2002d. Assemblies of God beliefs. http://www.ag.org/top/beliefs/contemporaryissues/issue_09_government.cfm (accessed August 17, 2002).

———. 2002e. Assemblies of God beliefs. http://www.ag.org/top/beliefs/contemporaryissues/issue_10_politics.cfm (accessed August 17, 2002).

———. 2002f. Assemblies of God beliefs. http://www.ag.org/top/beliefs/contemporaryissues/issue_12_civil_disbedien.cfm (accessed August 17, 2002).

Barry, A. L. 2001. *What about . . . pastors.* St. Louis: The Lutheran Church-Missouri Synod.

Beatty, Kathleen, and Oliver Walter. 1989. A group theory of religion and politics: The clergy as group leaders. *Western Political Quarterly* 42:129–58.

Bellah, Robert M., Richard Madsen, William M. Sullivan, Ann Swidler, and Steven M. Tipton. 1991. *The good society.* New York: Knopf.

Bendyna, Mary E. 2000. The Catholic ethic in American politics: Evidence from survey research. Ph.D. diss, Georgetown University.

Bendyna, Mary E., and Paul M. Perl. 2000. Political preferences of American Catholics at the time of election 2000. *CARA Working Paper Number 2.* Washington, DC: Center for Applied Research in the Apostolate, Georgetown University.

Blakeslee, Spencer, 2000. *The death of American anti-Semitism.* Westport, CT, Praeger.

Bloomquist, Karen L., and John R. Stumme, eds. 1998. *The promise of Lutheran ethics.* Minneapolis: Fortress.

Blumhofer, Edith L. 1985. *The Assemblies of God: A popular history.* Springfield: Gospel.

———. 1993. *Restoring the faith.* Urbana: Univ. of Illinois Press.

Blumhofer, Edith L., Russell P. Spittler, and Grant A. Wacker, eds. 1999. *Pentecostal currents in American Protestantism.* Urbana and Chicago: Univ. of Illinois Press.

Brackney, William H. 2000. Baptists reaching beyond toleration: A history of Baptists' experience. *American Baptist Quarterly* 19:290–97.

Bratt, James D. 1984. *Dutch Calvinism in modern America.* Grand Rapids: Eerdmans.

Brewer, Mark D. 2001. The electoral behavior of American Catholics: An examination and explanation. Ph.D. diss, Syracuse University.

Brooks, David. 2001. One nation, slightly divisible. *Atlantic Monthly* 288:53–65.

Brown, Willard D. 1928. *A history of the Reformed Church in America.* New York: Board of Publication & Bible Work.

Buddenbaum, Judith. 2001. The media, religion, and public opinion: Toward a unified theory of influence. In *Religion and Popular Culture: Studies on the Interaction of Worldviews,* edited by Daniel Stout and Judith Buddenbaum, 19–37. Ames: Iowa State Univ. Press.

Buehrens, John A., and Forrest Church. 1998. *A chosen faith: An introduction to Unitarian-Universalism.* Boston: Beacon.

Burns, Nancy, Donald R. Kinder, and the National Election Studies. 2000. National election studies, 2000 pilot study [dataset]. Ann Arbor: Univ. of Michigan, Center for Political Studies [producer and distributor].

Byrnes, Timothy A. 1991. *Catholic bishops in American politics.* Princeton: Princeton Univ. Press.

Calhoun-Brown, Allison. 1998. While marching to Zion: Otherworldliness and racial empowerment in the black community. *Journal for the Scientific Study of Religion* 37:427–39.

Carpenter, Joel A. 1997. *Revive us again: The reawakening of American fundamentalism.* New York: Oxford Univ. Press.

Catholic News Service. 2000. Catholics key swing vote this election. *Catholic Standard* 2:1.

Cavendish, James C. 2001. To march or not to march: Clergy mobilization strategies and grassroots anti-drug activism. In *Christian clergy in American politics,* see Crawford and Olson 2001, 203–23.

Center Conversations. 2001. *How the faithful voted: A conversation with John C. Green and John Dilulio.* Washington, DC, Ethics and Public Policy Center.

Chanes, Jerome A. 1999. *A primer on the American Jewish community.* New York: American Jewish Committee.

————. 2001. Who does what? Jewish advocacy and the Jewish "interest." In *Jews in American politics*, see Maisel and Forman 2001, 99–119.

Chaves, Mark. 1997. *Ordaining women: Culture and conflict in religious organizations.* Cambridge, MA: Harvard Univ. Press.

Childs, John Brown. 1980. *The political Black minister: A study in Afro-American politics and religion.* Boston: G. K. Hall.

Christian Church (Disciples of Christ). http://www.disciples.org

Christian Reformed Church. 1995. *Acts of synod.* Grand Rapids: Christian Reformed Church.

Church of the Nazarene. http://www.nazarene.org

Clegg, S. 1990. *Modern organizations: Organizational studies in the postmodern world.* Beverly Hills: Sage.

Clubb, Jerome M., and Howard W. Allen. 1971. The cities and the election of 1928: partisan realignment? In *Electoral change and stability in American political history*, edited by Jerome M. Clubb and Howard W. Allen, 235–54, New York: Free Press.

Cohen, Steven M. 1989. *The dimensions of American Jewish liberalism.* New York: American Jewish Committee.

Cone, James H. 1997. *Black theology and black power.* Maryknoll, NY: Orbis.

Converse, Phillip E. 1966. Religion and politics: The 1960 election. In *Elections and the political order*, edited by Angus Campbell, Phillip E. Converse, Warren E. Miller, and Donald Stokes, 96–124. New York: Wiley.

Corwin, Edward S. 1894. *A history of the Reformed Church, Dutch.* New York: Christian Literature.

Crawford, Sue E. S. and Laura R. Olson, eds. 2001. *Christian clergy in American politics.* Baltimore: Johns Hopkins Univ. Press.

Dawson, Michael C. 1994. *Behind the mule: Race and class in African American politics.* Princeton: Princeton Univ, Press.

Day, Katie. 2001. The construction of political strategies among African American clergy. In *Christian clergy in American politics*, see Crawford and Olson 2001, 85–103.

Djupe, Paul A., and Christopher P. Gilbert. 2001a. Congregational resources for clergy political action. Paper delivered at the annual meeting of the Midwest Political Science Association, Chicago, April 19–21.

Djupe, Paul, and Christopher P. Gilbert. 2001b. Are the sheep hearing the shepherds? An evaluation of church members' perceptions of clergy political speech. Paper presented at the annual meeting of the Society for the Scientific Study of Religion, Columbus, Ohio, October 18–21.

————. 2003. *The prophetic pulpit: Clergy, churches, and communities in American politics.* Lanham: Rowman & Littlefield.

Dollinger, Marc. 2000. *Quest for inclusion: Jews and liberalism in modern America.* Princeton: Princeton Univ. Press.

Eenigenberg, Elton. n.d. [c. 1959]. *A brief history of the Reformed Church in America.* Grand Rapids: Douma.

Ellul, Jacques. 1976. *The ethics of freedom.* Translated by Geoffrey W. Bromiley. Grand Rapids: Eerdmans.

Evangelical Free Church of America. 2002. Distinctives. http://www.efca.org/distinctives.html (accessed June 1, 2002).

Evangelical Lutheran Church of America. 2001. About the ELCA. http://www.elca.org/co/quick.html (accessed Oct. 2, 2003).

Fetzer, Joel. 2001. Shaping pacifism: The role of the local Anabaptist pastor. In *Christian clergy in American politics*, see Crawford and Olson 2001, 177–87.

Flowers, Ronald B. 2000. Toleration is a concession: Religious freedom is a right. *American Baptist Quarterly* 19:298–305.

Foster, Douglas A., Mel E. Hailey, and Thomas L. Winter. 2000. *Ministers at the millennium: A survey of preachers in Churches of Christ.* Abilene: Abilene Christian Univ. Press.

Gilbert, Christopher. 1989. The political influence of church discussion partners. Paper presented at the annual meeting of the American Political Science Association, Atlanta, August 31–September 3.

Gilens, Martin. 1999. *Why Americans hate welfare: Race, media, and the politics of antipoverty policy.* Chicago: Univ. of Chicago Press.

Gillespie, Michael Allen. 2000. Luther and the origins of modernity. Paper delivered at the Annual Meeting of the American Political Science Association in Washington, DC. August 30–September 3.

Ginsberg, Benjamin. 2001. Identity and politics Dilemmas of Jewish leadership in America. In *Jews in American politics*, see Maisel and Forman 2001, 3–27.

Goldberg, J. J. 1996. *Jewish power: Inside the American Jewish establishment.* Reading, MA: Addison-Wesley.

Goodwin, Everett C., ed. 1997. *Baptists in the balance: The tension between freedom and responsibility.* Valley Forge: Judson.

Goren, Arthur A. 1999. *The politics and public culture of American Jews.* Bloomington: Indiana Univ. Press.

Graber Miller, Keith. 1996. *Wise as serpents, innocent as doves: American Mennonites engage Washington.* Knoxville: Univ. of Tennessee Press.

Green, John C. 1996. A look at the "invisible army": Pat Robertson's 1988 activist corps. In *Religion and the culture wars*, see Green, Guth, Smidt, and Kellstedt 1996, 44–61.

Green, John C., and James L. Guth. 1991a. *The Bible and the ballot box: Religion and politics in the 1988 election.* Boulder: Westview.

Green, John C., and James L. Guth. 1991b. The Bible and the ballot box: The shape of things to come. In *The Bible and the ballot box*, see Guth and Green, 1991a, 207–25.

———. 1998. United Methodists and American culture: A statistical portrait. In *The people(s) called Methodists: Forms and reforms of their life*, Vol. 2 of *United Methodism and American culture,* see Lawrence, Campbell, and Richey, 27–52.

Green, John C., James L. Guth, Corwin E. Smidt, and Lyman A. Kellstedt, eds. 1996. *Religion and the culture wars: Dispatches from the front.* Lanham: Rowman & Littlefield.

Green, John C., James L. Guth, and Cleveland Fraser. 1991. Apostles and apostates? Religion and politics among political activists. In *The Bible and the ballot box*, see Guth and Green, 1991a, 113-36.

Green, John C., and Margaret M. Poloma. 1990. The issue agenda of American Protestant clergy: An analysis of ministers across six denominations. Paper presented at the annual meeting of the Society for the Scientific Study of Religion, Virginia Beach, VA, November 9–11.

Greenberg, Anna, and Kenneth D. Wald. 2001. Still liberal after all these years? The contemporary political behavior of American Jewry. In *Jews in American politics*, see Maisel and Forman, 16–93.

Guth, James L. 1983. Southern Baptist clergy: Vanguard of the Christian right? In *The new Christian right*, see Liebman and Wuthnow, 1983, 117–130.

———. 1984. The politics of preachers: Southern Baptist ministers and Christian Right activism. In *New Christian politics*, edited by David G. Bromley and Anson Shupe, 235–49. Macon: Mercer Univ. Press.

————. 1990. Theology and politics among American Protestant clergy: An analysis of seven denominations. Paper presented at the annual meeting of the Society for the Scientific Study of Religion, Virginia Beach, VA, November 9–11.

————. 1996. The bully pulpit: Southern Baptist clergy and political activism, 1980–92. In *Religion and the culture wars*, see Green, Guth, Smidt, and Kellstedt, 1996, 146–73.

————. 2001. The mobilization of a religious elite: Political activism among Southern Baptist clergy in 1996. In *Christian clergy in American politics*, see Crawford and Olson, 2001, 139–56.

Guth, James L. and Helen Lee Turner. 1991. Pastoral politics in the 1988 election: Disciples as compared to Presbyterians and Southern Baptists. In *A case study of mainstream Protestantism*, see Williams, 1991a, 363–85.

Guth, James L., John C. Green, Corwin E. Smidt, and Margaret M. Poloma. 1991. Pulpits and politics: The Protestant clergy in the 1988 election. In *The Bible and the ballot box*, see Guth and Green, 1991a, 73–93.

Guth, James L., John C. Green, Lyman A. Kellstedt, and Corwin E. Smidt. 1995. Onward Christian soldiers: Religious interest group activists. In *Interest Group Politics*, 4th ed., edited by Allan Cigler and Burdett Loomis, 55–76. Washington DC: CQ Press.

Guth, James L., Cleveland R. Fraser, John C. Green, Lyman A. Kellstedt, and Corwin E. Smidt. 1996. Religion and foreign policy attitudes: The case of Christian Zionism. In *Religion and the culture wars,* see Green, Guth, Smidt, and Kellstedt, 1996, 330–60.

Guth, James L., John C. Green, Corwin E. Smidt, Lyman A. Kellstedt, and Margaret M. Poloma. 1997. *The bully pulpit: The politics of Protestant clergy.* Lawrence: Univ. Press of Kansas.

Guth, James L., Linda Beail, Greg Crow, Beverly Gaddy, Steve Montreal, Brent Nelsen, James Penning and Jeff Walz. 2003. The political activity of evangelical clergy in the election of 2000: A case study of five denominations. *Journal for the Scientific Study of Religion* 42 (4): 501–14.

Haberer, Jack. 2001. *God Views: The convictions that drive us and divide us.* Louisville: Geneva.

Hadden, Jeffrey K. 1969. *The gathering storm in the churches.* Garden City: Doubleday.

Handy, Robert. 1955. Fundamentalism and modernism in perspective. *Religion in Life* 24:381–94.

Hanson, Calvin B. 1990. *What it means to be free: A history of the Evangelical Free Church of America.* Minneapolis: Free Church.

Harrell, David Edwin Jr. 2002. The sectional origins of the Churches of Christ. In *The Stone-Campbell movement: An international religious tradition*, edited by Michael W. Casey and Douglas A. Foster. 2002. Knoxville: Univ. of Tennessee Press.

Harris, Fredrick C. 1999. *Something within: Religion in African American political activism.* New York: Oxford Univ. Press.

Hatch, Nathan O. 1989. *The democratization of American Christianity.* New Haven: Yale Univ. Press.

Heitzenrater, Richard P. 1995. *Wesley and the people called Methodists.* Nashville: Abington.

————. 1997. Connectionalism and itinerancy: Wesleyan principles and practice. In *Connectionalism: ecclesiology, mission, and identity.* Vol. 1 of *United Methodism and American culture,* see Lawrence, Campbell, and Richey, 23–38.

Hertzke, Allen D. 1993. *Echoes of discontent: Jesse Jackson, Pat Robertson, and the resurgence of populism.* Washington, DC: CQ Press.

Hofrenning, Daniel J. B. 1997. The vital evangelical in American presidential politics. Paper presented at the annual meeting of the American Political Science Association, Washington, DC, August 27–31.

———. 1998. The evolution of evangelical partisanship. Paper presented at the annual meeting of the American Political Science Association, Boston, September 3–6.

Hoge, Dean. 1976. *Division in the Protestant house: The basic reasons behind intra-church conflicts.* Philadelphia: Westminster Press.

Howe, Charles A. 1993. *The larger faith: A short history of American universalism.* Boston: Skinner.

Hudson, Winthrop S. 1981. *Religion in America: An historical account of the development of American religious life,* 3rd ed. New York: Scribner.

Hughes, Richard. 1991. Are restorationists evangelicals? In *The variety of American evangelicalism,* edited by Donald W. Dayton and Robert Johnston, 109–34. Downers Grove: InterVarsity.

Hunter, James D. 1992. *Culture wars: The struggle to define America.* New York: Basic Books.

Hunter, James D. and Kimon Sargeant. 1993. Religion and the transformation of public culture. *Social Research* 60:545–70.

Jacobsen, Douglas, and William Trollinger Jr. 1998. Introduction. In *Re-Forming the center: American Protestantism, 1990 to the present,* edited by Douglas Jacobsen and William Trollinger Jr., 1–14. Grand Rapids: Eerdmans.

Japinga, Lynn. 1992. The glue that holds us together: History, identity, and the Reformed Church in America. *Reformed Review* 45:181–201.

Jelen, Ted G. 1990. The clergy and abortion. Paper presented at the annual meeting of the Midwest Political Science Association, Chicago, April 18–20.

———. 1993. *The political world of the clergy.* Westport, CT: Praeger.

———. 1997. Culture wars and the party system: Religion and realignment, 1972–1993. In *Culture wars in American politics: Critical reviews of a popular myth,* edited by Rhys H. Williams, 143–57. New York: de Gruyter.

Jelen, Ted G. 2001a. Catholicism. In *Encyclopedia of American immigration,* edited by James Climent. Armonk, NY: Sharpe.

Jelen, Ted G. 2001b. Notes for a theory of clergy as political leaders. In *Christian clergy in American politics,* see Crawford and Olson 2001, 15–29.

Jones, Dale E., Sherri Doty, Clifford Grammich, James E. Horsch, Richard Horseal, Mac Lynn, John P. Marcum, Kenneth M. Sanchagrin, and Richard H. Tayler. 2001. *Religious congregations and membership in the United States 2000.* Nashville: Glenmary Research Center.

Jones, G. Daniel. 1999. Jubilee: To free the enslaved and proclaim liberty to the captives. *American Baptist Quarterly* 18:27–36.

Kauffmann, J. Howard. 1989. Dilemmas of Christian pacifism within a historic peace church. *Sociological Analysis* 49:368–85.

Kauffmann, J. Howard, and Leo Driedger. 1991. Mennonite Church member profile, 1989. Survey Data Set Accessed at the American Religion Data Archive, http://www.thearda.com.

Kelley, Dean. 1977. *Why conservative churches are growing: A study in sociology of religion.* New York: Harper & Row.

Kellstedt, Lyman A., and John C. Green. 1993. Knowing God's many people: Denominational preference and political behavior. In *Rediscovering the religious factor in American politics,* see Leege and Kellstedt, 1993, 53–71.

Kellstedt, Lyman A., Corwin E. Smidt, James L. Guth, and John C. Green. 2001. Cracks in the monolith? Evangelical Protestants and the 2000 election. *Books and Culture,* May/June, 7–9.

Kellstedt, Lyman A., John C. Green, Corwin E. Smidt, and James L. Guth. 1996. The puzzle of evangelical Protestantism: Core, periphery, and political behavior. In *Religion and the culture wars*, see Green, Guth, Smidt, and Kellstedt, 196, 240–66.

Kenski, Henry C., and William Lockwood. 1991. Catholic voting behavior in 1988: A critical swing vote. In *The Bible and the ballot box*, see Guth and Green, 1991a, 173–87.

Kersten, Lawrence. 1970. *The Lutheran ethic: The impact of religion on laymen and clergy.* Detroit: Wayne State Univ. Press.

Kirkpatrick, Clifton, and William Hopper Jr. 1997. *What unites Presbyterians: Common ground for troubled times.* Louisville: Geneva.

Kirschner, Hubert. 1972. *Luther and the peasants' war.* Translated by Darrell Jodock. Philadelphia: Fortress.

Klein, Christa R. 1988. Lutheranism. In *The encyclopedia of American religious experience: Studies of traditions and movements* 3:431–50. New York: Scribner.

Klein, Christa R., and Christian D. von Dehsen. 1989. *Politics and policy: The genesis and theology of social statements in the Lutheran Church in America.* Minneapolis: Fortress.

Koller, Norman B., and Joseph D. Retzer. 1980. The sounds of silence revisited. *Sociological Analysis* 21:155–61.

Kosmin, Barry A., and Seymor P. Lachman. 1993. *One nation under God: Religion in contemporary American society.* New York: Harmony.

Kuenning, Paul P. 1988. *The rise and fall of American Lutheran pietism: The rejection of an activist heritage.* Macon: Mercer Univ. Press.

Lagerquist, L. DeAne. 1999. *The Lutherans. Denominations in America series.* Mystic, CT: Greenwood.

Lawrence, William B., Dennis M. Campbell, and Russell E. Richey, eds. *United Methodism and American culture.* 4 vols. Nashville: Abingdon.

Layman, Geoffrey C. 2001. *The great divide: Religious and cultural conflict in American party politics.* New York: Columbia Univ. Press.

LCMS News Release. 11 September 2001. LCMS president responds, offers prayers in wake of today's tragedies.

———. 18 July 2001. Kieschnick delivers formal acceptance.

Leege, David C., and Lyman A. Kellstedt, eds. 1993. *Rediscovering the religious factor in American politics.* New York: Sharpe.

Leege, David C., Lyman A. Kellstedt, and Kenneth D. Wald. 1990. Religion and politics: A report on measures of religiosity in the 1989 NES pilot study. Paper presented at the annual of the Midwest Political Science Association, Chicago, April 5–7.

Liebman, Robert C., and Robert Wuthnow, eds. *The new Christian right: Mobilization and legitimation.* New York: Aldine.

Lincoln, C. Eric, and Lawrence H. Mamiya. 1990. *The Black church in the African American experience.* Durham: Duke Univ. Press.

Lipset, Seymour M. 1995. The political profile of American Jewry. In *Terms of survival: The Jewish world since 1945*, edited by Robert S. Wistrich, 147–67. New York: Routledge.

Luidens, Donald. 1993. Between myth and hard data: A denomination struggles with identity. In *Beyond establishment: Protestant identity in a post-Protestant age*, edited by Jackson Carroll and Wade Clark Roof, 248–69. Louisville: Westminster/John Knox.

Luidens, Donald, and Roger Nemeth. 1987. The RCA today: Beliefs and behaviors. *The Church Herald*, February 27, 12–14.

Luther, Martin. 1974. Temporal authority: To what extent it should be obeyed. In *Luther: selected political writings,* see Porter, 1974, 51–69.

Lynn, Mac, Comp. 2000. *Churches of Christ in the United States.* Nashville: 21st Century Christian.

Maddox, Randy L. 1999. An untapped inheritance: American Methodism and Wesley's practical theology. In *Doctrines and discipline.* Vol. 3 of *United Methodism and American culture,* see Lawrence, Campbell, and Richey, 19–52.

Maisel, L. Sandy, and Ira N. Forman, eds. 2001. *Jews in American politics.* Rowman & Littlefield.

Marsden, George. 1975. From fundamentalism to evangelicalism: An historical analysis. In *The evangelical: What they believe, who they are, where they are changing,* edited by David Wells and J. Woodbridge, 142–62. Nashville: Abingdon.

Marty, Martin. 1970. *Righteous empire: The Protestant experience in America.* New York: Dial Press.

McKinney, Jennifer M., and Roger Finke. 2002. Reviving the mainline: An overview of clergy support for evangelical renewal movements. *Journal for the Scientific Study of Religion* 41:771–84.

McRoberts, Omar M. 1999. Understanding the "new" Black Pentecostal activism: Lessons from ecumenical urban ministries in Boston. *Sociology of Religion* 60:47–70.

Mead, Frank S. 1990a. *Handbook of denominations in the United States,* 9th ed. Revised by Samuel S. Hill. Nashville: Abington.

Mead, Frank S. 1990b. Assemblies of God, general council of. In *Handbook,* see Mead, 1990a.

Mead, Frank S. 1990c. Methodist. In *Handbook,* see Mead, 1990a.

Mead, Frank S. 1990d. Unitarian-Universalist Association. In *Handbook,* see Mead, 1990a.

———. 1995. *Handbook of denominations in the United States,* 10th ed. Revised by Samuel S. Hill. Nashville: Abingdon.

Meeter, Daniel. 1993. *Meeting each other in doctrine, liturgy, and government: The bicentennial of the celebration of the Constitution of the Reformed Church in America.* Grand Rapids: Eerdmans.

Melton, J. Gordon. 1993. *Encyclopedia of American Religions,* 4th ed. Washington, DC: Gale Research.

Menuge, Angus. 1999. Niebuhr's *Christ and culture* reexamined. In *Christ and culture in dialogue: Constructive themes and practical applications,* edited by Angus Menuge, 31–55. St. Louis: Concordia.

———. 2001. Promoting dialogue in the Christian academy. Presentation for the CUW faculty retreat, Green Lake, WI, August 20–21.

Miller, Donald E. 1997. *Reinventing American Protestantism: Christianity in the new millennium.* Berkeley: Univ. of California Press.

Mitchell, Joshua. 1992. Protestant thought and Republican spirit: How Luther enchanted the world. *The American Political Science Review* 86:688–95.

Moore David W. 2001. Little change in philosophy among rank-and-file Republicans in past eight years. http://www.gallup.com/contents/login.aspx?ci=4426

Moore, James W. 2002. What's so great about being a United Methodist? Pamphlet. Nashville: United Methodist Publishing House.

Moore, R. Laurence. 1986. *Religious outsiders and the making of Americans.* New York: Oxford Univ. Press.

Morris, Aldon D. 1984. *The origins of the civil rights movement: Black communities organizing for change.* New York: Free Press.

Myers, Edward P. 2002. Churches of Christ (A Cappella): Are we evangelical? In *Evangelicalism and the Stone-Campbell movement*, edited by William R. Baker, 50–67. Downers Grove: InterVarsity.

Nafzger, Samuel H. 1994. *An introduction to the Lutheran Church Missouri Synod*. St. Louis: Concordia Publishing House.

Nelsen, Hart, and Sandra Baxter. 1981. Ministers speak on Watergate: Effects of clergy role during political crisis. *Review of Religious Research* 23:150–66.

Niebuhr, H. Richard. 1951. *Christ and culture*. New York: Harper & Row.

Niebuhr, Reinhold. 1943. *Moral man and immoral society: A study in ethics and politics*. New York: Scribner.

Noll, Mark. 1992. The Lutheran difference. *First Things* 20:31–40.

Novak, Michael. 1985. The wisdom of Madison. In *James Madison on religious liberty*, edited by Robert S. Alley, 299–302. Buffalo: Prometheus.

Ohlmann, Eric H. 2000. American Baptist churches, USA. *American Baptist Quarterly* 19:197–207.

Olson, Laura R. 2000. *Filled with spirit and power: Protestant clergy in politics*. Albany: State Univ. of New York Press.

Olson, Laura R., and Sue E. S. Crawford. 2001. Clergy in politics: Political choices and consequences. In *Christian clergy in American politics*, see Crawford and Olson, 2001, 3–14.

Payne, Charles M. 1995. *I've got the light of freedom: The organizing tradition and the Mississippi freedom struggle*. Berkeley: Univ. of California Press.

Pelikan, Jaroslav. 1988. Lutheran heritage. In *The encyclopedia of American religious experience: Studies of traditions and movements*, 3:419–30. New York: Scribner.

Penning, James M. and Corwin E. Smidt. 2000. The political activities of Reformed clergy in the United States and Scotland. *Journal for the Scientific Study of Religion* 39:204–19.

————. 2001. Reformed preachers in politics. In *Christian clergy in American politics*, see Crawford and Olson, 157–73.

Penning, James M., Corwin E. Smidt, and Donald Brown. 2001. The political activities of Reformed clergy in the 2000 election. Paper presented at the annual meeting of the Southern Political Science Association, Atlanta, November 7–10.

Plantinga, Jr., Cornelius. 2002. *Engaging God's world: A Christian vision of faith, learning and living*. Grand Rapids: Eerdmans.

Poloma, Margaret M. 1989. *The Assemblies of God at the crossroads*. Knoxville: Univ. of Tennessee Press.

Pomper, Gerald M. 2001. The presidential election. In *The election of 2000: Reports and interpretations*, edited by Gerald M. Pomper, 125–54. New York: Chatham House, Seven Bridges.

Porter, J. M., ed. 1974. *Luther: Selected political writings*. Philadelphia: Fortress.

Prendergast, William B. 1999. *The Catholic voter in American politics: The passing of the Democratic monolith*. Washington, DC: Georgetown Univ. Press.

Presbyterian Church in America. 2000. *2000 yearbook*. Atlanta: Office of the Stated Clerk of the General Assembly of the Presbyterian Church in America.

Presbyterian Church in America. Date. A brief history: Presbyterian Church in America. http://www.pcanet.org/general/history.htm (accessed April 25, 2002).

Quebedeaux, Richard. 1978. *The worldly evangelicals*. New York: Harper & Row.

Quinley, Harold E. 1974. *The prophetic clergy: Social activism among Protestant ministers*. New York: Wiley.

Redekop, Calvin. 1989. *Mennonite society*. Baltimore: Johns Hopkins Univ. Press.

Reid, Daniel G., ed., 1990. *Dictionary of Christianity in America*. Downers Grove: InterVarsity.

Render unto Caesar . . . and unto God: A Lutheran view of church and state. 1995. St. Louis: A Report of the Commission on Theology and Church Relations of the Lutheran Church–Missouri Synod.

Rogers, Jack B. 1995. *Claiming the center: Churches and conflicting worldviews.* Louisville: Westminster/John Knox.

Roof, Wade Clark, and William McKinney. 1987. *American mainline religion: Its changing shape and future.* New Brunswick: Rutgers Univ. Press.

Sanders, Cheryl Jeanne. 1996. *Saints in exile: The Holiness-Pentecostal experience in African American religion and culture.* New York: Oxford Univ. Press.

Sargeant, Kimon H. 2000. *Seeker churches: Promoting traditional religion in a nontraditional way.* New Brunswick: Rutgers Univ. Press.

Schoolland, Marian M. 1958. *Children of the Reformation: The story of the Christian Reformed Church, its origins and growth.* Grand Rapids: Eerdmans.

Smidt, Corwin E. 2003. Clergy in American politics: An introduction. *Journal for the Scientific Study of Religion* 42:495–99.

Smidt, Corwin E., John C. Green, Lyman A. Kellstedt, and James L. Guth. 1996. The Spirit-filled movements and American politics. In *Religion and the culture wars,* see Green, Guth, Smidt, and Kellstedt, 1996, 219–38.

Smidt, Corwin E., Lyman A. Kellstedt, John C. Green, and James L. Guth. 1999. The Spirit-filled movements in contemporary America: A survey perspective. In *Pentecostal currents in American Protestantism,* see Blumhofer, Spittler, and Wacker, 1999, 111–30.

Smith, Frank J. 1999. *The history of the Presbyterian Church in America: Silver anniversary edition.* Lawrenceville: Presbyterian Scholars.

Smith, Harold Ivan. 1983. *The quotable Bresee.* Kansas City, MO: Beacon Hill.

Smith, R. Drew, and Corwin E. Smidt. 2003. System confidence, congregational characteristics, and black church civic engagement. In *New day begun: African American churches and civic culture in post-civil rights America,* edited by R. Drew Smith, 58–85. Durham: Duke Univ. Press.

Stark, Rodney, Bruce D. Foster, Charles Y. Glock, and Harold E. Quinley. 1970. Sounds of silence. *Psychology Today* 3 (April) 38–41, 60-61.

———. 1971. *Wayward shepherds: Prejudice and the Protestant clergy.* New York: Harper & Row.

Svonkin, Stuart. 1997. *Jews against prejudice: American Jews and the fight for civil liberties.* New York: Columbia Univ. Press.

Sweet, William Warren. 1939. *The story of religion in America.* New York: Harper & Bros.

Swierenga, Robert P., and Elton J. Bruins. 1999. *Family quarrels in the Dutch Reformed churches in the nineteenth century.* Grand Rapids: Eerdmans.

Tays, Dwight. 1990. Church participation in referenda and the first amendment. *Journal of Church and State* 32:391–409.

Thomas, Cal, and Ed Dobson. 1999. *Blinded by might.* Grand Rapids: Zondervan.

Torbet, Robert G. 1969. *A history of the Baptists,* 7th ed. Valley Forge: Judson.

Troeltsch, Ernst. 1931. *The social teaching of the Christian churches.* 2 vols. Translated by Olive Wyon. New York: Macmillan.

Tropman, John E. 1995. *The Catholic ethic in American society: An exploration of values.* San Francisco: Jossey-Bass.

UMC. 2002a. Beliefs. http://www.umc.org/aboutheumc/beliefs (accessed December 2002).

———. 2002b. Mission. http://www.umc.org/aboutheumc/mission (accessed December 2002).

———. 2002c. Policy Statements. http://www.umc.org/aboutheumc/policy (accessed December 2002).

———. 2002d. Doctrinal History. http://www.umc.org/churchlibrary/discipline/doctrinalstandards/doctrinalhistory/htm (accessed December 2002).

Unitarian-Universalist Association. 2000. Unitarian-Universalist Association directory 2000–2001. Boston: Unitarian-Universalist Association.

———. 2002. Principles and purposes. http://www.uua.org/aboutuua/principles.html (accessed June 2002).

Van Til, Henry R. 1959. *The Calvinistic concept of culture.* Grand Rapids: Baker Academic.

Vara, Richard. 2000. *Judaism: A primer.* The Houston Chronicle. August 12, star edition: Religion, p. 1.

Verba, Sidney, and Norman H. Nie. 1972. *Participation in America: Political democracy and social equality.* New York: Harper & Row.

Verba, Sidney, Kay Lehman Scholzman, and Henry E. Brady. 1995. *Voice and equality: Civic voluntarism in American politics.* Cambridge, MA: Harvard Univ. Press.

Vidich, Arthur J. and Joseph Bensman. 1968. *Small town in mass society: Class, power, and religion in a rural community.* Princeton: Princeton Univ. Press.

Wald, Kenneth D. 1991. Ministering to the nation: The campaigns of Jesse Jackson and Pat Robertson. In *Nominating the president,* edited by Emmett Buell Jr. and Lee Sigelman, 119–49. Knoxville: Univ. of Tennessee Press.

———. 1992. Religious elites and public opinion: The impact of the bishops' peace pastoral. *Review of Politics* 54:112–43.

———. 2003. *Religion and politics in the United States,* 4th ed. Lanham: Rowman & Littlefield.

Wald, Kenneth D., Dennis E. Owen, and Samuel S. Hill Jr. 1988. Churches as political communities. *American Political Science Review* 82:531–48.

———. 1990. Political cohesion in churches. *Journal of Politics* 52:197–215.

Walker, Williston. 1959. *A history of the Christian church.* New York: Scribner.

Walton, Hanes Jr. 1985. *Invisible politics: Black political behavior.* Albany: State Univ. of New York Press.

Weber, Max. 1963 [1922]. *The sociology of religion.* Translated E. Fischoff. Boston: Beacon.

Welch, Michael R., David C. Leege, Kenneth D. Wald, and Lyman Kellstedt. 1993. Are the sheep hearing the shepherds? Cue perceptions, congregational responses and political communication processes. In *Rediscovering the religious factor in American politics,* see Leege and Kellstedt, 1993, 235–54.

Welch, Michael R., Lyman A. Kellstedt, David C. Leege, and Kenneth D. Wald. 1990. Pastoral cues and congregational responses: Evidence from the 1989 NES pilot study. Paper presented at the annual meeting of the American Political Science Association, San Francisco, August 30–September 2.

Weston, William J. 1998. The "fidelity and chastity" amendment: A competition to renew the Presbyterian Church." In *Reformed vitality: Continuity and change in the face of modernity,* edited by Donald Luidens, Corwin E. Smidt, and Hijme Stoffels, 33–50. Lanham: Univ. Press of America.

——— 1997. *Presbyterian pluralism: Competition in a Protestant house.* Knoxville: Univ. of Tennessee Press.

——— 2001. What is now normal in the Presbyterian Church (U.S.A.)? In *Reformed encounters with modernity,* edited by H. Jurgens Hendriks, Donald Luidens, Roger Nemeth, Corwin E. Smidt, and Hijme Stoffels, 117–24. Cape Town, South Africa: International Society for the Study of Reformed Communities.

———. 2003. *Leading from the center: Strengthening the pillars of the church.* Louisville: Geneva.

Wilcox, Clyde. 1989. The fundamentalist voter: Politicized religious identity and political attitudes and behavior. *Review of Religious Research* 31:54–67.

Wilcox, Todd A. 1999. Who left the gate open? Explaining the partisan realignment among white evangelicals. Paper presented at the annual meeting of the Midwest Political Science Association, Chicago, April 15–17.

Williams, D. Newell. 1991a. *A case study of mainstream Protestantism: The Disciples' relation to American culture, 1880–1989.* St. Louis: Chalice.

Williams, D. Newell. 1991b. Future prospects of the Christian Church (Disciples of Christ). In *A case study of mainstream Protestantism,* see Williams 1991a, 561–74.

Willow Creek Association. About the WCA. http://www.willowcreek.com

Willow Creek Community Church. http://www.willowcreek.org

Wilson, John F. 1989. Religion at the core of American culture. In *Altered landscapes: Christianity in America, 1935–1985,* edited by David W. Lotz, 362–76. Grand Rapids: Eerdmans.

Wolin, Sheldon S. 1956. Politics and religion: Luther's simplistic imperative. *The American Political Science Review* 50:24–42.

Wright, C. 1989. *A stream of light: A short history of American Unitarianism.* Boston: Skinner.

Wuthnow, Robert. 1983. The political rebirth of American evangelicals. In *The new Christian right,* see Liebman and Wuthnow, 1983, 167–85.

———. 1988. *The restructuring of American religion: Society and faith since World War II.* Princeton: Princeton Univ. Press.

———. 1989. *The struggle for America's soul: Evangelicals, liberals, and secularism.* Grand Rapids: Eerdmans.

Wuthnow, Robert, and John H. Evans, eds. 2002. *The quiet hand of God: Faith-based activism and the public role of mainline Protestantism.* Berkeley: Univ. of California Press.

Index

General Conference Mennonite Church,
207, 208
German Evangelical Lutheran Synod,
128
gifts of the Spirit, 180, 181, 183, 264
Gingrich, Newt, 104, 317
Gothard, Bill, 168
government role in education, 27, 38,
39, 53, 54, 67, 68, 80, 95, 109, 110,
122, 136, 149, 162, 163, 174, 175,
191, 202, 203, 205, 215, 230–231,
242, 243, 245, 255, 268, 269, 281,
282, 293
government role in social programs, 14,
27, 39, 53, 54, 67, 70, 79, 80, 82,
94, 95, 109, 110, 122, 136, 149,
162, 163, 174, 175, 178, 191, 194,
202, 203, 205, 215, 216, 231, 242,
243, 254, 255, 268, 281, 293, 294,
331
Great Migration, 247, 261
gun control, 123, 174, 325
Guth, James, 3, 5, 6, 7, 12, 25, 31, 36,
42, 50, 71, 73, 76, 79, 84, 87, 90,
94, 96, 97, 101, 108, 112, 151, 154,
156, 159, 179, 184, 186, 189, 192,
207, 233, 235, 277, 279, 280, 302,
303, 305, 324, 329

Halakha, 226, 229, 230
health-care policy, 14, 27, 38, 39, 53,
54, 67–68, 79, 80, 94, 95, 109, 110,
122, 136, 149, 162, 163, 174, 175,
191, 202, 203, 215, 216, 231, 242,
243, 254, 255, 268, 281, 282, 293,
326
Heart Holiness, 167, 168, 172
Heidelberg Catechism, 71
Henry Institute for the Study of
Christianity and Politics, 13, 131
heterodox, 324
historical criticism of Bible, 9–10, 43,
50, 209
historicity of Adam and Eve, 14, 25, 35,
36, 50, 51, 64, 65, 76, 77, 92–93,
107, 118, 119, 133, 146, 147, 159,
165, 172, 188, 189, 200, 212, 240,
252, 253, 265, 266, 279, 290, 291,
324, 330
Holiness Movement, 85, 86, 167, 168,
170, 175, 178, 180, 266
Holy Club, 84

Holy Communion (see Lord's Supper)
homosexuality, 14, 27, 38, 39, 53, 54,
62, 65, 67, 68, 80, 94, 95, 104, 108,
109, 110, 122, 123, 136, 138, 147,
149, 162, 172, 175, 178, 185, 191,
201, 202–3, 209, 210, 213, 215, 219,
242, 243, 255, 268, 269, 276, 281,
282, 293, 330
Hybels, Bill, 286

immanent nature of God, 10
immigration, 10, 43, 46, 47, 49, 71, 73,
85, 128, 154, 155, 158, 165, 195,
196, 208, 224, 236
in essentials, unity; in all else, charity,
169
individual sanctification, 11, 14, 26, 36,
51, 64, 65, 76, 77, 86, 87, 88, 92,
93, 107, 118, 120, 133, 134, 138,
147, 159, 160, 165, 168, 172, 173,
178, 183, 189, 200, 205, 212, 240,
241, 252, 253, 259, 260, 262, 265,
266, 279, 290, 291
industrialization, 10
inerrancy of biblical texts, 10, 14, 25, 35,
36, 50, 51, 56, 62, 64, 65, 76, 77,
92–93, 107, 118, 133–34, 142, 143,
159, 160, 165, 172, 188, 189, 197,
200, 205, 212, 240, 252, 253, 265,
266, 279, 288, 2990, 291, 303, 323,
324, 330
Interfaith Alliance, 277, 328
Israel, 27, 39, 54, 67, 68, 80, 95, 108,
109, 110, 122, 136, 149, 162, 163,
174, 175, 191, 192, 203, 205, 215,
223, 224, 226, 230, 231, 232, 234,
242, 243, 255, 268, 269, 281, 282,
293, 294

Jefferson, Thomas, 102
Jesus' return to earth, 25, 36, 51, 64, 76,
92, 107, 118, 119, 132, 133, 146,
147, 159, 165, 168, 172, 178, 183,
184, 188, 189, 200, 211, 212, 240,
252, 253, 265, 266, 279, 290, 291,
303, 330
Jewish faith (see Jews)
Jews (see also Orthodox, Reform,
Reconstructionist, Conservative), 4,
10, 13, 223–34, 275, 323
Johnson, Lyndon, 42
Jones, Absalom, 248